Money

Guide to a Secure Retirement

by the Editors of Money Magazine

Compiled and Edited by
Junius Ellis

Oxmoor House®

Library of Congress Catalog Number: 89-061924
Hardcover ISBN: 0-8487-0761-3
Softcover ISBN: 0-8487-1004-5

Manufactured in the United States of America
First Printing 1989
Second Printing 1990

Published by arrangement with Oxmoor House, Inc.
Book Division of Southern Progress Corporation
P. O. Box 2463, Birmingham, AL 35201

Vice President and Editorial Director: Candace N. Conard
Production Manager: Jerry Higdon
Associate Production Manager: Rick Litton
Art Director: Bob Nance

Money Guide to a Secure Retirement
Compiled and Edited by Junius Ellis

Editor: Clark Scott
Editorial Assistant: L. Amanda Owens
Designer: Larry Hunter
Cover designer: Nancy Johnson
Cover photograph by: Colleen Duffley

To order *Money* magazine, write to: *Money*,
P. O. Box 54429, Boulder, CO 80322-4429

Think about it. The book you are holding will be your primary source of information for the longest and potentially most rewarding period of your life.

You survived adolescence and young adulthood, to be sure. But those chapters of your life are but fleeting intervals compared to the astonishing variety of experience and satisfaction that awaits you in a time we label with a word that is woefully out-of-date: retirement.

Increasingly, Americans are beginning to plan—and daydream—at younger and younger ages about making the most of the period of their lives after they complete their child rearing. Many of us begin to think about retirement around age 40, and almost everyone does by 50. But, if you are like most of us, you may have more questions than answers.

What opportunities await me?

Will I have the means to take advantage of them?

Where will I live?

How much money will I *really* need?

The purpose of this *Guide to a Secure Retirement*, the latest in the series of books the Editors of *Money* have prepared with Oxmoor House, is to help you achieve the financial independence you need to enjoy a fulfilling retirement. You will find here sophisticated investing advice for planning your retirement, as well as practical tips for after you retire. We will help you make the most of your company's retirement plan, manage your long-term investments, draw upon the equity in your house, find the right medical policies—and then make sure you have provided for your family.

In short, this will be *your* time and the choices you make will be *your* responsibility. We are pleased to have this opportunity to help you achieve your dreams.

Landon Y. Jones Jr.

Landon Y. Jones
Managing Editor, *Money*

Contents

Introduction

*I*n contrast to previous generations of Americans, people in the third quarter of life today are more likely to view retirement as a time of renewal and adventure than a restful reward for a long career. Indeed, the evidence is overwhelming that we are now in the golden age of retirement. Social Security benefits have never been higher. The number of company pensions and savings plans has more than doubled since 1974. Innovations such as Individual Retirement Accounts and Keoghs were unknown to retirees of earlier generations. Not only do prospective pensioners stand a better chance of living better than they ever could, but they also are freer to choose when to call it a career. Although the standard retirement age remains 65, both early retirement and late retirement are catching on.

Contributing to an early departure from work are attractive financial packages that growing numbers of companies offer to older employees. Working longer is on the upswing for quite different reasons. Since 1978, federal law has prohibited companies from making retirement mandatory for anyone except top-level executives. Career switching and part-time work late in life are more acceptable—and available—than before. Experts attribute the expanding job pool for older people to the national shift from a manufacturing economy to a service economy. The result is greater opportunities to start a new career in your sixties and to capitalize on your lifetime of experience and skills.

What's more, the generation now nearing or in retirement is the wealthiest in United States history. These are the people who bought houses cheap after World War II, prospered during the postwar economic boom, saw the value of their homes inflate during the 1970s, and paid far less into pension plans and Social Security than they will take out. Much of their wealth is in real estate; nearly three-fourths of people over 65 own their own homes. Half of the couples retiring today have a pension from a public or private employer. That can give you remarkable

freedom to decide just how much you want to work, and
when, and where. You can yield to passions and causes
that you may have put off for years, from travel adven-
tures to a whole new world of post-graduate study.

The goal behind both the acquisition of family wealth
and saving for retirement is financial independence—and
the opportunity to make the most of it. Alas, the price of
this unprecedented opportunity is the increasingly complex planning required to build, protect, and pass on your
bundle to the next generation. And success today is based
on a premise that used to be unthinkable: Americans
want to provide for their families and then retire with no
reduction in their standard of living.

The purpose of this book is to help you achieve that
lofty goal, regardless of your age. We will not beguile you
with the notion that it is easily attained. To the contrary,
you face many vexing issues and tough decisions. How
much will you need and how much can you reasonably
expect to have to finance life after work? What can you
really count on from Social Security? How much protection does your company pension offer? Where should you
invest your IRA, Keogh, and company-sponsored savings
plans? You will find answers to these and other key
questions in this guide. But keep in mind that retirement
planning is no longer a concern of only those persons
within a few years of reaching these goals. Every stage of
your life—from your thirties to your forties and fifties—
requires different strategies and a keen appreciation of
emergent trends that will directly affect the elderly and
their families.

For example, a baby born in America this year will turn
65 in a geriatric society in which one in every five persons
is that age or older. This will be the inexorable result of
major demographic changes that are unfolding all around
us. The age seesaw of our population, once weighted by
the young, will gradually tilt heavily toward the old because the baby boomers are maturing and the average life
span is increasing. Since 1965, median life expectancy at
birth has jumped from 70 to more than 75 today and could
reach 80 by the year 2000.

This trend means that extended families will no longer
be primarily horizontal, comprising brothers and sisters
and cousins. Instead, they will gradually turn vertical:
three and four generations of a single family will be alive

at once. Already the average married couple in the U.S. has more living parents than children. It means that spouses will spend more years together after their children have left home than they did raising them. It means that the average woman today will spend more years caring for her aging mother than she will have spent caring for a child.

Even more significantly, it means that a whole new set of hazards line the twisting path to a secure retirement. Most notably, families now stand a greater chance than ever before of having a disabled elderly relative to support. Those who do not prepare accordingly risk undermining the financial planning of two or even three generations. Given increased longevity, more and more parents are likely to have children who themselves are over 65. One-quarter of the aged need some type of long-term care—and the age group that most often does, those over 85, is the fastest growing. The number of disabled elderly Americans is expected to more than double between 1985 and 2020.

In the past, almost all of them would have been taken care of by families, frequently by a daughter in her mid-fifties. But the ability of families to care for the elderly is weakening now that some 60% of women 45 to 54 are working. Indeed, the most reliable predictor of a disabled older person's chances of entering a nursing home is the absence of living children or their presence in the labor force.

How sturdy is your present nest egg? If you are in the most intense retirement planning years—between ages 45 and 64—see whether this profile sounds anything like you:

● You look forward to a full life after work. In fact, you're not at all afraid to bid the workaday world good-bye, and you even intend to let go before you reach age 65.

● You are a superior saver, putting away an impressive 14% of your annual income (versus only about 4% for the U.S. population at large).

● You don't plan to move to a less costly house after retirement, yet you don't expect your standard of living to drop in step with your income.

● You haven't done much planning, which could be dangerous. For instance, your biggest worry is inflation, but your major form of investment is a savings account, the least inflation-resistant of all.

These attributes are all shared by most of the 600 pre-retirees interviewed in a 1988 study commissioned by Merrill Lynch and released to *Money*. The most encouraging finding: Nearly one in five people saves 20% or more of his or her income, a figure that rises with age. Says Merrill Lynch consumer markets president John Steffens: "While that's good, the other four need to start saving for the increasing costs of living longer. It won't be long before people live as many years in retirement as they worked."

According to the study, pre-retirees' greatest fears center around having enough money to carry them through their retirement. And inflation is the greatest threat to the purchasing power of fixed-income pensions and annuities. For instance, if inflation were to rise from a recent 5% rate to 7%, your income would drop by half in 10 years. Fret as they may, however, 53% of pre-retirees prefer to stash their retirement savings in inflation-eroding passbook accounts. Only 27% buy stocks, historically the best inflation hedge, and 47% say they have little or no confidence in the market. Notes Paul Westbrook, a retirement planner in Watchung, New Jersey: "When people think of saving for retirement, they think security and often resist suggestions that they aim for long-term growth."

The great majority of pre-retirees see long-term health care as an important issue. Yet, nearly two-thirds are untroubled about their ability to pay for long-term care. The only plausible explanation for such optimism is that respondents believe employers and the government should be responsible for three-quarters of long-term health-care costs. While long-term care is on the congressional agenda, employers are unlikely to expand benefits. "The first rule of survival is not to depend on the kindness of strangers," says Don Underwood, vice president of Merrill Lynch's Retirement Plans Department.

Pre-retirees think that the responsibility for providing their retirement income should be divided about equally among themselves, their employers, and the government. Most believe that they will collect the Social Security benefits to which they are entitled. But the younger ones, the 45- to 49-year-olds, are least sanguine. Only half of them feel that they can count on Social Security, compared with three-quarters of the 60- to 64-year-olds. Whatever your views, don't assume that what you collect from the government and your pension will equal your savings contributions. Many experts say that you will be lucky indeed if Social Security and your pension provide half of your retirement income.

On average, pre-retirees estimate that they will need 70% of their current income for a comfortable retirement. The figure is in line with guidelines that retirement planners generally recommend. But Bruce Paine, a retirement consultant in Leonia, New Jersey, contends that most early retirees will need 75% to 80% of their pre-retirement income. Says he: "You're going to have 3,000 additional hours to fill each year, and most 55- to 65-year-olds aren't ready for the rocking chair."

Whenever you decide to retire, you are bound to encounter some sleepless nights. You and your spouse have to worry about whether there will be enough money to live on until the end of your lives. If you are to get a pension lump sum, you must suffer the anxieties that you might invest it poorly and live out the latter years of your life as a burden to your children. Even if you invest wisely, you will have to contend with the nightmare of all retirees: No matter how smart and provident you are, inflation hurts you in the end. If you move too hastily to some putative paradise, you might wind up repenting your mistake at excruciating leisure. In addition, you must wonder how you can expect to escape the paralyzing boredom that afflicts so many who no longer have jobs to go to.

Fortunately, the survival strategies for the future are at hand. Those families that learn to talk to one another candidly about some sensitive topics—Does Dad have a will? Shall we ask the children about moving?—will thrive. So will people who see retirement as a glorious mixture of work, play, and learning. Growing old can be viewed as a kind of second adolescence. Like the first one, it is fraught with exhilaration and fear of the unknown. The difference is that this time you are bringing wisdom with you, and the experience should be that much sweeter.

The Dream of Financial Independence

Chapter One

*D*oes anybody remember leisure time? Not long ago, this delightful free period ran from about 5 p.m. to 11 p.m. Monday through Friday and then made a return appearance lasting all weekend long. It was the time to read, garden, muse, to do what you wanted to do. Today, leisure time is scarcer than a 9% credit card. A 1988 Roper poll, which found that half the population feels pressed for time, noted that participation in hobbies has plunged. For example, only 37% of those polled cited music as one of their hobbies, compared with 47% six years earlier.

Are frazzled workers destined to fizzle? Not a chance. Many are just knocking themselves out now so they can afford to retire earlier and make leisure their next full-time activity. As the average life expectancy has risen—to 72 for men and 78 for women—the age at which people retire has tumbled. Today, the average retirement age is 61; in 1970, it was 65. Millions of Americans these days are declaring their independence in their fifties, forties, and even thirties. For them, retirement has come to mean almost anything except shuffling off to play shuffleboard. Youthful retirees often run part-time businesses, volunteer at social service agencies, take their hobbies seriously, and travel widely.

Take Paul and Vicki Terhorst, both 40, who have roamed the globe and written a book since Paul's 1984 resignation from a high-powered accounting post in San Francisco. Or Ken and Shelley Cassie, 52 and 53. They quit their high school teaching jobs in 1988 so Ken could spend more time making pottery at their Brielle, New Jersey home and the couple could sell the work at crafts shows. "It's given us a chance to start again while we're young," says Ken. "Yes, we're aiming to make a certain amount of money, but the biggest thing is that this is fun. We do what we want when we want. I see this as a luxury we've earned."

You have probably thought about how you would spend the time *you* earned after retiring early. Whatever your dream, the chances of attaining it are far better than you might imagine. Financial lures abound for people who cut loose while still fairly young. A 1987 survey of 763 large employers by the Wyatt Company, a benefits consulting firm, shows that 93% of the companies paid pensions to retirees at age 55 or earlier if they had served at least a specified number of years, usually 10 or 15. In addition, more Americans are eligible to receive pensions as a result of recent federal legislation that requires companies to cut vesting time from 10 years to either five or seven. Company-sponsored savings programs, Individual Retirement Accounts, and Keogh plans also offer tax-advantaged ways to build cash for an early retirement. And Social Security benefits may not be substantially reduced if you stop working before 62, the age when you can start getting the government checks.

Early retirement is obviously not for everyone. Many can't afford it. In *Money*'s 1988 *Americans and Their Money* survey, having enough money for retirement was the No. 1 financial worry for people 35 to 49. You might not be able to get out early if you are facing tuition bills for your children's education well into your fifties. Your pension may be inadequate—or nonexistent—if you hopped jobs or worked for a small firm. Others are unprepared psychologically for early retirement (see "Are You Really Ready to Retire?," page 22). You may not be ready either to give up the camaraderie of business associates or to spend a lot more time with your mate. Sometimes, one spouse wants to retire early but the other doesn't. More often these days, it's the woman who wants to stay on because she entered or re-entered the work force late or only recently got a challenging job. Fear of boredom is genuine for those who can't figure out how they would occupy days without deadlines.

For those intrigued by the concept of early retirement, the main prerequisites are preparation, creativity, and dedication. You will have to reposition your investments while working to amass the pot needed at the early-retirement age you select. Quitting early means that your savings must last longer than otherwise. Assuming a 4% average annual return after inflation, someone planning to retire at 55 has to sock away $560,000 to collect $30,000 a year until age 90, compared with $468,000 for someone waiting until he is 65. The younger retiree also has 10 fewer years to accumulate that 20% additional cash

reserve. You may have to make sacrifices either before or
after you retire, like cutting back on luxuries or entertainment expenses.

The more creative you are earlier, the less Spartan you
will have to be later. Try to devise ways of building your
own retirement annuity, not through an insurance company but through your own skills. Ask yourself: What
could I do now that will bring in steady annual income
after I retire? The answer might be consulting, the most
popular form of post-retirement entrepreneurship, or
honing a hobby that you will turn into a sideline business
in retirement. It might be buying rental real estate today
with a mortgage you will have paid off by the time you
retire, thus practically guaranteeing a tidy, positive cash
flow. Or it might be picking up a new skill by taking night
classes (see "Working After Retirement," page 25).

Even if you are not contemplating a second career, you
should start gearing up today to make sure you have
enough money to carry you through retirement. First,
estimate how much annual income you will need after
stopping work. You will have to replace only about 70% to
80% of your current earnings, because you will no longer
rack up such costs as commuting. But don't forget to
factor in inflation between now and your target date—a
calculation that might require help from an accountant or
a financial planner. Then, find out what annual income
you can count on from pensions and Social Security. Your
employee-benefits department can help with the former.
Call the Social Security Administration at 800-234-5772
for the latter. Remember, your pension probably won't be
increased annually with inflation as Social Security
checks are. The total will leave you with an annual
shortfall that your investments, including any company
savings plans, will help fill. Next, add in money you
expect to get from any personal annuity you create.

Most early retirees make their break thanks to corporate pensions. Though many large companies reduce pensions by as much as 50% if you quit work at 55, about half
let employees leave at 62 without any cut in their pensions. It generally pays, however, to keep working until
you reach the age when your employer removes or
sharply scales back its early-retirement penalty. Say you
are 55, have worked at the company for 30 years, and earn
$50,000. Assume your company calculates your annual

pension benefit as 1% of your final salary times the years you worked there. But it will pay half that amount if you quit before 60. Retire now and your annual pension will be $7,500. But if you wait until 60, when yearly raises of 5% would boost your salary to $63,800, your yearly pension will be $22,300, or about three times as much.

Even though your pension check will almost always increase the longer you work, leaving your job before 65 may not cost as much as you think. David Wise, a Harvard professor of political economics who has studied hundreds of retirement plans, says that working past 60 can actually *cut* the total value of your future benefits in current dollars. Pension formulas typically increase your annual benefit more slowly after age 60. As a result, the only financial benefit you might receive from working an extra year would be that year's salary. Ask your company benefits counselor what your pension will be if you leave at various ages, both on an annual basis and as a lump sum. Then, have your accountant or financial planner figure out when your pension will stop growing enough to make working longer worthwhile.

Lately, many companies have offered special early-retirement packages that sweeten pensions for employees who accept these offers. Some deals are worth grabbing, but others are strikingly stingy. (For guidance on how to evaluate such arrangements, see "Taking Charge of Your Company Retirement Plans," page 75.) A new pension penalty included in the 1986 tax reform law may discourage some high earners from retiring early, however. Today, anyone retiring at 55 cannot collect more than $38,000 a year from a traditional pension you might get upon retiring from a $150,000 job. The ceiling rises to $72,000 for people who retire at age 62 and $90,000 for those taking pensions starting at 65. Companies often skirt these ceilings by paying any higher obligations out of company reserves, rather than pensions.

Social Security is less Scroogelike to early retirees than you might expect. True, your checks at 62 could be 20% smaller than if you waited to start receiving them at 65. But a closer look at the numbers shows that the government actually promotes early retirement when computing Social Security benefits. Consider a middle-aged manager with a typical earnings history. If he retired at 55 last year, in seven years he would begin getting a Social Security benefit of $660 a month in 1988 dollars. If he keeps working until 62, his monthly benefit will be $725, only 10% more. Thus, if this man works seven more years, his extra payoff from Social Security will be peanuts.

The outlook for early retirement in the future is partly cloudy. On the sunny side, this year's speedup in pension vesting may help some people retire early, though probably not by a lot. Few workers accrue sizable benefits after only five or seven years on the job, the new vesting requirement. And since a company plan will typically freeze your pension amount from the time you leave until its regular retirement date, inflation will melt a portion of your benefits. The aging of the U.S. population will also bring with it some ominous thunder for younger workers. The ratio of employees to retirees at many major corporations has slipped from about 15 to 1 in the 1970s to 4 to 1 today. That means as the baby-boom generation nears retirement at the turn of the century, companies will need to hang on to as many employees as possible. Early-retirement packages may be curtailed lest businesses end up paying retirees almost as much as employees.

Congress has already approved the scheduled changes that will snip the Social Security benefits for early retirees in the next century (see "Social Security Simplified," page 44). But by then, nearly a generation of Americans will have struggled throughout their youth for the delicious opportunity to quit their jobs. Their reward will be spending a full, idyllic third of their lives in well-plotted leisure. And the pleasure of leisure is something no government check can match—as the Terhorsts' and Cassies' stories illustrate:

The Terhorsts: Taking Off at Thirtysomething

Paul Terhorst is an early bloomer. At age seven, he asked for a file cabinet for Christmas, getting a jump-start on his eventual career as a certified public accountant. At 30, Terhorst rocketed through the ranks at the accounting firm Peat Marwick Main to become a partner based in San Francisco. Five years later, in 1984, Terhorst again roared ahead of his peers by chucking it all to become a full-fledged retiree.

Terhorst has since provided envious readers with an

insider's guide to very early retirement, *Cashing In on the American Dream: How to Retire at 35* (Bantam, $16.95). He wrote most of the eat-your-heart-out book while sojourning in Hungary and Yugoslavia with his wife, Vicki. Paul describes the book as advice on "living life now instead of postponing gratification." To learn what life is really like for a pair of 40-year-old, childless retirees, *Money* caught up with the Terhorsts last fall as they trekked through Baja California, the 760-mile-long Mexican strip of mountains, desert, and beaches stretching south from Tijuana.

The Terhorsts typically travel from March through October. They spend the rest of the year in a $20,000 one-bedroom condominium near the beach in Buenos Aires, Argentina. They take their hobbies everywhere. Paul picked up the saxophone, and Vicki, who formerly worked as a music teacher and painter, is intrigued by New Age crystals and spiritual healing. They retired on a net worth of $500,000 from three sources: Paul's Peat Marwick lump-sum partnership payout, the sale of four investment apartments in California, and money-market mutual funds. He also received a $9,000 advance for the book and its audiotape, and his first royalty check for $10,000. "When people in bars ask me how it works," muses Terhorst, "my short answer is sell your assets, put the cash in the bank, move to a cheap part of the world, and live off the interest."

Quitting a job, he finds, can make life far more affordable: "It's not the cost of living that's so expensive but the cost of working." As the former accountant figures it, when you stop toiling for pay, you owe income taxes only on your investments. Social Security taxes, which can amount to as much as 15.3% of your employment income in 1990, will disappear altogether. Terhorst also recommends selling your house. Then, he says, rent or buy an inexpensive apartment in a foreign country where Americans can live cheaply, such as Brazil, or in a little town Stateside, perhaps in Kentucky or South Carolina. "You spend 80% of your income on what I call infrastructure costs, such as taxes and mortgage payments," he reckons. "When you denounce the privilege of working, you can live on 20% of your income."

The Terhorsts were once a perfectly corporate couple heavily into infrastructure costs. They lived in a $225,000 two-bedroom, San Francisco condominium, employed a full-time maid, took cabs routinely, and spent five weeks a year vacationing in such faraway spots as Rio, Rome, Puerto Vallarta, and Madrid. But in 1981, the firm transferred Paul to Buenos Aires to handle audits for American companies with offices there. That's when the couple's values began to shift. "In Argentina," explains Paul, "they don't take jobs so seriously. People at parties ask you what you do for fun instead of what you do."

In 1982, Paul began toying with the idea of retiring, although the prospect of exiting his career was scary. He recommends that anyone pondering early retirement spend at least two years thinking about and planning for it. Adds Vicki: "The financial details were important for Paul because he needs security. He wanted to never have to go back to work again." She shared the question asked by many wives of retirees—would her husband be underfoot all day? "My fear was that I would have to give up my own independence," Vicki recalls. Both of them finally concluded that they could have the time of their lives in retirement, even though doing so meant Paul would give up his inside lane on the fast track. So when Paul was asked to transfer to Los Angeles in 1984, he resigned instead. The couple inaugurated their new life by spending three months in a rented house on the beach in Pinamar, Argentina.

The Terhorsts wanted a simple, worry-free investment strategy to match their life-style. So they converted their $500,000 in assets into federally insured bank certificates of deposit at eight institutions. The CDs have one-year maturities and come due every month or so, yielding on average about 8%. Their investment adviser argued strongly for a portfolio of stocks and bonds, but Paul objected. "I just don't think I could earn superior returns in the stock market. It's risky and it's a hassle," he says. Paul rejected bonds because inflation can erode their value. He knows that if inflation flares and interest rates rise, he won't be locked into low rates for long. (Since the cost-of-living index in Argentina sometimes zooms by a rate of more than 25% a month, they keep their money in U.S. dollars to take advantage of the devaluation of the Argentinian austral. The favorable exchange rate helps offset inflation increases.)

For all their apparent hedonism, the Terhorsts live

frugally. The price they pay for their freedom is what Terhorst calls "downscaling." They fund their retirement by adhering to a tight budget that wouldn't suit everyone's taste. The couple generally keep their daily living expenses down to $50 or less, including housing but not air fare. When traveling, they often spend only $25 a day, unless they splurge or happen to be in the U.S., a relatively pricey destination. The Terhorsts visit their parents and siblings at least every two years.

The Terhorsts figure they spend approximately $24,000 a year. Their CDs produce an annual income of about $50,000, leaving them plenty of spare change to counter inflation and even come out with a year-end surplus. In fact, says Paul, "My net worth has increased by almost $100,000 since I retired." Neither Vicki nor Paul think about the possibility that the money will run out. But if it did, Paul says, "I'd go back to work." Doing what? "Who knows?" he shrugs.

Moreover, Terhorst maintains that anyone can do as he has with far less than $500,000 if you adopt what he calls a "bare-bones retirement" in which you might need to work part time. Just determine your net worth and figure how much the amount can earn every year after you convert it to cash. For example, a net worth of $300,000 (including home equity, Individual Retirement Accounts, and cars) and an 8%-a-year return can produce about $24,000 of annual income. If you are a parent, this whole scheme may sound rather farfetched. But Terhorst insists that it's quite realistic as long as you are willing to forsake private schools, expensive colleges, and such extras as piano lessons, summer camp, and the latest clothes. He believes the extra time a retired parent has for his children is worth the material sacrifice. "Do you want to give your kids everything they could possibly want," he asks, "or play with them and be a part of their lives?"

Paul doesn't pretend that everyone who dreams about early retirement can—or will—do it. "The real point is that you have options," he concludes. Establish your priorities in life. Decide exactly what it is that makes you happy. And do it—today.

Are You Really Ready to Retire?

While you may be all set for a financially secure retirement, you may not realize how much life after work can draw on your emotional reserves. If you suddenly find yourself with 40 or more hours a week of free time that you haven't adequately prepared for, you could be headed for trouble.

The following questions, based on the findings of gerontologists and psychologists, will help you determine how well prepared you are for the day when the alarm clock no longer rules. Answer "yes" or "no" to each question that applies to you. Then, tally the number of points assigned to each answer for your score. At the end, see what the specialists think.

	Yes	No
1. Will you be able to cut back your hours at work gradually instead of all at once? *Change may exact a toll if it's too abrupt. Making the transition slowly gives you time to adjust at your own pace.*	☐ +3	☐ −3
2. Are you married? *Being unmarried can reduce life expectancy more than smoking or being overweight.*	☐ +4	☐ −4
If you're married: a) Is your marriage satisfying? *Retirement can put a strain on your relationship with your spouse. If you don't get along before you retire, chances are things will get worse afterward.*	☐ +2	☐ −2
b) If your spouse is working, will he or she retire at about the same time as you? *An increasingly common problem occurs when the husband retires while his younger wife continues to work; it often reduces his self-esteem and creates confusion about household duties.*	☐ +3	☐ −3
If you're not married: a) Do you live with someone? *Although being in a satisfying marriage is the best way to overcome feelings of isolation, living with anyone is a close second.*	☐ +3	☐ −3
b) If you live alone, do you have daily contact with family or friends? *This is another substitute for a live-in companion.*	☐ +2	☐ −2
3. Do you have a place at home or outside of it where you can have total privacy? *Togetherness is fine—up to a point. Everybody needs a retreat.*	☐ +2	☐ −2
4. Do you have at least one person outside of the office—for example, your spouse, a friend, even your banker or broker—in whom you can confide? *Even if you rarely share intimacies, just the presence of a confidant is essential.*	☐ +4	☐ −4
5. Do you try not to hang around the office after the workday is over? *If you're spending too many hours at work, you may be dependent on the job for your social life. Letting go will be hard for you.*	☐ +3	☐ −3
6. Have you made any new friends outside of work this year? *Don't make the mistake of assuming your work colleagues will still have time for you after you retire.*	☐ +3	☐ −3

	Yes	No

7. Are you involved with community, church, or cultural groups? □ +4 □ −4
Such activities may prove to be the center of your post-work days. Don't wait until retirement to get involved outside your job.

8. Do you schedule activities—fishing trips, museum visits, picnics—to fill up your free time? □ +3 □ −3
Retirement may well be the first time in 40 years that you will control your own time. You should know how to plan your days without a boss looking over your shoulder.

9. Have you taken part in an intellectual pursuit, such as attending a class or lecture, or a physical one, such as a competitive sport, in the past month? □ +2 □ −2
Aim for a variety of activities. Just because you like fishing doesn't mean that after retirement you will enjoy it every day.

10. Have you learned something new—say, a foreign language or gourmet cooking—in the past five years? □ +2 □ −2
Taking on new challenges shows an openness to change.

11. Were you able to adjust easily when your children left home or during other periods of major change? □ +4 □ −4
If you have been able to weather most of life's changes, you'll almost surely adjust well to retirement.

12. Are you looking forward to retirement? □ +3 □ −3
Your attitude can cast a shadow over everything. A negative one could become a self-fulfilling prophecy.

If you score 18 points or above, you're on solid footing. Between zero and 18, you have some catching up to do. Below zero, you need to work hard on improving your emotional preparation for retiring. The American Association of Retired Persons can help. Write for a list of its guidebooks to AIM Guidebooks, P.O. Box 19269-A, Washington, D.C. 20036.

The Cassies: Making a Hobby Work

When Ken Cassie, 52, took early retirement in 1988 after teaching Russian for 26 years in New Jersey public schools, a friend gave him a T-shirt declaring, *i'm going to pot*. That's exactly what he is doing, with his wife, Shelley, 53, who also quit her job teaching high school English to become his business manager. The Cassies couldn't have retired so young if they hadn't methodically molded Ken's pottery hobby into a profitable sideline, selling his wares at local craft shows. Ken enjoys having time now to pursue an activity "where the product of my labor will be visible." For Shelley, retirement is freedom. "We are now the masters of our own time," she exults. "It's really a dream come true."

It all began in 1976 when a friend lent Ken a potter's wheel. Two years later, he and Shelley began selling creations that now include 62 items ranging from tiny vases for $3.95 to $135 birdbaths. Ken's artistic flair is only half the story. "Without Shelley's marketing skills, there would be no direction and I would just be up in the studio throwing pots," concedes Ken. Together, they created a way to evaluate a craft show's potential profitability through a nine-criteria test, ranging from the cost of hotels to the ease of unloading their van to the entrance fees. The couple generally avoid shows costing more than $350 to enter and those farther than four hours away.

The couple, who live in the shoreside community of Brielle, gave up combined annual wages exceeding $80,000 for a more modest and volatile income flow. They expect to gross about $20,000 annually from their pottery sales, netting $12,000. The Cassies also generate about $4,000 a year from two neighboring rental houses they bought with friends. Their pensions will bring in about $32,000 per annum. So all together, their income will be about $48,000 a year. In addition, Shelley has accumulated $100,000 in her tax-deferred school annuity, which they can tap anytime.

Although financing their brave new world worked on paper, the Cassies did a year's trial run before making the final decision to retire. They lived solely on Ken's salary—about $45,000—a bit below their expected retirement income. The couple found they had to economize. So they cut out luxurious lunches on the road, managed without a housekeeper, and shared expenses with a jewelry-designing couple while on the exhibition circuit.

Since retirement, Ken has been in his studio about 4½ hours a day, seven days a week, throwing, glazing, and firing. But he also jogs four miles and swims one mile every day. Shelley is close behind, running three miles and swimming half a mile. The Cassies plan to take a break from pottery in the craft-show circuit's off months of January and February. They expect to paint and wallpaper their house and visit their daughter, Elise, 25, a veterinary technician who lives in Fort Myers Beach, Florida. Beginning next year, the couple look forward to spending one winter month abroad.

Ken says he and Shelley look at their retirement not as a denouement, but as another stage of their "evolution." They'll keep turning out pottery only as long as it remains a labor of love. Says Ken: "We didn't leave one job to become slaves to another."

Working after Retirement

As in Ken Cassie's case, chances are there's another job—maybe even a whole new career—in your retirement, even if you won't need the pay. What with longer, healthier lives and earlier, richer retirements, middle-aged Americans face a prospect that would have startled their parents: decades of active, useful living after they receive the golden handshake. What sensible person whose life has largely been defined by work would want to laze through so many potentially fruitful years? Here are answers to some of the first questions you are apt to ask about that next big step:

Why should I work after I retire? To begin with, you may have no choice. Inflation, poor planning, and an inadequate pension may force the issue. And even if you don't need a job to make ends meet, you may decide you want one just to keep active and healthy—benefits that become more crucial as you get older.

Does it pay to keep working? If you're well off, you could wind up losing money by working. Social Security and tax code provisions penalize people who earn too much in retirement. For example, if you had gone back to work in 1989 and you were between the ages of 62 and 64, you would have lost one dollar of Social Security benefits for every two dollars you earned above $6,120. Between 65 and 69, the earnings limit is $8,400. Once you reach age 70, you can earn as much as you like without penalty. In addition, you have to pay federal tax on up to 50% of your Social Security benefits if the total of your adjusted gross income, tax-exempt income, and half your Social Security benefits exceeds $25,000 ($32,000 if you are married). On top of all this, your paycheck may push you into a higher tax bracket. However, if you keep working and put off collecting Social Security until you are 70, you will receive an extra 3% in benefits when you do get around to retiring.

How do I decide what type of job is right for me?
Like most retirees, you may want to stay with what you know, albeit on a part-time basis. If you have the zest for a change, do some homework at a library. Ask for *The Occupational Outlook Handbook* or *The Encyclopedia of Careers and Vocational Guidance*. Both provide detailed information on hundreds of careers. Some of the most successful second careers spring from a lifelong dream, a hobby, or an interest shared with a friend. Also talk with people who are working in occupations you think you might enjoy. Once you've made your choice, you can launch a job search.

When and how should I begin planning my retirement career?
Start as soon as you can—certainly well before you call it quits at your present job. If you want to change fields, begin planning at least five years before you retire. This will give you time to take classes and meet people in your field of interest. Even if you want to stay in the same field, it's a good idea to research potential employers a year or two before your planned retirement.

What is the best way to find a job?
Most career counselors answer this question with a buzz word: networking. Make a list of everyone you know—friends, relatives, business relations, old school chums, even distant acquaintances—who may be able to help you find a job,

whether it is in your old field or a new one. You often can make useful contacts at career seminars or by joining professional organizations. If you don't know anyone at a company you are interested in, try to find out the name of the person who has the power to hire you. Look in the *Reference Book of Corporate Managements* or *Standard & Poor's Register*, available at most libraries. Or phone the personnel department at the company. Then write a letter to that executive detailing your skills and interests. After a week or so, follow up with a phone call. Be cordial but persistent. Typically, you will have to be interviewed by 20 to 30 people, and it may take anywhere from three months to a year before a job offer materializes.

Will I be offered a lower salary because I am receiving a pension? The practice still exists at many companies, but habits are changing. Federal law protects older job seekers from arbitrary hiring and salary discrimination. And employers are coming to appreciate that older workers are usually well worth full pay. If you are asked your salary expectations, be assertive. To protect yourself from being shortchanged, find out what the average salary is for the position you want. Career counselors or library research can help. Should you meet all the job qualifications for a position in your old field, it's fair to request the middle to high end of the salary range. If you are changing fields and need training, you should expect your salary to be at the low end of the scale.

Should I prepare for conflicts with younger colleagues? Conflicts sometimes do occur, but the best preparation is the confidence of knowing that you're probably more experienced than younger workers. If you feel someone is treating you unfairly because of your age, discuss the matter in a friendly, professional manner. If your troubles continue, you can complain to your superior. If you are at least 40 years old and the person causing your difficulties is in a higher position, you can complain to your local Equal Employment Opportunity Commission office. The commission will investigate to determine whether your accusation has merit. If the EEOC finds your grievance valid, typically it will try to resolve it by conciliation before going to court. You can also sue independently, but that can take months.

Should I consider starting my own business? Probably not. While independence sounds exhilarating, don't forget that 66% of small businesses fail within five years, usually because of poor planning or lack of funds.

If you are convinced that you are an entrepreneur, seek advice from people who have started their own businesses. The Service Corps of Retired Executives, sponsored by the Small Business Administration, holds seminars on starting your own business and provides free advice. Look for SCORE's address in your local telephone directory under U.S. Government/SBA/SCORE or call 800-368-5855 for the number of the SCORE chapter nearest you.

Where can I go for job training and placement?
Your first and best source is your present employer. More and more companies offer job planning and counseling. Another option is to call your state job training or employment service (look in the telephone book under State Government Offices). Many have listings for older workers or can direct you to placement services in your area. Private career counselors provide occupational testing, one-on-one counseling, and training in job-search skills. But if your employer doesn't pay the fees for you, be prepared for charges that can run into the thousands.

Another excellent source of help is the growing number of nonprofit organizations set up to assist older workers. The American Association of Retired Persons is launching AARP Works, an employment planning program available in 12 locations. For information, write to the Worker Equity Department, AARP, 1909 K Street N.W., Washington, D.C. 20049. Operation Able offers help to seniors looking for employment in seven states (Arkansas, California, Massachusetts, Michigan, Nebraska, New York, and Vermont). Write to Operation Able, 36 South Wabash Street, Suite 1133, Chicago, IL 60603, to find the affiliate closest to you. You can also write for nonpaying consulting work to the National Executive Service Corps (257 Park Avenue South, New York, NY 10010), a volunteer placement service for retired executives. Small and medium-size businesses often recruit through its job search division.

How to Reach Your Goals

Chapter Two

*H*aving money in the family. What an idle dream it
seemed when you started out in your first apartment with
a few wedding presents and a batch of furniture the
Salvation Army would not take. Your rent seemed bigger
than the national debt and, to make ends meet, you drove
an Own-a-Wreck and survived on a diet of meatless
meat loaf.

Now that you have progressed in life and career, it is
easy to see how your standard of living has advanced.
And if you are in your forties or fifties, you may be
surprised to discover when you tot up your assets that
you have accumulated a stunning sum. If you are younger,
you may be equally amazed at your potential for doing so.
Indeed, wealth—a term once reserved for the few—is
beginning to touch the many. Internal Revenue Service
surveys of estates reveal that the number of millionaires
doubled between 1976 and 1982, the most recent year for
which figures are available. Another 850,000 people had
assets of at least $500,000, and half a million owned more
than $250,000.

Most people on their way to such wealth consider
themselves solidly middle-income folks who will work,
save, and invest their way to upper assetdom. Yet with
affluence comes responsibility. On the one hand, there is
the risk of mismanagement and loss; on the other, the
opportunity to enlarge your net worth, to secure your
retirement nest egg, and to pass some of it along to your
heirs. This chapter lays out the basic game plan for
evaluating and reaching these goals. Subsequent chapters
will discuss in detail how to tailor strategies to your
family's profile. Developing a plan that works best for you
demands time, discipline, and the guidance of specialists,
such as financial planners, experienced in negotiating the
maze of wealth management. But that's a small price to
pay for the luxury of knowing you and your children will
be provided for.

Start your asset-building program by making the most
of what you have. You should pay close attention to your

employee-benefits plans—particularly those to which you contribute. They have gained greatly in value because they allow you to stack up tax-deferred savings. Examine your investments: there may be sensible ways to invest that you have never thought of. Your house is probably the foundation of your family wealth because its value has boomed over the past decade or so. Yet it may diminish in relative importance in the future even though it keeps pace with inflation. By coordinating these three elements, you can achieve both security and growth:

Your benefits. The funds stored in your employee-benefits plans may well turn out to be the stars of your future personal finances. That is because these plans typically offer more opportunity for tax-free buildup and more choice of investments than you might otherwise have access to. While every company has its own wrinkles, employee-benefits plans fall into two major categories: defined benefit and defined contribution.

The first, which has been around for decades, is simply your pension plan. Defined benefit means that the company puts away money for you and decides what you get—based on a formula—when you retire. Spurred by tax breaks for themselves as well as their employees, more and more companies have added defined-contribution plans. These allow employees to put aside a portion of their salaries in a fund to which the company also adds. There are two types of such plans: matching programs, in which a company contributes a specified percentage—usually 50%—of what you invest, and profit-sharing arrangements under which your employer adds a portion of profits to your savings. Additionally, you may be offered an employee stock-ownership program (ESOP). Your employer will typically match up to 50% of the amount you invest in shares of company stock.

In both types of plans, defined-benefit and defined-contribution, funds accrete quietly and inexorably until they total surprisingly large sums. At the Bechtel Group, a $55,000-a-year design engineer who left after 21 years of service walked away with $314,000 from various plans. An ESOP would have added even more. The National Center for Employee Ownership in Oakland, California found that employees who earned $35,000 a year at companies with ESOPs can generally leave their jobs

after 20 years with proceeds from an ESOP of more than
$200,000.

Defined-contribution plans offer far more opportunity
for wealth building than do pension plans. If you leave
your company, you can take all your contributions with
you, and the company's contribution vests more quickly
than in pension plans—usually after one to three years of
employment. Furthermore, many companies let you contribute to these plans as part of 401(k) salary-reduction
programs. That is the best arrangement of all because it
puts you three giant steps forward. First, you can exclude
your contribution—up to $7,627 in 1989—from your tax-
able income. Second, you get an immediate gain on your
investment because your employer matches it. Finally,
the earnings are not taxed until you begin withdrawing
them at age 59½. If you change jobs before then, you can
roll over the funds into an IRA that continues the tax-
deferred buildup.

Perhaps even more important, defined-contribution
plans usually give you more than one investment option.
The choices may include your company's stock, diversified portfolios of stocks and bonds that operate much like
mutual funds, and guaranteed investment contracts—
loans to large insurance companies that promise a fixed
rate of return slightly higher than bank certificates of
deposit. With most plans you can choose between two
different types of investments, usually a growth fund and
an income fund. If you are close to retirement and are
leery of taking risks with your money, you will probably
want to choose an income fund or guaranteed investment
contract that pays steady dividends. If you have just
started your career, however, you may prefer to invest for
growth in stock funds. Although you may go for growth
when the stock market is about to take a deep dive, such
moves are at least partly offset by the company's matching contribution. The same holds true for your ESOP.
Even if your employer's stock sags, the match will compensate for temporary drops in value.

When you retire, your company may offer you several
payment options for your pension. The two most common choices are a monthly check or a lump sum, which is
typically based on your length of service, final five years'
pay, and life expectancy. Deciding which to take requires
detailed computations. The wealth-building point that

many Americans are learning to take with increasing seriousness: if you believe you can invest the lump sum profitably enough to equal the pension you would otherwise get, you can also leave behind a sizable legacy. An added incentive: the tax bite on lump sums taken at retirement can be moderate. Almost everybody who retires after age 59½ is eligible for five-year forward averaging, which lets you spread out the lump as though it were paid in equal installments over five years. While the entire tax bill must be paid the year you receive the lump sum, forward averaging will significantly lower your bracket.

Your investments. One factor you should take into account in designing your investment portfolio is the security of your income, notes Gerald Perritt, editor of the *Mutual Fund Letter*. That is because people's investment inclinations often mirror the way they earn their money. For example, a freelance writer, a musician, or a salesperson on commission might earn $35,000 one year, $60,000 the next, and $10,000 the third year. Yet these are the types of people, says Perritt, who tend to invest in chancy emerging growth stocks, risky venture-capital deals, and highly leveraged real estate projects. Such an individual might instead be better off hedging with safer vehicles—CDs, Treasury bills, or mutual funds with holdings in stocks that pay dividends and promise some growth. By contrast, a corporate employee with a secure job who earns $50,000 a year and has a generous, diversified portfolio in his employee-benefits plans is often inclined to invest his spare cash in a safe but stodgy mutual fund. In this case, advises Perritt, the person can obviously afford to look for a little more bang in his personal investments.

If your analysis of your income tells you that you should be investing some of your spare cash more aggressively, but you are the type of person who frets over every decision, you might adopt a strategy called dollar-cost averaging. With this technique, you merely pick a mutual fund that matches your investment goals and tolerance of risk and invest equal sums periodically. This way, you will be purchasing fewer of the fund's shares when securities prices are high and more when prices dip. To make dollar-cost averaging work, you have to have the discipline to keep writing those regular checks even when your investment plunges. No-load growth mutual funds are ideal vehicles for this approach.

Another wealth-building avenue is to invest in mutual funds inside tax-deferring envelopes such as rollover IRAs. (If you are covered by a company pension plan and earn more than $25,000—$40,000 for a couple—you can no longer fully deduct your contribution to a standard IRA.) Single-premium deferred annuities, sold by insurance companies, operate in a similar fashion. You buy an annuity—the lowest priced is $5,000—with after-tax dollars, but your gains accumulate tax-free. Some annuities promise a specified annual return; others may offer a choice among as many as 15 different funds and allow you to add small deposits monthly or quarterly so that you can dollar-cost average. You have to choose carefully, however, because many insurance companies extract hefty fees.

Your house. This remains the most valuable asset most families acquire. Indeed, in 1984, the Census Bureau estimated that a house represented about 41% of a typical family's worth. Housing economists, however, are not forecasting the same heady gains for houses that they enjoyed in the inflation-ridden late 1970s and early 1980s. Expect instead that the single-family house (median price today: $93,100) will track inflation over the long run. That means your home will more likely be a source of capital preservation rather than capital growth.

While boosts in housing prices generally have occurred more slowly in recent low-inflation years, they are expected to cool out before long. About two-thirds of all sales are trade-ups, a factor that has papered over the lackluster pace of first-home sales. John Tuccillo, chief economist for the National Association of Realtors, anticipates that the heavy demand for trade-up houses will continue only until the mid-1990s. New households will then be formed from among the less populous baby-bust generation. Demand will flatten, and inflation alone will dictate increases in house prices, he predicts.

Owning an asset whose value keeps pace with inflation is just one of the reasons for pursuing the American Dream of home ownership. For example, making regular payments on the mortgage is a method of disciplined savings that works well for those who would normally

spend every dollar they earn. Owning a house also qualifies you for one of the few remaining tax shelters available to individuals: deductions for property taxes and
mortgage interest. When you sell, you can defer taxes on
the profits if you put them into a new house within two
years. And at age 55, you can exclude $125,000 of your
gain from taxation.

However impressive the fortune you ultimately create,
you probably will have a harder time in the future ensuring that your family—and not the IRS or your state—is
your prime beneficiary. Currently, estate taxes do not
inhibit the passage of wealth within most families; the
federal tax code exempts $600,000 for individuals ($1.2
million for a husband and wife). Above those limits, the
IRS takes 40% to 55%. So if you and your spouse die at the
same time and leave $1,200,001, the most the estate will
owe in federal taxes is 40 % of $1—40 cents.

Those generous limits are being scrutinized by an increasingly stingy Congress, which is threatening to
toughen death taxes. Raising the percentage that the IRS
can claim, scaling back the exemption for individuals and
couples, and taxing appreciated assets are all ways that
Congress may choose to respond to the pressure to
increase revenues and help reduce the budget deficit.

No matter how confiscatory estate taxes become, it is
still better to have created a small family fortune than not.
And who knows what it might grow to in another generation or two.

Figuring What You Will Need

Of all the major milestones in life—graduating from
college, say, or getting married—retiring from work may
be the only one in which the decisive consideration is
whether you can afford to do it. Indeed, financial independence does not come cheap. It means being able to
support your pre-retirement standard of living for as long
as three decades in the face of an unpredictable economy
and implacable inflation. Financial security in retirement
is not a birthright; to get it, you have to plan for it.

The first step in setting your goals is to decide how
much income you will require in retirement. If you are
more than 10 years away from calling it quits, you

The Actual Costs of Retirement

The rule of thumb is that you will need an annual retirement income amounting to 70% to 80% of your current earnings.

Whatever the life style you envision, the best way to ensure that you can pay for it is to plan as far ahead as possible. The first step is to determine what your annual expenses are likely to be. The worksheet on the facing page will help you do that.

Despite the diversity in retirement living, financial planners surveyed by MONEY note at least some similarities in spending patterns after age 65. For example, most retirees spend about the same amount on food, gifts, charitable contributions, and personal care as they did while working. Medical and dental bills, on the other hand, are significantly higher, depending on how generous your company's retirement coverage is.

Here are guidelines to help you fill out the worksheet. The column listing the national average in 1986 expenditures of families earning $40,000 or more gives you a rough basis of comparison for your own spending.

Line 1: If you pay off your mortgage and take care of all necessary maintenance problems before you retire, housing costs should drop by as much as 25% to 30%. Count on even more shrinkage if you sell your house and buy a smaller one. Condominium owners and renters should factor in maintenance-fee and rent increases. And anyone who plans to spend more time at home should anticipate higher utilities charges.

Line 2: Financial planners estimate that if you are moving from business suits to jeans, you can expect to reduce clothing expenses by 20% to 35%.

Line 4: Scratch commuting costs. Otherwise, transportation expenses will increase if you intend to be very active.

Line 6: Most people keep giving the same amounts to charitable, political, and educational institutions, as well as to family members. But the overall figure drops, usually by the amount you used to give at the office.

Line 7: If your kids will be grown by the time you retire, you can eliminate education expenses, unless you plan to help pay your grandchildren's college bills. And if you intend to return to school yourself, check into reduced tuition costs for senior citizens.

Line 8: There will be little change in your payout for property, liability, and auto insurance, but retirees can generally reduce their life insurance coverage by at least 50% or, if their spouses are fully provided for under their pension plan, eliminate it altogether.

Line 9: If you are currently covered by a company health plan, expect medical and dental costs to spurt by about 50% because of increased illnesses combined with reduced insurance coverage. Medicare pays only about one-fifth of doctors' fees and less than one-third of hospital bills. Check your company's coverage for retirees. You will probably find you need additional Medigap coverage, which runs an average of $42 a month.

Line 10: You should plan to be debt-free by the time you retire, thereby eliminating loan repayment expenses.

Line 12: How much you spend for entertainment depends on how active you are. On average, expect such expenditures to increase by about 20% during your retirement.

Line 13: Budget for high veterinary bills if you will have an aging dog, cat, or other pet.

Line 14: While your contributions to pension plans cease at retirement, many financial planners encourage clients to continue setting aside about 10% of their income as a hedge against inflation.

Line 15: Unless you have some kind of job, it's farewell at last to Social Security (FICA) taxes. Also, check out the tax laws in your state because some don't tax income from retirement plans. The conventional wisdom that you will be in a lower tax bracket after retirement is no longer true under tax reform for people earning more than $75,000 annually. Moreover, married couples filing jointly whose total earnings exceed $32,000 ($25,000 for single retirees) could pay tax on up to 50% of their Social Security benefits.

Line 16: With more adult kids expecting financial help from Mom and Dad and Americans' increasing longevity, you could be contributing to the down payment on a child's first house while paying for a parent's nursing home.

Total current expenditures should equal 100% of your current before-tax income. By dividing your total expenditures at retirement by your current gross income, you will arrive at the percentage of your current income that you will need in retirement.

Expenditures	At retirement	Current year	National average
1 Housing. Rent, mortgage, property taxes, utilities (gas, oil, electricity, and water), telephone, home furnishings, household services, maintenance, improvements			$12,674
2 Clothing. Purchases and cleaning			2,354
3 Food. (including tobacco and alcohol)			6,242
4 Transportation. Car repair and maintenance, installment payments, gas, commuting costs, other			9,331
5 Gifts.			N.A.
6 Contributions.			1,785
7 Education.			676
8 Insurance. Life, medical, auto, property, liability			571
9 Medical and Dental Care. Premiums, deductible, and out-of-pocket costs			1,471
10 Loan-Repayment Costs.			N.A.
11 Personal Care. Grooming, health club, other			360
12 Entertainment. Vacations, dining out, movies, plays, concerts, sports events, cable TV, videocassettes, entertaining, sports, hobbies, other			2,282
13 Pet Expenses.			N.A.
14 Savings and Retirement. Contribution to company plans, IRAs, Keoghs, SEPs, other savings, investments			5,405
15 Taxes. Federal, FICA, state, local			6,660
16 Support of Relatives.			N.A.
Total Expenditures. (add lines 1 through 16)			49,811
Total Current Expenditures Divided By Current Gross Income.			100%
Total Expenditures At Retirement Divided By Current Gross Income.			

obviously won't be able to predict your retirement expenses accurately, but the worksheet on page 36 will help you form a reliable estimate. Then, you can compare this amount with figures on another worksheet on page 40, used by financial planners to determine how much you will need to maintain your standard of living later on. By measuring your income needs against the resources you will have in retirement, such as Social Security and your company pension, you can calculate how much capital you must accumulate. Equally important, you can use this information to implement a savings plan.

You can count on a lower tax bill in retirement. Leaving the payroll means you no longer have to pay the Social Security tax, which in 1989 siphoned as much as $3,380 from a worker's salary and $5,860 from self-employment income. Your Social Security benefit may be partly taxable if you take in more than $32,000 ($25,000 if you are single), but at least half your benefit still escapes the tax man. The pleasantly surprising conclusion is that you generally can expect to live as well in retirement as you do now on 70% to 80% of your current income.

The unpleasant surprise of retirement planning is that the combination of Social Security and pension benefits is unlikely to give you the income you need. Even if you spend a couple of decades with a fairly generous employer, you can generally expect the combination to replace no more than 40% to 60% of your salary in the first year you are retired. The rest will have to come from the capital you build up in your IRA, your Keogh plan, your personal investments, and any capital-accumulation plan offered by your employer, such as a profit-sharing or 401(k) account. How much capital will it take to make up that income gap? A married couple retiring at age 65 should figure on about $179,000 of capital for each $10,000 that their pension and Social Security benefits fall short of their yearly income needs. Thus, if you need to replace $25,000 of annual income in retirement, the price of a worry-free retirement would be nearly $450,000.

Part of the reason you require so much capital is that the money has to last as long as you do. The median life expectancy is 20 years for a man at age 60 years and 25 for a woman. Thus, you have a 50% chance of outliving the median life expectancy assigned to you when you retire. As a result, you may want to base your planning on the assumption that you will live longer than 85% of the people your age. So, a 60-year-old man could feel secure with savings sufficient to meet his income needs to age 90; a woman of the same age should lay in enough to reach 94.

The other contingency that boosts the cost of financial independence is inflation. Because your Social Security benefits increase in step with the consumer price index, your benefits will continue to provide the same proportion of your retirement income in later years as in the year you left work. Almost no private employers' pensions are indexed to inflation, however. Consequently, your capital must be large enough so that it earns more than you need to live on, leaving you a surplus to reinvest. Later, as inflation pushes your expenses ahead of your investment earnings, you will have enough stashed away to meet the added need by dipping into principal without having to worry about running out of money ahead of schedule.

While the sums you may have to save for retirement may seem imposing, the job of accumulating them need not be—if you start early. Assuming your investments grow at the conservative pace of three or four percentage points over the inflation rate—which recently was about 4.2% annually—you could build a retirement chest of $179,000 (in 1988 dollars) by saving only $6,600 a year. (The calculation includes the amounts your employer contributes to your capital-accumulation plan at work, if you began 20 years before you retire.) If you postpone saving until you are only 10 years from the finish line, you would have to set aside more than $15,600 a year.

Help from Planners

If you already have set unambiguous retirement goals and are confident that your assets and your current investment program will add up to what you'll require when you stop working, the advice you can get from a broker on investments, an attorney on estate planning, and an accountant on tax matters may be sufficient. But if you're a haphazard saver, or you don't relish coordinating advice from several professionals, then you should at least consider hiring a financial planner.

How Much Should You Save?

The worksheet at right will tell you roughly how much you need to start saving now to hold on to your standard of living in retirement. The multipliers used in lines 7, 9, and 11 allow for inflation by assuming your investments will grow at three percentage points over the inflation rate, before and after retirement. This keeps all figures in 1988 dollars.

Line 3: If you and your spouse are over 60, you can ask your local Social Security office to estimate the annual benefits you each have earned, or you can calculate them yourself with the help of a Social Security pamphlet called *Estimating Your Social Security Retirement Check.* (For a very rough estimate of your benefit, fill in $10,000 if you make $45,000 or more; if you make between $18,000 and $45,000, enter between $7,500 and $10,000.)

Line 4: Your company benefits department may be able to estimate your pension. Make sure the estimate assumes that you continue working until your retirement age at your current salary. That will somewhat understate your likely eventual payout but will keep the figure in 1988 dollars.

Line 7: The multipliers in column A incorporate the cautious assumption that men will live to 90 and women to 94—longer than 85% of them do now. Single men should use the multiplier under "men." Women and couples should use the one under "women," since wives usually outlive husbands.

Line 8: Your personal retirement portfolio includes any investments you have specifically earmarked for

1. Current gross income _____

2. Annual income needed in retirement, in 1988 dollars (70% of line 1) _____

3. Annual Social Security retirement benefits _____

4. Annual pension benefits _____

5. Guaranteed annual retirement income (line 3 plus line 4) _____

6. Additional retirement income needed (line 2 minus line 5) _____

7. Capital required to provide additional retirement income (line 6 times multiplier from column A at right) _____

8. Amount you have saved already

   _____ + _____ + _____ = _____
   personal   IRA/Keogh   employer-   total savings
   retirement   sponsored
   portfolio   savings plans

9. What your current investments will have grown to by the time you retire (total from line 8 times multiplier from column B at right) _____

10. Additional retirement capital required (line 7 minus line 9) _____

11. Total annual savings still needed (line 10 times factor from column C at right) _____

12. Annual employer contributions to your company saving plans _____

13. Amount you need to set aside each year (line 11 minus line 12) _____

AGE AT WHICH YOU EXPECT TO RETIRE	MULTIPLIER A	
	men	women
55	22.1	23.5
56	21.8	23.2
57	21.4	22.8
58	21.0	22.5
59	20.6	22.1
60	20.2	21.8
61	19.8	21.4
62	19.3	21.0
63	18.9	20.6
64	18.4	20.2
65	17.9	19.8
66	17.4	19.3
67	16.9	18.9

TIME UNTIL YOU EXPECT TO RETIRE	MULTIPLIER B	MULTIPLIER C
1 year	1.03	1.00
3 years	1.09	.324
5 years	1.16	.188
7 years	1.23	.131
9 years	1.30	.098
11 years	1.38	.078
13 years	1.47	.064
15 years	1.56	.054
20 years	1.81	.037

retirement, aside from your IRA or Keogh. For your employer-sponsored savings plans, check the most recent statement from your 401(k), profit-sharing, thrift, or stock ownership plan and total your vested balance in each.

Line 12: Consult the most recent annual statement from these plans to find the amount your company contributed on your behalf to each of the plans last year. Enter the total.

The kind of help you'll require and how much you should pay for it depend largely on what you can realistically afford and when you hope to retire. Some planners offer tax planning, legal counsel, and investment advice in addition to broad strategies for meeting your goals. Most will sell you such investments as insurance, for which they earn commissions. Fees are often steep. Full-blown initial plans, which typically cover every aspect of your financial life from here to the grave, cost from $500 to $5,000. Only wealthier clients, whose finances are complex, should have to pay the higher fees.

If you're still in your twenties or thirties, a financial planner can help you build assets to meet interim goals and give you a jump on building a retirement nest egg. Planning becomes more critical after you enter your forties. As your children scatter, your career progresses, and your assets accumulate, you can begin to set retirement goals based on more realistic projections of earnings, investment returns, and inflation. A financial planner can help you set more rigid guidelines for saving toward retirement.

The closer you are to calling it quits, the fewer your financial options—and the simpler your retirement-planning needs. You may be able to find answers to your most important questions for less than $1,000. Some first-rate planners offer formal pre-retirement studies for $500 or so. Others will sell you a chunk of their time, typically for $100 or more an hour. Write to the Institute of Certified Financial Planners (10065 East Harvard Avenue, Suite 3320, Denver, CO 80231) for a list of planners in your area.

Many large companies have pre-retirement seminars for employees, and if you're eligible you should attend. Otherwise, it might make sense to spend up to $250 or so for a computerized financial plan that many banks, insurance companies, and other institutions offer. Consumer Financial Institute (288 Walnut Street, Newton, MA 02160) offers such a detailed plan to people within five years of retirement. It costs $300.

Weaving a Sturdy Safety Net

Chapter Three

*A*lthough it is never too late to start saving for your
retirement, the ideal time to begin the process is soon
after you go to work. Like it or not, the government
automatically imposes the discipline with its payroll tax
for Social Security—the old-age safety net for most Americans. For all the concerns about the fiscal health of the
retirement program, you can still count on Uncle Sam to
pay benefits through at least the first decade of the next
century. After that, Social Insecurity could possibly arise
as the large baby-boom generation finally reaches retirement age.

The best conduits for personal retirement savings are
tax-advantaged accounts that magnify returns by allowing investment earnings to compound tax-free until withdrawal at retirement or upon disability. The old standby,
the Individual Retirement Account, may still make sense
if you are eligible to deduct annual contributions from
your taxable earnings. Better yet are fully deductible
contributions to company-sponsored savings plans (dis-
cussed in the next chapter) and their Keogh cousins for
self-employed workers and moonlighters. If your employer doesn't offer a tax-sheltering savings vehicle, your
insurance agent or stockbroker almost certainly does.
While you are working, you can stash savings in a deferred annuity and watch your principal grow unchecked
by taxes. After you retire, you can use that money or
other funds to buy an immediate annuity, which then
starts paying you monthly income for the rest of your life.
So-called cash-value life insurance is another alternative.

Social Security Simplified

Despite a persistently spreading fear that the government's retirement program will fold, Social Security is
here for the long term. True, the program has needed
bolstering in the 1980s to ensure benefits for workers
now nearing retirement. But the system will be on firm

footing when today's 40- to 60-year-olds retire. Theoretically, Social Security could go bankrupt early in the next century when today's young workers retire; politically, there's little chance that such a debacle will occur. Instead, the rules will change in ways no one can now predict with absolute certainty.

So try to put aside the rhetoric and start analyzing the benefit you almost certainly will get. In 1989, a 65-year-old can retire and receive up to $10,788 a year. Generally, you must work 40 quarters or 10 years before Social Security will pay you a retirement benefit. (People who are now 60 to 65 need 34 to 39 quarters.) Not everyone who works that long will get a Social Security check. If you are paid by a nonprofit organization, such as a museum or hospital, most of your working years probably won't count toward earning a Social Security benefit. Only employment since January 1, 1984 at a nonprofit institution will be used in the benefit formula, unless you've paid in Social Security taxes all along. About one-third of employees of state and local governments and all federal employees hired before January 1984 aren't covered by Social Security. Federal government workers hired since then are covered.

As do most companies, the Social Security Administration pays full benefits to employees who retire at 65 and cuts payouts for workers who quit earlier. You can't apply for your own retirement check until age 62, and it will be 80% of the amount you would get by waiting until age 65. Starting in the year 2000 and lasting through 2022, the early-retirement benefit for a 62-year-old will be nipped by about .8% a year. So by 2022, early-retirement checks from Social Security will be only 70% of full benefits.

Social Security rewards workers who put off their benefits past 65. Soon the lure will be more enticing. Today, Social Security enlarges your retirement check by 3% for each year you delay taking full benefits between age 65 and 70; that's in addition to the annual cost-of-living increase. The delayed retirement credit will inch up a bit for anyone turning 65 in 1990 or later. The credit will increase by one-half of 1% every other year until it reaches 8% in 2008. But don't put off taking your Social Security benefit at 65 just to get a larger check later. The extra money you receive from the delayed retirement credit won't equal the Social Security income you could have been accepting starting at 65.

The retirement program also sticks it to some people who just can't call it quits. The government cuts benefits by $1 for every $2 you earn in wages over a certain threshold between ages 62 and 69. That's done so the retirement funds won't overly subsidize people earning income. In 1989, the threshold is $8,880 for between 65 and 70, and it's $6,480 for those 62 through 64. So if you are 65 to 70 and earn more than $32,000 in 1989, you could lose all your Social Security benefit. In 1990, the penalty will be reduced. Then you will lose $1 for every $3 in earnings over the threshold, which will increase yearly with wage inflation.

Social Security won't start sending you a check until you notify the local office that you're ready. File an application three months before you want the first monthly check to arrive and be sure to bring or send in a certified copy of your birth certificate. If you expect a check for your spouse's benefit, you will need a certified copy of your marriage license. Divorcees filing for benefits have to present certified copies of marriage and divorce papers. In the January check, benefits automatically rise by the increase in the previous year's cost of living. If inflation is less than 3%, however, Congress must vote to raise Social Security checks by that amount.

If you're married but only one of you worked for pay, Social Security will send you one monthly check equal to 1½ times the worker's entitlement, provided the beneficiary doesn't start collecting until age 65. A nonworking spouse who collects Social Security at 62 will get only 37.5% of the worker's benefits. A working couple with only one spouse employed long enough to receive a full Social Security benefit at 65 will also get one monthly check of 150% of that spouse's entitlement. If the lower-earning spouse didn't earn enough to get a Social Security benefit equal to more than half the high-earning spouse's, the couple will also get a single check of 150% of the bigger benefit. Couples entitled to two full benefits are mailed separate checks, unless they request a single monthly payment. A divorced person can get the spouse's benefit at age 62, as long as the couple were married more than 10 years.

Women frequently can choose between collecting Social Security based on their own employment or taking a joint benefit based on their husbands' earnings. Financial planners urge working women to send for a statement of their Social Security earnings record once they reach age 55. (For details on obtaining your records, see "Sizing Up Your Future Check," page 50.) Then, the woman will know whether she has worked long enough to get a full benefit. If she hasn't, she might want to work a little longer to qualify. After that, she can compare her own benefit with her husband's to figure out whether they would be better off receiving one check based on his earnings or two checks based on their combined salaries.

From Social Security's inception in 1937 through 1983, all benefits were free of federal, state, and local taxes. Now, up to half your benefits could be subject to federal income taxes if the total of your adjusted gross income, tax-exempt interest, and half of your Social Security benefit exceeds $32,000 and you're married and filing jointly, or $25,000 and you're single. You will be taxed on half of any excess or half of your Social Security benefit, whichever is smaller. Say your adjusted gross income is $25,000, and this year you will get $10,000 in Social Security benefits and $5,000 in tax-exempt interest. You add half your benefit, or $5,000, and all the interest to your income for a total of $35,000. So if you're married, you will exceed the $32,000 cutoff by $3,000, and you will add half that, or $1,500, to your taxable income. Many states tax Social Security benefits, too. By the time the baby boomers, born between 1946 and 1964, reach retirement, at least half are likely to find their benefits taxed. Reason: The federal formula's thresholds aren't indexed to inflation, and in 30 years or so, many more retirees will have incomes exceeding $32,000.

No one knows exactly how Social Security will cope with the work force's evolution from yuppies to grumpies. By 2020, nearly twice as many people are expected to be collecting Social Security checks as today. Yet at that time, there should be only 2.4 workers paying Social Security taxes for each retiree. Today, the ratio is about 3 to 1; in 1945, it was 42 to 1. This much seems clear: Everyone who pays into the system will get a Social Security benefit. But analysts say these modifications are almost inevitable:

● Higher payroll taxes. In 1989, the Social Security tax

rate is 7.5% for salaried employees and 15% for the
self-employed (but a special tax credit drops their effective tax rate to 13%). The tax rates rise to 7.65% and 15.3%
in 1990, when self-employed workers will be able to
deduct from their gross income half their Social Security
taxes. Haeworth Robertson, former chief actuary of the
Social Security Administration, predicts the payroll tax
rate for employees will jump to between 12% and 20%
within 35 years. That would amount to a tax hike of
between 79% and 199%.

● A delay in the retirement age. Already, the age to get
full Social Security benefits is due to rise from 65 to 67 in
the year 2027. But don't rule out a retirement age of 68 or
even 69 if you now are in your twenties or early thirties.

● A cutback in the percentage of pay that Social Security
will replace. Today, a person consistently earning an
amount equal to the pay at which Social Security taxes
stop—$48,000 in 1989—will get 24% of his pre-retirement
pay from Social Security. In the next century, he might get
a benefit equal to 20%, and his benefit almost certainly
will be taxed.

Clearly, Social Security will get even more complicated.
The 1989 Guide to Social Security might help you understand the program better. You can get the $3 booklet,
published by William M. Mercer Meidinger Hansen Inc.,
one of the leading benefits consultants, by writing to the
company's Social Security division at 1500 Meidinger
Tower, Louisville, KY 40202. You should also keep up
with revisions in Social Security by stopping by the
agency's local office every few years once you reach your
mid-fifties and asking about any new laws or rules that
will affect your benefit. Starting a relationship early could
pay off later if you think your Social Security check might
be too small or too late.

Smart financial planning demands that you and your family understand how Social Security's retirement, survivor, and disability systems work. But Americans have become increasingly confused about the intricacies of the programs. The following questions and answers will help you sort through the tangle of Social Security rules:

What kind of benefits can I get? The Social Security system consists of three funds that pay benefits. The Old-Age and Survivors Insurance Trust Fund provides monthly checks to retirees, their families, and to families of deceased workers. The Disability Insurance Trust Fund pays benefits to disabled workers and their families. The Hospital Insurance Trust Fund pays Medicare claims.

I'm 30, expecting a baby, and planning to leave my job for a few years. How will that affect my benefits? As long as you eventually accrue 40 quarters of coverage, you will still get retirement benefits. The checks may be the same size or slightly smaller than if you did not take time off.

I'm married but have never worked for pay. Will I still get a Social Security retirement benefit? You will receive a benefit equal to 50% of your husband's or wife's by meeting three tests: you have been married at least a year, you have not earned enough Social Security coverage to get your own retirement benefit equal to more than 50% of your spouse's, and you wait until 65 to receive the benefits. If you start collecting the checks at age 62, your benefit will be only 37.5% of your spouse's, not 50%.

I was married for 15 years before I divorced my husband, and I have never worked for pay. Am I entitled to Social Security benefits as his former spouse? If you were married at least 10 years, have been divorced for at least two years, and remain single, you are eligible for spousal benefits at age 62. If you remarry at 60 or later and then retire, you will get benefits based either on your current spouse's earnings or your former spouse's, whichever are greater. If you tie the knot before

Common Questions about Social Security

60, however, your first marriage won't count for Social
Security purposes.

**I'm 35 and have a wife and a young daughter. If I
die tomorrow, what will Social Security pay them?**
Based on your age, your family will get special survivors
benefits if you have accumulated six quarters of earnings
out of the last 13—that is the equivalent of roughly $1\frac{1}{2}$
years of work. Your child under age 18 will receive 75% of
your retirement benefit until she turns 18, up to $9,600
annually. Your wife will get 75% of your benefit as long as
she is caring for a child under 16; she will receive your full
benefit when she is 65. Those survivor payments would
be smaller if you died at an older age, in part because
younger families tend to need more income. Social Security will also give your family a lump-sum payment of
$255 toward your funeral expenses, regardless of your
age at death.

Sizing Up Your Future Check

In the past, one of the biggest aggravations of Social
Security was getting an accurate estimate of the benefits
you could expect after retirement. If you knew the right
questions, you could write to the Social Security Administration, which months later would send back, piecemeal,
the scraps of information you had specifically requested.
No longer. In 1988, the agency began spelling out your
whole basket of benefits in an eight-page document called
Personal Earnings and Benefit Estimate Statement. To
get one, you simply call a toll-free number (800-937-2000)
and request Form SSA-7004. This is a questionnaire asking you for a number of facts about yourself, including
your name, Social Security number, date of birth, previous year's earnings, current year's estimated earnings, the
age at which you plan to retire, and your projected
earnings from now to retirement. About four to six weeks
after you send in the form, you can expect to receive this
list of estimated benefits:

• Your monthly retirement check from Social Security, in
today's dollars, at your stated retirement age. To arrive at
this figure, the Social Security Administration computer

assumes that your future annual earnings, net of inflation, will rise at the national average of 1% a year.

• The full benefit you could get by waiting until you are age 65 to retire. Under Social Security regulations, 65 will remain the standard retirement age until 1999. After that, the age for collecting a full benefit will start to rise at the rate of nearly one month per year. Someone born in 1939, for example, will have to wait four months after his or her 65th birthday to be eligible for a full retirement benefit. From that point on, the full-benefit retirement age keeps increasing until it gets to age 67 in 2027. There it will remain.

• The 33% larger benefit available to people your age who continue working until they are 70 years old.

• Your survivors' monthly benefits if you die during the current calendar year. Children of Social Security taxpayers are likely to be eligible for these benefits until they reach 18 or 19, depending, as a rule, on when they finish high school. A spouse who stays at home with the children can also collect survivors benefits until the youngest child is 16. By taking an outside job, however, a widow or widower will probably forfeit some Social Security income.

• Your disability benefits if you will be unable to work for at least a year or if you are terminally ill. Like survivors benefits, Social Security disability benefits include income for dependent children.

• A year-by-year statement of your earnings that were subject to Social Security taxes and of the Social Security taxes that you paid. Since the Social Security Administration has been known to make an occasional error in figuring benefits, you should check the numbers you get by matching them against your own earnings records. The Social Security statement also explains briefly, but clearly, what it takes to become eligible for benefits. Basically, you must work 10 years to earn retirement benefits, but generally only five out of the last 10 years to claim disability benefits.

What Social Security Pays

These figures represent the approximate yearly income from Social Security benefits for a single person and, on the following line, for a worker and a nonworking spouse of the same age, when they become eligible for full Social Security benefits at age 65 to 67. All of the amounts in the table are Social Security Administration projections in 1988 dollars, based on continuous employment throughout an adult lifetime.

Your age in 1988	Your earnings in 1987	$20,000	$25,000	$30,000	$35,000	$45,000 or above
25	Individual	11,796	13,548	14,568	15,600	17,652
25	Couple	17,688	20,316	21,852	23,400	26,472
35	Individual	10,896	12,540	13,476	14,436	16,296
35	Couple	16,344	18,804	20,208	21,648	24,444
45	Individual	9,972	11,496	12,360	13,104	14,412
45	Couple	14,952	17,244	18,540	19,656	21,612
55	Individual	9,048	10,344	10,920	11,352	12,036
55	Couple	13,572	15,516	16,380	17,028	18,048
65	Individual	8,100	9,216	9,564	9,792	10,056
65	Couple	12,144	13,824	14,340	14,688	15,084

▲___ Annual Social Security benefit ___▲

Should You Still Fund an IRA?

As with Social Security, the rules governing Individual Retirement Accounts can be confusing. Congress axed the full deduction for contributions by middle- and upper-income taxpayers in 1987. In their zeal to raise revenues, lawmakers cut in half the number of people who qualify for the full deduction and burdened people who make contributions to nondeductible IRAs with a lifelong snarl of paperwork. Left intact is the remaining nondeductible IRA benefit: tax-deferred compounding of investment earnings—an advantage that could be wiped out entirely if tax rates rise by the time you start withdrawing your funds.

If you are among those who still qualify for the deduction, putting the maximum $2,000 in an IRA—plus $250 in a nonworking spouse's account—may make sense. You get a tax-sheltered investment return for your retirement as well as more cash in your pocket from tax savings—$560 if you are in the 28% bracket. You can open an IRA at any bank, credit union, mutual fund, brokerage house, or insurance company. Institutions typically charge an annual maintenance fee, usually $25 or less, and may impose a start-up fee of $25 or so. People who qualify for the full deduction include couples filing jointly with adjusted gross incomes of less than $40,000; singles with incomes of less than $25,000; and anyone who is not covered by a pension, profit-sharing, or other tax-advantaged retirement plan, including simplified employee pensions and Keoghs. Partial deductions are allowed for couples earning between $40,000 and $50,000, or singles earning between $25,000 and $35,000. Their write-off drops $10 for every $50 they earn above $40,000 if married or $25,000 if single.

Whether the twin advantages—a current write-off and tax-deferred earnings—are sufficient to make a partially deductible, or even a fully deductible, IRA worthwhile depends on how soon you may need the money. If you take it out of your IRA before age 59½, you will have to pay a 10% penalty plus income tax on the withdrawal. (After age 70½, however, you will be penalized if you *haven't* begun withdrawals.) When those factors are taken into account, a person taxed at the maximum 33% who contributes $2,000 annually to a deductible IRA earning 8% would have to leave his money untouched for more than 11 years to beat the return he would have earned in a taxable investment at 8%. The break-even point for taxpayers in the 28% bracket is 12 years. The bottom line? Even if you can take the full deduction, an IRA is sensible only if you are sure that you won't need to tap it for at least a decade.

Another disincentive is the load of record keeping that now accompanies nondeductible IRA contributions. Each year, you must fill out an IRS tax form—No. 8606—to account for your deductible and nondeductible contributions. (See "How You Can Keep Tabs on Your IRA," on page 54.) These forms must be saved for the life of your IRA. The information on them will determine the tax on your withdrawals when you begin taking money out of your account. The nondeductible contributions will not be taxed upon withdrawal; the deductible contributions, plus all earnings in your IRAs, will be taxed at your regular income tax rate.

Furthermore, your bookkeeping headaches don't end once your withdrawals begin. Consider this migraine-maker: Every time you take money out of your IRA, you must calculate the proportion of nondeductible to deductible contributions and earnings in *all* of your accounts combined. Your withdrawal must then contain this proportion of nondeductible contributions and will be taxed accordingly. Say that your combined IRAs total $20,000—$2,000 or 10% of which represents nondeductible contributions. The other $18,000, or 90%, represents deductible contributions plus earnings. If you withdraw $1,000, you will owe taxes on 90% of that amount, or $900.

Some financial advisers argue that the disadvantages of nondeductible IRAs are outweighed by the benefits of tax-deferred compounding of earnings in your account over the long term. But James B. Cloonan, president of the American Association of Individual Investors, a nonprofit educational organization, disagrees. He calculates that deferring taxes on an investment for 15 to 25 years is equivalent to earning an additional percentage point of annual yield. But you could lose that extra yield if your tax rate when you retire is higher than it is today. Cloonan believes the current 33% top rate is probably the lowest maximum we'll see for a long time. So the yield advantage is almost certain to disappear.

How You Can Keep Tabs on Your IRA

Taxpayers who persist in making nondeductible contributions to an Individual Retirement Account must now start laying a long, toilsome trail of paperwork so that they will know what percentage of future withdrawals is not taxable. For 1988 and later, no IRA contributions were deductible if you were eligible for an employee retirement plan, unless your income was below $35,000 for single filers or heads of household, $50,000 for joint filers. Naturally, the IRS has devised another new tax form, this one numbered 8606, to isolate taxed and untaxed contributions. If you made nondeductible contributions in 1989 or if you might make them in the future, work through this simplified version of the new form. Then, faithfully preserve copies of Form 8606 each year.

1. The value of all your IRAs as of Dec. 31, 1989 _____

2. Distributions or withdrawals from your IRA in 1989 (excluding rollovers) _____

3. The total 1989 value of your IRAs (line 1 plus line 2) _____

4. Nondeductible contributions made in calendar year 1989 _____

5. The proportion of after-tax contributions to total contributions in your IRAs (line 4 divided by line 3) _____

6. Nontaxable 1989 distributions and withdrawals (line 5 times line 2) _____

7. Net nondeductible contributions made in 1989 (line 4 minus line 6) _____

IRA Updates

If you do decide to continue participating in an IRA, this form will help you keep track of your contributions.

1986 and earlier Contributions	Where invested	Maturity date (if any)	Rate of return	Withdrawals	Balances at year end

1987 Contributions	Where invested	Maturity date (if any)	Rate of return	Withdrawals	Balances at year end

1988 Contributions	Where invested	Maturity date (if any)	Rate of return	Withdrawals	Balances at year end

1989 Contributions	Where invested	Maturity date (if any)	Rate of return	Withdrawals	Balances at year end

1990 Contributions	Where invested	Maturity date (if any)	Rate of return	Withdrawals	Balances at year end

The 59.5 Solution

As Andy Rooney might ask: Didja ever wonder why you have to wait until age 59½ to get your IRA money without paying a penalty? Why not 60? Or 55? It's like this: In 1962, Congress created Keogh retirement accounts for the self-employed and chose the day you turn 59½ as the time when participants could start withdrawing money from their Keogh plans penalty-free. That age originated because it was halfway between 55 (the typical corporate, early-retirement age) and 65 (the age for receiving full Social Security benefits).

Well, sort of. Congress took a cue from the actuarial tables, long used by insurers, which deem that age 60 starts when you turn 59½ because you have survived more than six months of your 60th year. The logic may be Byzantine, but at least this wasn't a bureaucrat's bungle. In any case, the date has become a critical milestone for anyone planning retirement. Here's why:

● Money taken out of an IRA or Keogh plan after age 59½ is no longer subject to a 10% early-withdrawal tax penalty.

● You must normally wait until you have reached 59½ to withdraw cash from an employer savings plan without having to pay the 10% penalty. But if you are older than 55 and are retiring, you can avoid the penalty by either rolling over the savings account into an IRA or collecting the payments as a lifetime annuity. The Internal Revenue Service also will not impose the 10% penalty if you are disabled or if you need the money for any medical expenses that exceed 7.5% of your adjusted gross income. The process of withdrawing your savings-plan cash is complex, however, as explained in the next chapter.

● You will owe the 10% penalty before 59½ on even some withdrawals from *after-tax* company thrift-account plans. These include cash from the plan's investment earnings and company matching contributions.

● The 10% penalty also applies to any investment earnings on annuities sold by insurance companies, if you withdraw the money before you reach age 59½. Again, disabled investors are exempt from this requirement, as are those who collect their money in annual payments extended over their lifetime.

● If you take your lump-sum pension payout before 59½, then you cannot take advantage of the technique known as forward averaging, a calculation that significantly reduces the income taxes due on the amounts that are not rolled over into an IRA.

Why Keoghs Make Sense

Keogh plans can produce much more dramatic results than IRAs for people who are self-employed or who moonlight for extra income. Investors who commit to putting a fixed annual percentage of their self-employed earnings in a Keogh can make fully tax-deductible contributions of up to 20% of their yearly net income or $30,000—whichever is smaller—even if they are already covered by an employer pension or have an IRA. As with an IRA, these Keogh contributions compound tax-deferred until withdrawal, can be withdrawn without penalty at age 59½, and must be tapped beginning at age 70½. But unlike IRAs, your withdrawals from a Keogh at retirement or upon disability are eligible for a tax-saving technique called forward averaging (for details see "How to Make Your Payout Less Taxing," on page 86).

You can open a Keogh at most banks, brokerage houses, insurance companies, and mutual funds. But act soon if you want to shelter any of this year's earnings. Only contributions to an account that exists on December 31 can be deducted from current-year income. Once an account is established, however, you can take a deduction for money you put into it up to the April 15 deadline for filing your return.

Although the federal government sets no minimum opening balances, institutions establish their own—typically $250 to $1,000. Start-up and annual management fees range from nothing to $25. Make sure the institution has received or applied for a letter of determination from the IRS declaring that its Keogh plans meet federal guidelines. If the institution doesn't, the IRS could disqualify it, which means all the assets in the account would immediately be taxed as ordinary income. If you own a business

and have employees—or expect to in the near future—
setting up a Keogh is more complicated. Consult a tax
accountant or pension consultant.

The simplest Keoghs to set up are defined-contribution
plans, so called because the maximum annual payment is
fixed. There are two varieties of defined-contribution
Keoghs—money-purchase and profit-sharing plans. You
can put as much as 20% of your income, to a maximum of
$30,000, into a money-purchase plan each year. But be-
fore opening one, be certain you can afford it. You'll have
to contribute that percentage every year unless your
business shows a loss. The IRS will fine you 5% of the
amount of any underfunding and notify you to make up
the difference within 90 days or be assessed a penalty of
100% of the shortfall.

To avoid the risk of such penalties, you may be better
off with a profit-sharing plan. You can contribute only 13%
of your self-employment income or $30,000, whichever is
smaller, but you can pick a different percentage each
year, or not contribute at all. If you want to stash away
more than 13% but are wary of committing yourself to
higher contributions, you can set up two separate plans—
one of each type—as long as your combined contributions total no more than 20% of your self-employment
income or $30,000. If your Keogh accounts are at different
institutions, however, you should file Form 5310 with the
IRS, which will determine whether the combined plans
conform to Keogh rules.

You may be able to salt away even more—up to 100% of
your self-employment income—with yet another type of
Keogh. Called a defined-benefit plan, it lets you deduct
whatever you need to achieve an annual retirement income equal to the average of your highest earnings in
three consecutive years. The target income can be as
much as $90,000 if you plan to start withdrawing your
funds at age 62 or $75,000 if you intend to retire at age 55.
Obviously, the older you are the more you'll have to put
away each year to reach your income goals. Detailed
actuarial computations also are required because contributions to a defined-benefit plan vary according to such
factors as your age, your life expectancy, and the rate at
which you assume your investments will grow. Each year,
you must submit to the IRS a form on which an actuary
certifies as correct the calculations that led to your de-

duction. Lawyers generally charge $500 to $1,500 to set up a defined-benefit plan for an individual, and an actuary's certification generally costs $300 to $1,000 yearly.

If there's a major disadvantage to Keogh plans, it's the onerous disclosure forms that account owners must file annually with the IRS. The most cumbersome is form 5500-C, a lengthy questionnaire steeped in bureaucratic jargon. The deadline for filing Form 5500-C is July 31—or, if your Keogh plan is tied to your fiscal year, the last day of the seventh month following the close of your fiscal year. You can get an extension by—you guessed it—sending the IRS another form, No. 5558. The penalties for late filing are steep: $25 a day, up to $15,000. Fortunately, you have to file a 5500-C only in the year you start a Keogh and every third year after that. In each of the intervening years, you file the less intimidating 5500-R or 5500-EZ (for plans that cover sole proprietors or partners in a partnership). Some accountants and institutions that manage Keoghs will fill out the forms for a fee, usually $95 to $250 for each document.

If you are self-employed or moonlight but are daunted by the thought of wading through a Keogh's paperwork, consider a simplified employee pension, or SEP. Essentially, a SEP is an IRA with higher deduction limits. With a SEP, you can contribute and deduct roughly 13% of your self-employment income or $30,000, whichever is smaller.

You can open a SEP at the same places that handle IRAs. In fact, you can use the same application form for both types of accounts. Make sure the institution knows it's a SEP; otherwise, you might have trouble putting more than $2,000 a year in the account. You can set up and contribute to a SEP as late as April 15 and take a deduction for the previous year, just like with an IRA. As with both IRAs and Keoghs, you can begin withdrawing your SEP funds at age 59½, and you must start withdrawals by age 70½. But if you take your SEP money in a lump sum, you can't use forward averaging to reduce your taxes, as you can with a Keogh.

Shifting Your Tax-Deferred Accounts

Every spring, banks, brokerages, and mutual funds face off with one another over shares of the estimated $25 billion that pours into tax-deferred retirement accounts before the mid-April tax deadline. Even if you swore off putting new money into IRAs after tax reform, this annual hype fest is still a good time to assess your existing tax-deferred accounts and see what reallocation may be in order. Is it time to ease some cash into stocks, for example, or to lock in the interest rates on Treasury notes? If so, make your move. But mind the following rules which apply equally to IRAs, SEPs, or Keoghs.

The process is quite simple if you are planning to convey tax-deferred money from one mutual fund to another within a fund family, or from one investment to another within a brokerage account. In that case, simply call your fund or broker. Just make sure that the superior (or safer) returns you project on your new investment compensate you for any sales charges and commissions you may incur.

The process is more complicated if you want to shift some or all of an account from one custodian to another—for example, from a brokerage to a fund or from one fund company to another. First, you have to decide whether to have the two custodians carry out the move—a process known as a transfer—or to withdraw the money yourself and redeposit it in a new account. This is called a rollover.

By transferring rather than rolling over, you avoid most of the tax-related pitfalls of moving tax-deferred money. For example, the law allows you to transfer assets as often as you wish, while it restricts rollovers to one per account within a 12-month period. In addition, when you withdraw money in a rollover, you must redeposit it in a new tax-deferred account within 60 days. Otherwise, the money turns into a pumpkin on which you will owe income taxes and, if you are under age 59½, a 10% early-withdrawal penalty. In a transfer, by contrast, your tax deferral is never in jeopardy because you never take possession of the funds.

On the other hand, you can execute a rollover in a matter of days, while transfers between custodians can take up to four weeks. Until the process is completed, the money remains invested in the original account, gaining (or losing) ground accordingly. Thus, a rollover may make sense if you are trying to catch a move in the stock market or if you are switching money out of a certificate of deposit. Most banks allow you to withdraw assets from a CD without penalty only during a seven-day window following the certificate's maturity. After that, the bank simply plows the funds into another CD. So unless you initiate a transfer two to four weeks before your CD matures, a rollover may be the only way to be sure of extracting your money before it's reinvested.

The mechanics of transfers and rollovers are quite simple. To request a transfer, ask the bank, brokerage, or fund company to which you plan to relocate your money for an IRA application form and a so-called letter of acceptance. This paperwork establishes a tax-deferred account with the new custodian, and that company then sends your current custodian your signed letter of acceptance, directing that the specified amount be sent to your new account.

To avoid delays, check with the institution holding your current account to find out whether you face other requirements before the money can be sent. For example, most companies charge a fee for closing a discretionary tax-deferred account—that is, one in which you can switch among different investments. You have to pay $10, for instance, to pull your money out of the T. Rowe Price no-load fund group and $50 to get out of the brokerage Shearson Lehman Hutton. These fees are not tax deductible, and it is better to pay them out-of-pocket rather than from your account so that the fee does not deplete the earning power of your savings.

To carry out a rollover, notify the custodian of your account that you wish to withdraw all or part of your money. You can do this either in person or by letter. (If you write, you will need to have your signature guaranteed by a bank or broker.) The company will issue you a check within five days, and you then have 60 days from the date you receive it to open a new tax-deferred account wherever you choose. You can also split the old account into several different new ones. But if you open more than one Keogh, you will have to submit a separate IRS Form 5500 every year for each plan. It is much simpler to establish your Keogh at one mutual fund family or brokerage firm where you can take advantage of a variety of investments in one plan.

Stockpiling Money in Annuities

Annuities offer another vehicle for deferring taxes on your savings—but there are good reasons to be cautious. At first glance, single-premium, deferred annuities seem to deliver everything risk-averse investors crave: an attractive fixed rate of return, recently as high as 11%; a guarantee that your investment will not be zapped by plunging stock or bond prices; and a tax shelter for earnings on investments earmarked for retirement. Trumpeting these advantages, an army of insurance agents, financial planners, and stock brokers sold an estimated $10.4 billion of single-premium deferred annuities in 1987. Some companies reported sales increases of more than 60%.

What they are selling is a vessel into which you pour one payment ranging from $1,000 to $500,000. There is no immediate payout and no definite date for payouts to start. You decide years later whether to use the money and its earnings for lifetime annuity income or to withdraw it all at once. Unfortunately, some of the highly touted guarantees are about as ironclad as campaign promises. Those secure high rates of return, for example, typically vanish after one year. While marketing brochures stress that your annuity account's balance won't drop if the stock or bond market does, the sales literature glosses over the stiff tax penalties and early-withdrawal fees that can drain your assets as severely as another Wall Street crash. Furthermore, some annuities generate their enticing rates from junk bonds—high-yield, high-risk, corporate issues that are most vulnerable to default should hard times befall the firm or the economy.

Annuities, like IRAs, are often pitched as tax shelters. But, in fact, both work best as ways of stockpiling retirement money. The difference is that you are limited to yearly contributions of $2,000 to your IRA, while there is practically no limit on how much you can sock away in an annuity. Thus, the ideal candidate for an annuity is someone who wants to put aside a lot of money as soon as possible and be able to use it years later to generate a comfortable monthly income.

In contrast, various penalties and restrictions make annuities ill-suited to investors who are just looking to shelter investment earnings at a high rate of return. Don't confuse a tax-sheltered return with the *tax-free* return on municipal bonds, which lately paid a 7.8% after-tax return. Since you must eventually pay taxes on the earnings in an annuity, the after-tax return on a plan paying 8% for 10 years could fall as low as 6.3%—only a little bit more than that of a comparable taxable investment, such as a bank certificate of deposit. To reap even this modest reward of tax deferral, you must not dip into your investment before age 59½. If you withdraw your funds earlier, a 10% penalty on all your earnings, on top of regular income taxes, will ordinarily wipe out most or all of the benefit of tax deferral.

The theory behind single-premium annuities is simple and reassuring. An insurance company invests your money in its portfolio of bonds, mortgages, stocks, and real estate and assumes full market risk. You are guaranteed a set rate of return for a specific period, usually one year but sometimes as long as five years. After that, the company declares a new interest rate each year. When you are ready to start drawing on the account, you can postpone the tax bite by annuitizing—that is, converting the balance into a monthly income stream. At that point, the portion of payout representing the growth of your original investment is taxable.

Annuities bristle with hidden and undisclosed costs that make comparison shopping tricky. The tallest tariffs are company-imposed surrender charges for early withdrawal; these penalties usually kick in if you tap more than 10% of your account value in a year. Typically, these charges start at 6% to 8% for the first year or two and then decline by a point or so each year until they disappear. One noteworthy exception: Withdrawals from annuities sold through the mail by USAA Life in San Antonio were subject to only a 4% charge, plus $25, in the first three years. After that, you paid just $25 for each withdrawal.

Sales brochures seldom reveal how seriously taxes and surrender charges can erode the return on your investment. A bar chart in a brochure of Keystone Provident Life of Boston shows that $100,000 invested in its annuity and earning 8.5% for 10 years would grow to $226,098, while the same amount in a taxable investment yielding 8.5% would be worth $181,122. The annuity is a clear winner—except there's no way you could put your hands on the full $226,098. Income tax for those in the 28% bracket would siphon off $35,307. If you were under 59½, the 10% tax penalty would take another $12,610. That leaves $178,181—or less than you would net from the taxable investment.

For greater flexibility in cashing out, seek an annuity with a more favorable escape clause, called a bailout provision. Some insurers agree to waive surrender fees if the renewal yield falls one percentage point or more below the rate initially guaranteed. Others give you the right to exit without penalty when the initial guarantee expires, which enables you to switch profitably to a competitor's annuity paying a higher rate. Note that you can escape taxes through something called a 1035 exchange, which is similar to a tax-free rollover (or transfer) of money from one IRA to another.

Your return in an annuity can also suffer from sales charges and administrative expenses. While these costs are seldom collected up front, agents nevertheless earn commissions of 3% to 7% of your original investment (some insurers pay them as much as 10%). The money comes from the proceeds of high surrender fees or from your portfolio earnings. Before you buy an annuity, don't be embarrassed to ask the agent what commission he will earn on the sale. If he balks, go to another agent. At least one company, USAA Life, operates without a sales force and offers true no-load annuities.

The biggest challenge for shoppers is choosing an annuity that consistently will pay a competitive interest rate. All annuities guarantee a rate for the life of the plan, but it is a trifling 3% to 5%. To sell their plans lately, insurers have been promoting one-year rates of 8% to 11%. When the initially guaranteed rate expires, your renewal rate will be whatever the insurer decrees. In setting it, most companies look to the current and forecast yields on their investment portfolio and rival instruments such as CDs. But companies also know they don't necessarily have to be competitive in renewals, because some investors don't keep track of their rates. To avoid getting trapped in an annuity with a lagging return, ask the salesman for a history of the company's rate renewals. A competent salesman who regularly deals with one or two different companies should be able to produce at least a partial record.

High rates also require some scrutiny; they could be a sign of a high-risk investment strategy that could lead to the financial failure of the insurance company. In general, avoid companies with more than 20% of their bond portfolio in issues rated BB or lower. You can size up an insurer's portfolio in *Best's Insurance Reports*, which is available in the business section of major libraries. This fact-crammed reference also rates the company's overall financial stability. Only a few years ago, one major annuity issuer, Baldwin United, filed for bankruptcy, jeopardizing $3.4 billion in annuities held by 165,000 investors. The annuity holders didn't lose their principal, but many were unable to touch it for several years and wound up getting lower yields than they were promised. So stick to companies that are rated A+ (superior) or A (excellent) by Best. If the rating later slips, consider a tax-free exchange to another annuity, even if it means you have to pay a surrender charge.

The questions of solvency, rate guarantees, and surrender charges that preoccupy you when you are shopping for an annuity give way to other concerns as you near retirement. Then, the major question becomes when and how you should start drawing from your account. Annuities provide a great deal of flexibility. You can take a lump sum and pay taxes immediately or you can choose one of several life-income options. Among the alternatives: a straight life annuity, which pays a fixed, monthly benefit for the rest of your life; a period-certain plan, which pays you for life but continues paying your beneficiary if you die before a set number of years; and a joint and survivor annuity, which promises a monthly check as long as you or your beneficiary lives.

Built into almost all annuity contracts at purchase are guaranteed payout rates based on ages and benefit options. But these guarantees are so low they are largely irrelevant. Instead, when you are ready to annuitize, compare the *current* payment rates being offered by your company with those of others and roll over your money if the differences are substantial. In 1988, for example, a 65-year-old man who had amassed $233,048 in a Northwestern Mutual Life annuity could have converted it to a monthly lifetime income of $2,268. The same account balance at Family Life, a Merrill Lynch subsidiary, would have generated just $2,072 a month. Given such wide disparities in rates, you should never automatically take the annuitization deal offered by your present company. By doing a little shopping around, you could easily increase your monthly income by more than 10%.

Your Life as a Tax Shelter

Once upon a time there was plain, old, whole life insurance for which you paid a fixed premium every year to provide for your family in the event of your untimely death. While you were still kicking, the policy offered a savings account, called the cash value, that grew tax-deferred at a slow but certain 4% or so a year. In a financial pinch, you could retrieve your cash value and give up the policy. Or you could borrow from it at low interest and never repay the loan (the balance due would be subtracted from the policy's death benefit). If you did not cash in your insurance, your beneficiary would get the policy's proceeds free of federal income taxes when you died.

Protection and savings in the same package—could anything be simpler or more comforting? But times changed, as did the ways your cash value could be invested by insurers. Now, tax reform has made life insurance that doubles as an investment one of the most enticing shelters for your retirement stash. Yet many insurance shoppers remain wary, wondering whether they should instead buy low-cost term insurance, which provides a death benefit but no savings or investment account, and do their investing on their own. Do cash-value policies really deliver? The answer, according to many financial experts, is a cautious yes.

One reason is that term policies get more expensive as you age. With cash-value policies, however, your premium dollars buy far less insurance than they do with a term policy. So if you need $250,000 of coverage but cannot afford a cash-value policy that large (typical cost: $1,750 a year for a 50-year-old, male nonsmoker), buy term ($425 in the first year, rising to $1,120 in the fifth year). Term is also the answer if your insurance need is only temporary—say, you want coverage for 10 years until your children are educated.

One of the most popular forms of cash-value policies is universal life, which is essentially a combination of term insurance and a savings account that the insurer usually invests in fixed-income assets, such as bonds. Another possibility is variable life, which lets the policyholder choose among a broad range of investments, from zero-coupon Treasury bonds to stock funds. A third choice is variable universal, a hybrid that combines the investment options of variable life with the flexible premium and death benefit of universal life. Yet another option is single-premium life, which requires a buyer to pay the entire premium, from $5,000 on up, at the outset. In October 1988, however, Congress took away one of single-premium's great attractions—tax-free loans against a policyholder's investment account—on policies bought after June 20, 1988. Now tax-free borrowing is permitted only from cash-value policies that require you to pay premiums over at least seven years.

Here is a closer look at the main varieties of cash-value policies:

Universal life. Policyholders can change both the premiums and the face amount of the policy from year to year. With universal life, money is deducted periodically from your investment account to pay for the company's administrative expenses and the cost of insurance on your life. As a result, this choice suits couples with fluctuating incomes or those who are not certain how much insurance coverage they will need.

Recently, however, this plan has worked less smoothly than insurers expected. Many universal policies were sold in the early 1980s, when market interest rates were running at 12% a year. Today, companies are experiencing "negative good will," as agents delicately put it, because current market rates allow them to pay only 8% or 9% on their investment accounts. Consequently, some purchasers have had to pay higher premiums to keep their insurance coverage intact. Policyholders often complain that their agents didn't always make clear that if interest rates went down, premiums could go up. The alternative is a drain in cash value, a reduced death benefit, or even cancellation of coverage. If you are shopping for a universal policy, a good question for you to ask the agent is: At what interest-rate assumption will your universal policy outperform a comparable, whole life policy? The answer ought to be 6% or 6.5%—midway between the average 8.5% rate policies were paying in early 1989 and the guarantee, which is 4% or 4.5%.

Variable and variable universal. These policies make sense for people with reasonable risk tolerance and long-time horizons. Generally, these policies offer all the conveniences of a large mutual fund family, including telephone switching among funds for free or at nominal cost. Thus, policyholders can assume as much or as little investment risk as they desire, allocate their money among different kinds of funds, and turn aggressive or defensive as market conditions change. The insurers' portfolios are often managed by well-known mutual fund companies, such as Fidelity, Scudder Stevens & Clark, and Oppenheimer.

Single premium. This option is recommended for people who need some insurance and want to park a lot of cash in a safe place. Single premium comes in as many forms as there are cash-value policies; the only difference is you pay all your premiums up front. Elimination of the tax-free borrowing benefit has caused these policies to more closely resemble single-premium annuities, which pay out periodic income for a certain number of years or for life, but provide no death benefit. Single-premium insurance is probably the better buy if you plan to hold the contract until death; single-premium annuities are better suited to a retirement fund. Reason: To pay for the protection, the life insurance policies typically offer returns that are one to 1.5 percentage points lower than those of the annuities.

Before deciding which cash-value insurance policy suits you best, be clear about two points. First, do not commit funds that you will need any time soon. Companies charge stiff surrender fees to discourage buyers from cashing in policies early. Anyone holding a cash-value life insurance policy for less than 10 years can expect to get an uncompetitive return. Second, determining whether a contract has inexpensive insurance and good investment returns is a Herculean task. You can turn for help to the National Insurance Consumer Organization (121 North Payne Street, Alexandria, VA 22314), which will calculate the average rate of return on an insurance contract for five, 10, 15, and 20 years; the fee is $30 for the first policy and $20 for each additional policy.

Diligent consumers can make use of two cost indexes in evaluating policies of the same type—for example, comparing one universal policy with another. Many states require companies to calculate these indexes for you. The interest-adjusted payment index is a measure of the average premium for $1,000 worth of coverage. The lower the number, the cheaper the policy. The interest-adjusted, surrender-cost index measures the current cost of cash-value policies if you were to cancel them in 10 or 20 years and take your money. This tells you your actual cost if you have to get out. Index amounts will vary with the size of a policy and the age of the policyholder, however, so a policy that represents good value for you may be a poor choice for your older sibling.

Besides the cost of insurance and the level of administrative expenses, you will also want to know how your policy's investment funds perform. (See the table on page 72 for the 10 policies whose equity funds have done best so far this year.) The newsletter, *Insurance Investing*, reports on the performance over the past 12 months of a wide range of equity, gold, and international portfolios held within insurance contracts and suggests switching strategies. (For a sample copy, write P.O. Box 2090, Huntington Beach, CA 92647; 714-893-7332; $117 for 12 issues.) Most insurance investment funds are less than five years old, but so far insurers' common-stock funds have run nose-to-nose with the major market indexes.

After you have determined the kind of insurance you need, and how much, you still have to decide where to get it. Agents push primarily one company's products, but if you don't like the insurer's wares, many agents will hunt for more attractive alternatives offered by other companies. Financial planners typically charge $50 to $150 an hour, but the consultation fees may be offset by sales commissions on the policy they sell you. Most planners rely on a handful of companies whose products they know well. Some favorites whose names were mentioned repeatedly by well-regarded planners: First Colony Life

Insurance Company (804-845-0911), the Life Insurance
Company of Virginia (804-281-6000), North American
Company for Life & Health (312-648-7600), and Pan-Amer-
ican Assurance (504-566-1300). Some of the best deals in
universal life can be bought directly from low-loads such
as USAA Life Insurance Company (800-531-8000),
Ameritas Marketing Corporation (800-255-9678), or Lin-
coln Benefit Life (800-525-9287). For $25, the Council of
Life Insurance Consultants (800-533-0777), a Chicago
trade group, will send you a packet of information on
low-load life insurance, including the names of available
distributors in your area.

What to Ask an Insurance Agent

Few financial products are more confounding than
cash-value policies, which give you both life insurance
protection and an investment account. The following
questions and answers can help you find the best deal:

How can I make sense of the agent's sales pitch?

Your agent probably will hand you a sales tool known as
the illustration—columns of numbers that purport to
clarify the potential and guaranteed earnings of the policy, given your age and health. Glenn Daily, an insurance
analyst with Seidman Financial Services, offers drastic
advice: "Throw away the illustration. Get the agent to
explain the product without reference to the numbers on
the page." This will test the agent's understanding of the
policy and enable you to analyze fundamentals, undis-
tracted by the salesman's pie-in-the-sky projections.

Sooner or later, however, you must look at the illustration—very carefully. One column of an illustration's projection of cash-value earnings assumes that current rates,
most recently as high as 11%, will continue through the
life of the policy. Don't believe it. Current rates may drop
after just one month and change monthly thereafter.
Another column shows the worst case for future earnings, based on the insurer's guaranteed minimum rate of
return, usually 4% or 4.5%. For a more realistic view of
future earnings, ask the agent for a projection based on a
rate of return between the guaranteed and current rates,
say 6%.

What fees do I pay for a policy? Start-up fees on cash-value life insurance, including the agent's commission, can be as much as 125% of the first year's premium. Rather than take the entire bite at the outset, insurers nibble away at your account for as long as 15 years. For instance, a company keeps a certain percentage, typically 1.5%, of the earnings on your investment account. The insurer also charges you slightly more for the policy's insurance coverage than the protection actually costs. In addition, insurers might charge 2% to 8% of the annual premium plus monthly fees of $3 to $5 for administrative costs. Finally, if you cash in a policy early, the insurer could penalize you with a stiff surrender charge, as much as your entire investment in the first year or two.

Can I reduce these charges? One way is to buy low-load policies directly from companies such as USAA Life and Ameritas Marketing Corporation. These policies' start-up costs consume only about 40% of first-year premiums. But even with low-load policies, you might pay $3 to $5 monthly and 2.5% to 3.5% of the premium to cover administrative expenses and the premium tax levied by every state. You can often cash in a low-load policy early at no charge.

Should I buy a policy from a company that promises to pay me dividends? With few exceptions, such dividends are paid by mutual companies to owners of whole life policies. The dividends can be taken in cash or as additional paid-up insurance or used to reduce premiums. Nonparticipating policies, which are sold by stock companies, generally have lower premiums. Mutual companies won't guarantee future dividends, but they do make projections based on their anticipation of investment performance and mortality experience.

How can I be sure the company is healthy? Buy policies only from companies that earn ratings of A + or A in *Best's Insurance Reports*, available in most large libraries.

Top Performing Insurance Mutual Funds

Below are the 10 top-performing equity portfolios offered through variable and variable universal insurance contracts that are currently available to the public. The figures cover the 10 months to Nov. 1, 1988. Despite good results, customers, frightened by Black Monday, shunned variable policies. Sales fell 63% in the first half of 1988.

COMPANY	Policy	Portfolio Manager	Fund	Returns to 11/1/88
Northwestern National Life	Select Life	Fidelity	Equity income	26.03%
Monarch	Future Reserves	Fidelity	Equity income	23.85
Equitable Life Assurance	Incentive Life, SP-Flex, Champion	Equitable	Growth	22.37
Charter National	Life Invest	Scudder Stevens	Capital growth	20.04
Monarch	Captn	Oppenheimer	Growth	19.86
SMA Life	Vari-Exceptional	SMA	Growth	18.86
MONY Life	Monyvestor	MONY	Equity income	17.89
Provident Mutual	Options	Newbold's Asset Mgmt.	Growth	17.62
Northwestern National Life	Select Life	Fidelity	Growth	17.55
Century Life	2000	Century	Growth	16.89

Source: Lipper Analytical Services

Why Disability Insurance Is So Crucial

Contrary to what life insurance agents may tell you, the coverage you need most isn't whole life, universal life, variable life, or even universal-variable life. It's disability income insurance. This often overlooked coverage pays you a monthly income if you are unable to work because of injury or illness. Statistics show that disability is far more probable than death, especially if you are young or middle-aged. At age 42, for example, you are about four times more likely to be disabled for at least three months before retirement than you are to die. In fact, disability is sometimes called "living death," since your family's financial needs continue but you can't meet them unless you have insurance.

Unfortunately, there are plenty of temptations to put off obtaining coverage. It is expensive: the premium on an individual policy offering a $2,200-a-month benefit for a 40-year-old, nonsmoking manager could run as high as $1,459 a year. Also, you may mistakenly think you are fully protected by Social Security and possibly by your employer's group disability policy. But Social Security's disability criteria are so strict that only about 35% of those who apply for benefits actually qualify for them. And even if your employer offers insurance—as do 99% of large companies but less than 25% of businesses with fewer than 50 employees—there may still be holes in your coverage.

Some group policies don't cover you until you have worked for your employer for a year or two; others limit benefits to $2,000 a month. You can learn these details from the summary that federal law requires your employer's benefits administrator to make available. If your group plan seems skimpy, you can supplement it with an individual policy.

How much coverage do you need? In general, insurance experts recommend that disability insurance equals 60% to 70% of your before-tax earnings. Benefits should start 90 days after you become disabled (your savings presumably can carry you until then) and continue if necessary until you reach age 65. You probably cannot buy much more insurance than that, anyway. To avoid attracting phony claims, most insurers will cover you only to the point at which your disability income from all sources, including Social Security and company benefits, would equal 70% of your current before-tax earnings. Still, that's better than it sounds. Benefits from a policy you buy with after-tax dollars are tax-free in contrast to income from a policy paid by your employer.

Equally important as the amount of coverage is the way your policy defines disability. Under the most generous definition, known as "own occ," insurers agree to pay full benefits if you can't work in your own occupation as long as you are under a physician's care. In contrast, a policy using the narrower "any occ" definition would pay only if you are unable to work in any occupation for which you are clearly suited. Under the any-occ rubric, for example, practicing lawyers would not lose their benefits if they refused to work as a taxi driver. But they would be cut off if they could teach law and declined, even if teaching would pay them an inadequate salary.

Insurers commonly compromise by splitting the definition and paying benefits under own-occ rules for the first one to five years of a disability and under any-occ rules thereafter. Not surprisingly, pure own-occ policies are 5%

to 15% more expensive. The most expedient way to
minimize the cost of your coverage is to prolong the
so-called elimination period—the time you have to wait
for benefits to begin after you become disabled. A 40-
year-old, nonsmoking manager would pay as much as
$400 a year in additional premiums if he or she took a
30-day waiting period rather than the more usual 90-day
wait. Savings are less dramatic for longer waits: stretching from 90 days to 180 would typically cut premiums
only about $100 a year.

Most financial advisers recommend that you choose a
policy that stops paying benefits at age 65 because pension and Social Security retirement benefits kick in at that
age. For premiums about 20% higher, you can select a
benefit period that continues until you die. Such a policy
would make sense if you are young and there is a possibility that a long-term disability would prevent you from
building retirement benefits.

As with their other products, insurers tend to offer lots
of options on disability policies. The most valuable (and
often standard in a top-of-the-line policy) is a residual-
benefits provision, which may add 20% to 25% to your
premium. This option supplements your income if you are
well enough to go back to work but not yet healthy
enough to work at full capacity and earn full pay. Read
your contract carefully, though. Some less generous policies pay so-called partial benefits—usually 50% of your
full benefit—if you are partially disabled. Unlike residual
benefits, which continue as long as needed, partial benefits typically terminate after three to six months.

Another valuable option is a cost-of-living adjustment
(COLA), which will boost your premium 25% or so. With
this rider, monthly benefits increase automatically to
counter inflation, rising either at a specified rate or at the
same rate as the consumer price index, up to a specified
annual maximum. And you should insist on a policy that
is at least guaranteed renewable, which means that the
insurer cannot cancel your coverage as long as you pay
your premiums and cannot raise your premium unless it
boosts premiums in general. A preferable alternative is a
noncancelable policy. This guarantees that your policy
cannot be revoked and that your premium cannot be
increased at all.

Taking Charge of Your Company Retirement Plans

*L*ike most employees, you can rattle off your company's policy on vacations and sick days, perhaps even the medical expenses covered by its group health insurance. But also like most employees, you probably haven't a clue about the inner workings or potential benefits of the retirement package where you work. Don't blush, brush up. A thorough evaluation might reveal that your company's pension and tax-deferred savings plans are so chintzy you may as well start that long-postponed job search—or at least begin building a separate nest egg of your own. You might also be surprised to discover that your retirement plans are much more generous than you had imagined. This chapter will help you size up your package, weigh your options, and prepare for the taxing decisions and terminology that will attend the eventual payouts of your retirement money. Suffice it to say that what you don't know now could cost you and your family dearly when you finally decide to call it quits.

For example, Wall Street's October 1987 crash rudely reaffirmed some tired truths about the stock market—and some fresh ones about the retirement packages of millions of employees. Chief among the lessons is that old-fashioned, corporate paternalism is waning, and with it the cozy promise that if you put in your time, your company would look after your retirement. Today, the amount of money you take with you when you retire depends partly on how well *you* manage your interest in company savings plans—including profit-sharing and 401(k) accounts, in which the employee, not the employer, bears the investment risk. Over the past decade, these thrift plans have grown three times as fast as traditional pensions, the bedrock of company retirement benefits. The 401(k) has spread most rapidly; more than 82% of large and medium-size companies now offer one, up from less than 2% in 1983.

As long as the stock market kept going up, the growing significance of these plans was easy to overlook. But not anymore. The crash was a powerful lesson in how crucial your management of the plans can be in achieving a successful retirement. Fortunately, Black Monday sent a far more forgiving message about the other half of many employees' retirement package, their pension. No matter how hard you were hit in your company plans, the crash did not cost you a penny in pension benefits. That's because your employer guarantees your pension benefit, boom or bust.

The two types of retirement plans thus demand very different strategies. With regard to your pension, your task is simply to understand how your benefits build and to use that knowledge to capitalize on a valuable asset. In your savings plans, the challenge is a more active one of balancing investment risks with your desire for high, tax-deferred returns on your contributions and those of your employer.

The Importance of Your Pension

Your employer typically calculates the size of your pension by multiplying a percentage of your final salary— say, 1%—by the number of years you were on the payroll. There is little you can do to manage your interest under this arrangement. Almost all employers fund their pensions entirely out of their own pockets, and all of them bear the responsibility both for investing the pension fund and for ensuring that the money to pay your retirement benefits is there when you need it, regardless of the fund's investment performance. In the rare event that your company were to go bankrupt with an underfunded pension, a quasi-governmental insurance agency, the Pension Benefit Guaranty Corporation, would guarantee your benefits up to $1,900 a month.

A far more serious threat to many employees' future retirement income is their own readiness to change jobs. In the past, workers covered by company pensions typically were entitled to a certain retirement payout—that is, they became vested—after 10 years. Starting in 1989, however, companies must begin to vest employees fully after their fifth year or gradually between their third and seventh year of service. The shorter vesting schedule will help job hoppers become vested in more pensions, but it may not boost their retirement income appreciably.

That's because when you leave a pension in mid-career, your benefits are frozen as of your departure. When you eventually start collecting checks from that pension, generally no earlier than age 55, inflation may have drastically eroded its value. So if you are within a decade of retirement, you should not change jobs or accept an early-retirement package without taking into account the value of the pension benefits you would forfeit.

How can you tell the value of what is essentially just a series of monthly checks beginning at some time in the future? The answer: Your pension's current worth is the amount of money your employer would theoretically have to set aside today to pay you your promised monthly checks over your expected life span in retirement. Ask your employee-benefits department to tell you what your

The Choices in Retirement Plans

The nine varieties of retirement plans listed here are all that most wage earners need to concern themselves with. With the exception of the defined-benefit pension, all of the plans require some care-taking—from occasional to intense.

PLAN TYPE	Major source of funding	Usual form of benefits
Defined-benefit pension	Employer	Annuity
Money-purchase pension	Employer: employee contributions sometimes allowed	Lump sum or installments
Profit-sharing plan	Employer: employee contributions usually optional*	Lump sum
Savings plan	Employee*: company usually matches a portion of employee contributions	Lump sum
Employee stock-ownership plan (ESOP)	Employer	Single payment of stock shares
Tax-sheltered annuity (TSA or 403[b] plan)	Employee**: employer may contribute in some plans	Employee's choice of lump sum or annuity
IRA	Any salary or wage earner	Lump sum or periodic withdrawals
Keogh plan	Self-employed people	Same as IRA
Simplified employee pension (SEP)	Company: employee contributions may be optional††	Same as IRA

*Employee contributions are tax deductible if the plan is set up as a 401(k).
**Employee contributions are tax deductible.
†Those not covered by a company retirement or Keogh plan or who have adjusted gross income less than $25,000 ($40,000 for married couples)
††Employee contributions are tax deductible in some SEPs.

benefit would be if you retired now and what it would be
if you retired at the time you had planned to leave. For
example, a 56-year-old executive currently earning
$70,000, who had been with a typical company for 15
years, might normally be entitled to $1,300 a month. That
benefit would require a pension reserve of $156,000. If the
executive were to stay on the job until age 62 and
received raises of 7% a year, he would retire on $3,310 a
month. The fund would then need $343,000 when he
reached age 62. That's the equivalent of $222,000 today,
assuming the money was invested at 7.5%. An early-retirement package would have to offer him an additional
$66,000 ($222,000 minus $156,000) just to compensate
him for foregone pension benefits.

The moral is that each year you continue working you

Where invested	Remarks
Diversified among stocks, bonds, cash and sometimes real estate	Benefits depend on salary and length of service
Same as defined-benefit pension	Benefits depend on size of contributions and investment performance of pension fund
Usually employee's choice of diversified stock fund, fixed-income account or company stock	Company contributions depend on size of company profits
Same as profit-sharing plan	Employees may be permitted to borrow a portion of vested benefits
Company stock	Starting at age 55, employees must be given a choice of other investments for a portion of their account balance
Usually employee's choice of mutual funds or insurance company annuities	Offered only by schools and nonprofit institutions
Account with bank, brokerage, insurance company, mutual fund, credit union, savings and loan or trustee	Contributions are tax deductible for some IRA holders†
	Contributions are tax deductible
	Designed for small businesses

earn far more in pension benefits than you might think. In a typical plan, the value of your pension would quadruple between ages 55 and 65. The reason is that every year you work, your payout grows because it is based on an ever-larger percentage of an (presumably) ever-larger salary.

Weighing an Early Retirement Offer

Suppose your boss asks you to consider taking early retirement in exchange for a package of tempting pension and fringe-benefit incentives. You probably will have only one to two months to decide whether to accept or reject such an offer. Dozens of companies—including CBS, IBM, and Metropolitan Life—have dangled early-retirement packages before at least 100,000 employees since 1986. And others are likely to do so, according to benefits specialists, as firms look for ways to cut payroll costs.

When evaluating an offer, you will need to answer the following questions: Am I ready to retire? If I turn down the package, will I be laid off anyway? Can I trust the company to live up to its promised fringe benefits? Some employees have little alternative but to accept a package. Others may view an offer as the long-awaited inducement to clear their desks and leave a dead-end job. Either way, the paperwork can be staggering. Some companies send a targeted employee a stack of 20 or more documents. Take the package to your financial planner or accountant for help in assessing its pluses and minuses. Expect to pay $100 to $200 an hour for five to 30 hours of work, depending on the complexity of the proposition in these key areas:

Pension. Consider as generous a package that offers to pay you a pension equal to or greater than the one you would get by retiring as previously planned. The most fetching offers have such "sweetened pensions," in which the company calculates your benefit adding on three to five years to your age or tenure. Both types of sweeteners can increase your pension by as much as 30% over what you would have received by retiring early without a special arrangement. Be cautious about accepting an offer that would require you to take more than $117,529 in pension benefits this year. Under tax reform, you could owe a 15% tax to the Internal Revenue Service on distributions exceeding that amount. (See "Beware the New Pension Tax," page 90.)

Health insurance. A 1986 law, the Consolidated Omnibus Budget Reconciliation Act (COBRA), requires that your employer at the very least continue your group health insurance coverage at your expense for up to 18 months after retirement, regardless of your age. (COBRA doesn't cover dental insurance.) Most firms keep paying the premiums when you retire early, but your dental coverage will almost certainly expire the day you quit. Employer-provided coverage will be more comprehensive than a policy you could buy on your own—but also more expensive. You can expect to pay $1,000 to $2,000 a year, depending on whether you cover dependents.

Early retirement deals that are the most appealing, but growing scarcer by the day, let you keep your employer's health insurance coverage for the rest of your life. If you are one of the fortunate few whose company will keep you covered, check whether the premiums, deductibles, and benefits for an early retiree are the same as those for employees. Companies aren't required to put aside money to finance health insurance coverage for retirees and probably won't have to in the future. But under an impending accounting rule change that will likely take effect in 1992, corporations will have to start listing their future health insurance costs as current liabilities. That would add as much as $2 trillion in red ink to the nation's corporate balance sheets, according to a congressional study. Businesses of all sizes will probably soon begin limiting their health-care coverage for former employees.

Retirees under 65 are especially vulnerable because their insurance isn't supplemented by Medicare, making it considerably more expensive for employers. The annual cost of a health plan for a retired couple under 65 ranges from $2,800 to $4,000, compared with $1,200 to $2,000 for a couple over 65. But aren't companies obligated to finance your health insurance in retirement if they vowed to provide it? A number of court decisions have split fairly evenly on the question. Most collective bargaining agreements include escape clauses that let businesses alter their insurance coverage, and the courts have ruled based on the precise language that is found in each individual contract.

Life insurance. The most liberal offers give early retirees the same life insurance coverage they had as employees. Without this option, you can generally switch from the company's group life policy to an individual policy costing, at age 55, about $400 a year per $10,000 of coverage. But converting this way could be more expensive than buying your own policy elsewhere. Another option from some employers is just slightly better than no insurance at all. Here, you get a death benefit that's less than 50% of what you had as an employee. This benefit often shrinks each year, paying little more than burial expenses if you live to age 70.

Parlaying Your Company Plans

Unlike pensions, company-sponsored savings and profit-sharing plans do not guarantee any particular retirement income. Instead, your employer establishes an investment account on your behalf and promises only to chip in a specified sum periodically. Otherwise, the responsibility for managing your account falls largely on you. You decide how to invest your account in the plan, and you take the consequences. If your investments go sour, no corporation stands by to make up the loss.

A consolation for shouldering the investment risk is that you can change jobs without gutting your payout. The sum that has built up in your account—usually tax-deferred—simply leaves with you. To preserve your shelter, you can either roll it over into an Individual Retirement Account or into the savings plan offered by your new employer, if that plan permits. Whichever you choose, your money continues to grow free of taxes until withdrawal at retirement or upon disability.

The first decision you need to make in piloting a company savings plan is whether to get on board at all. There is a reason to hesitate aside from the investment risk. Once you have money in the plan, it is quite difficult to get it out. In 401(k)s, for example, you can withdraw tax-deductible assets only in the case of financial hardship, and even then, if you are younger than 59½, you will owe the tax man a 10% penalty tax on top of his usual cut.

Financial planners brush this demurral aside, however. One way or another, you have to save for your own retirement, they point out, and these savings plans give you impressively more benefit for the buck than other methods. At the very least, they allow your money to grow tax-free, which builds capital faster than similar investments outside the shelter of a company plan. In a 401(k) plan, moreover, the first $7,627 you stash away in 1989 is fully deductible from your taxable income. (The maximum tax-free contribution rises annually with inflation.) That means that if you are in the 28% tax bracket, it effectively costs you only $72 of spendable income to save $100. The 401(k) advantage turns even more enticing if your contributions are matched by your employer. In the most common formula, the employer kicks in 50 cents for each dollar you contribute—an instant, guaranteed 50% return.

Assuming that you do decide to participate in the plan, which investments should you choose? Generally, you must select among two to four funds. These might include some relatively risky growth investments—such as a diversified stock fund or a fund invested entirely in the employer's stock—and one or two safer choices, such as a government securities fund or one consisting of guaranteed investment contracts (GICs), which are virtually risk-free investments similar to bank certificates of deposit but backed by an insurance company. Rather than trying to manage your retirement savings to take advantage of—or reduce your exposure to—changing market conditions, you are better off adopting a conservative, diversified portfolio and sticking to it. Don't think of your company plan in isolation; ideally, the investments in the plan should blend in with your outside holdings to create an overall retirement portfolio that reflects your risk tolerance and your goals (see "Managing Your Investments for a Lifetime," page 96).

If your personal holdings are large enough, it makes sense to keep most of your stocks there and to put safer, income-producing investments in your company plan. That way, you can soften the impact of setbacks in the stock market by writing off capital losses on your income tax return. You don't have that option if you suffer losses inside tax-sheltered retirement plans. Because of the limited investment choices that company plans offer, they may not blend smoothly with the rest of your portfolio. This is particularly true if—as is the case for many corporate employees—your company's plans make up the bulk of your retirement portfolio and absorb most of your annual retirement savings. In that event, you must construct a diversified portfolio that matches your goals as best you can with the choices available to you.

If you are more than a decade from retiring, your focus should be on building your assets; your best course then is to keep half to two-thirds of your account in a growth-oriented fund and the rest in fixed income. As you move to within five years of retirement, shift two-thirds or more of your account into the income fund. Note that you probably will not be able to make the move all at once. Most company plans forbid you to rearrange your account more often than quarterly. Many also limit the fraction of your account that you can move between investments at one time. In this case, however, such restrictions can have a benign effect. By forcing you to make portfolio switches gradually, they may prevent you from cashing out at what later turns out to have been a temporary market bottom.

How Good Are Your Benefits?

Although wise management of your employer's retirement plans will improve your eventual payoff, nothing beats having an openhanded package to begin with. To help you judge yours, *Money* asked employee-benefits experts what features distinguish a solid-gold handshake from a brass imitation. Their answers:

A generous pension formula. Pension plans usually compute your retirement benefits by multiplying a percentage of your salary by the number of years you worked for the company. The best formulas, known as final-pay pensions, typically use your salary during your highest-paid three to five years. About one in six companies bases its pension payout on your average salary over your entire career, a formula that tends to penalize employees who rise through the ranks. In practice, however, many of these companies voluntarily update their plans to make them competitive with final-pay pensions.

A representative final-pay formula would award you retirement income equal to 1% of your average salary during your three to five highest-paid years times the number of years you spent with the employer. Be pleased if the pension gives you 1.5% or more for each year of service. On the other hand, if your plan follows a career-average pay formula, a typical multiplier of 1.5% would produce only about as much retirement income as a three-quarters of 1% to 1% final-pay pension, because the salary used in the formula would be smaller. Few companies using career-average pay plans go much higher.

If you are tempted to leave work before your company's standard retirement age, note that most formulas will reduce your pension. If you have been with your employer for 30 years, for example, three out of four companies can be expected to trim your benefits—by 4% a year on average—if you left before age 62.

Adjustments for inflation. Less than 5% of pension plans guarantee periodic inflation raises to retirees. And although many companies voluntarily increased pension payments during the roaring inflation of the 1970s, the practice has faded in recent years. Companies have either adopted a new, tough corporate philosophy or simply no longer fear inflation as much. If your employer has boosted retirees' income in the past five years of comparatively low inflation, take it as an encouraging sign.

More than one plan. Since even a long-term employee can expect his combined pension and Social Security benefits to replace only about 40% to 60% of his salary, it helps to have a supplementary savings plan, such as profit sharing or a 401(k). Multiple plans are far more prevalent among large employers—92% of such companies backed employees with at least a pair of plans, according to one study. In more than two-thirds of the 401(k) plans surveyed, the employer offers to chip in a certain percentage of your contribution, most commonly 50 cents on the dollar. One in five of them matches you dollar for dollar, however, and one in 100 gives you more.

How to Make Your Payout Less Taxing

So you served your time, built up your pension credits, religiously stashed a part of your paycheck in the company savings plan, and tended it wisely all these years. Now comes the gut-wrenching part: deciding how to take the money. At stake is probably the bulk of your retirement wealth. And since most choices open to you are irrevocable, if you choose wrong, you are stuck with the consequences for the rest of your life. For these reasons, you probably will want to have a financial planner or accountant help you wrestle with the numbers and keep you from tripping over the tax laws. Together, you might consider the following questions:

Should you take your payout as a lump sum or an annuity? If your only company retirement plan is a pension, this decision has probably already been made for you. That's because most pensions pay benefits only in the form of a monthly annuity, which means equal monthly payments for the rest of your life. Only about one in five pension plans allows employees to take a lump sum instead. You are most likely to face the choice if your retirement package includes a savings plan such as profit sharing or a 401(k). Though such plans normally pay benefits as lump sums, your company may let you convert your account balance into an annuity. And even if your savings plan requires you to take a lump sum, you can always use the money to buy an annuity from an insurance company.

With an annuity, you don't have to worry about squandering your retirement money on a bad investment or spending it all before you die. The annuity is guaranteed to last as long as you do. On the other hand, even with moderate inflation of 5% or so, fixed monthly payments will decline in purchasing power over the years. A 5% annual price rise will halve the real value of your checks after only 14 years. If you take a lump sum, however, you could put a portion in growth investments to preserve the purchasing power of your assets. Also, you may lean toward a lump sum if you want to leave money to your heirs.

In converting your benefits to a lump sum, a pension plan's administrator calculates the amount it would take

Option	Initial tax	Net sum invested	Income age 65*	Income age 75*	Balance age 75	Age when income ends
Pension (annuity)	$0	$0	$17,280	$10,608	$0	Death
Lump sum with 10-year averaging	50,770	199,230	17,280	17,280	87,552	79
Lump sum with five-year averaging	60,110	189,890	17,280	17,280	70,053	78
IRA rollover with immediate withdrawals	0	250,000	17,280	17,280	148,759	80
IRA rollover with no withdrawals for five years	0	250,000	0	17,280	389,638	93

*In after-tax 1988 dollars, assuming inflation of 5% a year

to pay you a check every month for the rest of your expected life, as determined by actuarial tables, assuming the money earns a particular rate of interest, say, around 8%. But pension payments stop at the end of your life (or your surviving spouse's), not at the end of the actuarial life expectancy assigned to you at retirement. Thus, an annuity turns out to be a bargain if you manage to live longer than average, while a lump sum wins out if you die shortly after you retire. So if you are chronically ill, you should consider taking a lump sum; conversely, if you or your spouse are descended from a long line of nonagenarians, you might lean toward the annuity. If you're somewhere in between, read on.

Note that in calculating lump-sum conversions, employers use unisex life expectancy tables that understate life expectancies of women, who as a group live longer than men. All else being equal, that makes an annuity a better deal for a woman than for a man. Interest rates can also determine whether a lump sum or an annuity is more advantageous. The higher the rate the plan's actuaries assume it can earn, the smaller the lump sum needed to pay a benefit. For example, in July 1984, when interest rates were around 10.5%, a pension of $1,000 a month for a 60-year-old man translated to a lump sum of $93,000. In March 1988, when interest rates were 8%, the same benefit produced $109,000.

Many pension managers assume a conservative interest rate at the beginning of the year and stick with it. Thus, in

Choosing Between a Lump Sum and an Annuity

You and your spouse are both 65 and set to retire on January 1. You can take a $2,000 check monthly for life or a $250,000 lump sum. What's a couple to do? Unless one of you is a math whiz, you might go to an accountant or financial planner, who would project both options for you. As the table at left shows, the safe annuity course would shrink your annual income of $24,000 ($17,280 after taxes) to $10,608 in 1988 dollars by the time you reach 75 if inflation were to run at a modest 5% a year.

By taking a lump sum instead, you would have four options, under which you would invest the $250,000 either in a tax-free bond fund paying 7.3% a year or in a taxable bond fund yielding 9%. In each case, you could withdraw $17,280 after taxes the first year and increase that 5% a year to keep up with inflation. If you needed income, you could pay income tax on the $250,000 right away using 10-year forward averaging, as explained in the accompanying story. Then you could put the remaining money in the tax-free fund, and it would last until you were 79. The next two options—using less favorable five-year averaging or rolling the money into an IRA with immediate withdrawals—would provide income until you were 78 and 80, respectively. The last course is best: roll the money over into an IRA and let it grow for five years untouched. Then the sum, invested in the taxable fund, would last until age 93.

a year of rising interest rates, a lump sum offered by your plan late in the year could be disproportionately large. One simple way to tell would be to ask your life insurance agent how large an annuity benefit you could buy with the lump sum your pension is offering. To be competitive, an insurance company has to change its interest-rate assumptions frequently to match prevailing rates in the economy. So if interest rates are rising, you might be able to obtain a higher monthly payment from an insurer's annuity than from your pension, in spite of the insurer's sales charges and profit margin.

If you want an annuity, what kind should it be? The most common annuities are life only, which pays you a certain monthly amount until your death; joint and survivor, which assures that if you die first your spouse will continue to receive a certain amount until he or she dies; and life and period certain, which pays benefits for your lifetime or a specified period—whichever is longer.

The option you choose will affect the size of your monthly checks. Life-only annuities pay the largest pensions but stop once you die; the other options continue to provide checks for your beneficiaries at the cost of reducing your income by 10% to 15% during your lifetime. One possible compromise: Select the life-only option and buy a life insurance policy. Then when you die and the pension payments cease, the insurance benefits will provide for your spouse. (Under federal law, a married person cannot choose the life-only option without the written consent of his or her spouse. To make the insurance tactic work, get a notarized waiver of the joint-and-survivor option from your spouse.)

Take the example of a 63-year-old manager who must choose between a life-only pension of $30,000 or a $25,700 joint-and-survivor pension with his 63-year-old wife as beneficiary. Say that he selected the life-only option and then bought a whole life policy that has an initial face value of about $130,000. (Level-premium whole life is required because term insurance becomes prohibitively expensive at older ages.) The couple could pocket an extra $50 a month in retirement income after subtracting the cost of the insurance. Upon his death, his wife would get the same income as under the joint-and-survivor pension option. To reduce the cost of this

strategy, insist on a policy with minimum cash value
buildup and a face value that decreases over time. That
way, as your beneficiary ages, he or she needs less life
insurance proceeds to provide the same income because
his or her life expectancy is growing shorter.

Which tax option should you take for a lump sum?

A lump-sum distribution need not be very large to push
you into the top tax bracket of 33%, which in 1989 was
triggered by a taxable income of $43,150 if you were
single, $71,900 if you were married. Luckily, the tax code
lets you use one of two tax-saving tactics. First, if the
lump sum makes up at least 50% of the value of your
interest in a specific plan, such as a 401(k), you can roll
over the distribution into an Individual Retirement Account within 60 days after receiving it. Your money will
compound tax-free until you make withdrawals, which
will be taxed as ordinary income. Thus, if you don't need
to begin withdrawing money from the IRA for three to
five years, the rollover is probably the better choice.

Second, you can use a tax-saving device called forward
averaging if you meet these conditions: your payout represents your entire interest in a plan; you have participated in the plan for at least five years; and you are 59½. If
you are 52 or older in 1989, you get a special break: you
don't have to wait until you reach 59½ to use forward
averaging. But if you aren't at least 55, you will be socked
by a 10% early-withdrawal penalty.

If your lump sum makes it past all these checkpoints, it
is taxed as if you had received it over five years instead of
all at once. This is known as five-year forward averaging.
If you were born before January 1, 1936, you can choose
an even more capacious break, 10-year forward averaging. In both cases, you pay the total tax in the year you get
the money, but at a much lower rate than if the sum were
taxed the way the rest of your income is. For example,
with five-year forward averaging, a married couple with
$30,000 of other income who received a lump sum of
$150,000 would pay $30,398 in taxes—an effective tax
rate of 20%—instead of the $45,867 (31% rate) they would
pay under ordinary tax tables. With 10-year forward
averaging, you figure your taxes at 1986 rates, when
brackets were as high as 50%. The couple in this example
would pay a tax of $24,570 on their lump sum—an

effective rate of about 16.4%.

People over age 52 who participated in their employer's pension plan before 1974 have yet another option. They can elect to have the portion of the sum attributable to their pre-1974 contributions taxed as capital gains at the top 1986 rate of 20%. Your company benefits department can tell you exactly how much qualifies as capital gains. Taxpayers in this category can then use five-year or 10-year forward averaging for the remainder of their payout.

What methods give you the least tax? If none of your distribution qualifies as capital gains, the answer is easy: 10-year averaging if your payout is less than $473,700. Above that amount, the lower tax rates used in five-year averaging outweigh the greater bracket-lowering power of 10-year averaging. For other situations, the only way to choose between forward averaging and a rollover is to project the consequences of both into the future and see which alternative rewards you with the most after-tax income.

Beware the New Pension Tax

Taxes, by nature, are complicated and sneaky, but this one is ridiculous. It's a 15% excise tax that will be applied in addition to any income tax you might owe on what are called "excess distributions from qualified retirement plans." If you have worked for 20 years or more for a company with generous benefits, take a hard look at this potentially very expensive new tax immediately. Despite what you may have heard—that it will affect only superearners like Lee Iacocca and Michael Milken—in fact, it can hurt you and many other people who may have earned more than $40,000 a year.

The potential pain traces, not surprisingly, to the Tax Reform Act of 1986, which decreed that certain amounts paid out of pension and profit-sharing plans, Keoghs, and Individual Retirement Accounts are "excessive." So a 15% excise tax will be levied on any retirement distributions a taxpayer receives in a given year that exceed $150,000. Or if a taxpayer wants to draw out all of his accumulated money from a fund in a lump sum, he may take up to five times the $150,000, or $750,000. Anything beyond $750,000 gets hit with the 15% tax.

Recognizing that this tax could retroactively punish millions of taxpayers who had been innocently accumulating sums greater than $750,000, Congress tossed in a lifesaver. It said that if you had accumulated $562,500 or more in all of your plans from benefits *vested or non-vested* by August 1, 1986, you would be allowed to grandfather those funds so that you could take them all out as a lump sum and the extra 15% tax would not apply to them no matter how much they totaled. Further, you could elect to take them on an annual basis and still avoid the 15% tax, but only if you followed certain formulas and rules.

Here is where things get very complicated. In addition to any lump sum you may have grandfathered—an election you were supposed to have made on Form 5329 of your 1988 return—you may draw out $112,500, indexed for inflation (which would be $117,529 for 1988, up to about $122,000 for 1989). Anything over that is taxed at 15%—unless you are clever in the method you elect to draw out those funds. When you make your election, you must select one of two ways of recovery. The first, the attained-age method, combines the worst features of the other and is so difficult to calculate that you probably should dismiss it. The other possibility is "discretionary." With it, you may have either 10% or 100% of your annual withdrawals of grandfathered funds excluded from the 15% tax. One more point: After the election, you may shift from the 10% method to the 100% method, if your needs require, but once you do that, you will stay at 100% from then on.

So, you ask, why not simply make the election to grandfather and take the 100% option, which on the

Defending Against the Retirement Tax

By making the right choices, you could save thousands of dollars on the new, maddeningly complicated 15% excise tax on excess retirement plan withdrawals. The table below shows what might happen to a long-term employee who plans to retire in 1991 at age 60. He had accumulated $800,000 in his plans, plus IRAs, by Aug. 1, 1986, and he may elect to grandfather all of those funds, as explained in the accompanying story. By 1991, when he starts to draw out money, the funds will have increased to $1.2 million, assuming an 8% annual rate of return. He then decides to take out all of his money in large chunks over six years. The table shows the amount of excise tax he would have to pay if he did not grandfather compared with what he would pay if he did (plus the effect of four different ways of withdrawing the funds, as described above). The choices really matter: results range from a $46,000 tax savings to a $3,000 tax bill.

THE OPTIONS	With grandfathering	No grandfathering	Tax saving (loss)	Explanation
10% to 100% mixed	$33,000	$79,000	$46,000	Uses 10% method for first year, then switches to 100% method
100% recovery	34,000	79,000	45,000	Uses 100% recovery method for each year
10% to 100% mixed	52,000	79,000	27,000	Uses 10% method for first two years, then switches to 100%
10% recovery	82,000	79,000	(3,000)	Uses 10% recovery method for each of the six years

Source: Seidman Financial Services, Houston

surface would seem to exclude everything from that infernal new tax? Because life in the world of taxes is not what it seems. The straight 100% option could be a very expensive mistake, depending on your retirement plans and needs.

If you are thinking that you couldn't possibly have accumulated $562,500 in your retirement plans by mid-1986, think again. For example, a refinery operator for Exxon who never earned more than $40,000 a year, but who worked for that company for 30 years, is going to have to make the grandfather decision. The message is clear: Check out all the amounts you have accumulated in each of your plans, both vested and nonvested as of August 1, 1986. The administrator of your plans, in most cases your company, is required by law to make these valuations and report them to you, but only if you request them. Do so today and be sure not to overlook any plans. After Ron Meier, managing director of Seidman Financial Services in Houston, reviewed one client's case, he told the man and his wife that they didn't have to file anything because they had accumulated a bit less than the $562,500. But on the way out of the office, the woman asked whether their IRA counted. It sure did—and it pushed them well over the tax threshold.

To sort through and analyze all of this and apply it to your particular condition and future needs, you should work with a professional, even if you normally do your own tax return. Choose well, since it is likely that many tax pros lack the ability to fathom this new tax as well as to re-evaluate not only your retirement but also your estate plans. (Yes, excessive distributions and the 15% tax can even find their way into your estate.) A terribly time-consuming headache, you say, that may cost you an adviser's fee as high as $1,500. True, but never forget that one false move—or nonmove—could cost you instead, say, $46,000.

When you get around to tapping your retirement savings, the accepted wisdom is to take out money in two consecutive waves. First, you draw on funds outside your Individual Retirement Account, company retirement plan, or any other tax-deferred investments, sheltering as much money in them as you can for as long as possible. Only later do you dip into these holdings. But tax law tampering by Congress, as with so many other facets of financial life, has complicated this simple approach.

The Internal Revenue Service has new guidelines for starting mandatory, taxable withdrawals at 70½ from all of your tax-sheltered accounts—even if you are still working. That includes IRAs, pensions, profit-sharing accounts, 401(k)s, and 403(b)s, a type of plan for employees of tax-exempt organizations. (An exception: Most employees who turned 70½ before January 1, 1988 may wait until they actually retire to start payouts from a company plan.) Laws requiring withdrawals to begin at 70½ have been on the books in various forms for years. The new rules, however, contain precise timetables for taking money out and revamped life expectancy tables for computing the amount. They also include a strong incentive to comply; underwithdrawals may be punished by a draconian tax equal to 50% of the shortfall. As you approach the 70½ mark, the following pointers can help you steer clear of the IRS and still manage your tax-favored accounts to your best advantage:

When. You must start withdrawals for the year you turn 70½. If your 70th birthday falls between July 1, 1989 and June 30, 1990, you must calculate a minimum withdrawal for this year. Generally, the deadline for taking your cash out is December 31. But you may postpone your first withdrawal until April 1 of the following year. Bear in mind, however, that an April 1, 1990 payout would cover only 1989. You would have to make a second withdrawal by December 31 to cover 1990. That second payout is computed using your balance as of December 31, 1989, minus the April withdrawal.

How much. The amount of the minimum withdrawal is based on both age and the total in each tax-deferred

The Art of Withdrawing Gracefully

account at the beginning of the year for which you are
making the withdrawal. Assume, for example, that you
turned 70½ and that your IRA was worth $100,000 on
January 1. To determine the minimum withdrawal, you
must divide this balance by the number given for your age
in the life expectancy tables found in IRS Publication No.
575, *Pension & Annuity Income.* Should you have a
beneficiary, the appropriate table lists his or her age to
arrive at a single number representing your joint life
expectancy (see the accompanying table).

For your first withdrawal, you use age 71 for yourself
and, let's say, 70 for your beneficiary. (The calculation is
based on your ages at the end of the year for which the
withdrawal is being made.) Thus, your first mandatory
withdrawal must be at least $4,950 ($100,000 divided by
20.2, the life expectancy for a 71-year-old IRA owner with
a 70-year-old beneficiary). If you also have money in a
company retirement plan, your employer will compute
the amount of the payout. It is your responsibility, however, to make sure that the IRS minimum is met. To avoid
the penalty, ask your company's benefits supervisor for a
statement that will ensure you of compliance.

Taking the optimum. The above calculations are the
easy part. Like many retirees, you may be in the 15% tax
bracket: 1989 earnings of up to $29,750 for married cou-
ples filing jointly, $17,850 for singles. But two minimum
payouts in 1990—one in April for 1989 and one at the end
of December—could well push you into the 28% bracket.
A too large minimum payout could also backfire on your
Social Security benefits. If your adjusted gross income
plus your tax-exempt income and half your Social Security exceed $32,000 a year for married couples filing
jointly ($25,000 for singles), up to one-half of your Social
Security benefits are taxable.

Massaging the tables. If continued tax-deferred growth
is your objective, your choice of a beneficiary can result
in a higher actuarial life expectancy and, consequently,
lower annual payouts. If you have no beneficiary, for
instance, your life expectancy at 71 would be 15.3 years,
yielding an initial payout of $6,536 on a $100,000 account.
But the joint life expectancy of a husband and wife, both
71, is 19.8 years; at 72, it is 18.9 years, with respective

minimum payouts of $5,051 and $5,291. The IRS allows a maximum 10-year spread in age between you and your beneficiary, regardless of your actual age difference. This maneuver prevents you from drastically reducing your payouts by naming, for example, a grandchild as your beneficiary. If the beneficiary is your spouse, however, real ages are always used.

A few new wrinkles help you keep the minimum withdrawals down by stretching out your actuarial life expectancy. The new tables use updated, unisex figures. They permit you to recalculate your life expectancy each year, extending your payouts—and your tax shelter—over a longer period. This also helps ensure that you don't outlive your funds. This practice is based on the reassuring principle that the longer you live, the longer you are expected to go on living.

If you are	And your beneficiary is									
	65	66	67	68	69	70	71	72	73	74
	Your joint life expectancy is									
70	23.1	22.5	22.0	21.5	21.1	20.6	20.2	19.8	19.4	19.1
71	22.8	22.2	21.7	21.2	20.7	20.2	19.8	19.4	19.0	18.6
72	22.5	21.9	21.3	20.8	20.3	19.8	19.4	18.9	18.5	18.2
73	22.2	21.6	21.0	20.5	20.0	19.4	19.0	18.5	18.1	17.7
74	22.0	21.4	20.8	20.2	19.6	19.1	18.6	18.2	17.7	17.3
75	21.8	21.1	20.5	19.9	19.3	18.8	18.3	17.8	17.3	16.9
76	21.6	20.9	20.3	19.7	19.1	18.5	18.0	17.5	17.0	16.5
77	21.4	20.7	20.1	19.4	18.8	18.3	17.7	17.2	16.7	16.2
78	21.2	20.5	19.9	19.2	18.6	18.0	17.5	16.9	16.4	15.9
79	21.1	20.4	19.7	19.0	18.4	17.8	17.2	16.7	16.1	15.6
80	21.0	20.2	19.5	18.9	18.2	17.6	17.0	16.4	15.9	15.4

Source: Internal Revenue Service, Publication No. 575

Timing Your Withdrawals

To take money from your accounts correctly, you can use this table. See the story for instructions.

Managing Your Investments for a Lifetime

*T*here was once a time when investing for retirement was a simple process of figuring out how much income you would need and then building a portfolio of high-quality bonds to deliver it. No longer. Bond coupons may give you reliable income, but they offer scant protection from inflation's erosion of your principal's purchasing power. Indeed, no single investment or technique can provide piece of mind *and* a topnotch return in the face of today's jittery stock market, volatile interest rates, resurgent inflation, and fears of recession. Instead, a lifetime plan for prudently investing your wealth and conquering risk requires deft asset allocation—that is, determining the proper mix of investments that should not only preserve your capital but make it grow over time.

Donald and Bernice Graeb of Glenshaw, Pennsylvania, a Pittsburgh suburb, are a case in point. In the early 1980s, the couple had saved $140,000 with well over a decade to go before Donald reached retirement age. He had built a stock portfolio worth $80,000 and invested the rest in cash and an insurance-backed annuity through his employer's 401(k) plan. But the Graebs were worried that their stock portfolio was a hodgepodge of individual issues assembled with help from stockbrokers but without regard for overall diversification. "Brokers just recommended whatever happened to be in favor at the time," recalls Donald. Understandably, the couple feared that their total portfolio was overexposed to stock market fluctuations.

Beginning in 1982, the Graebs took their first steps to solve these problems. They consulted a local money manager who helped them overhaul their portfolio and create a textbook example of proper diversification. The couple sold off most of their individual stocks and substituted a combo of investments carefully diversified among mutual funds that invest in blue-chip, growth, and small-company stocks as well as foreign shares, gold, and commodities. They also added a real estate partnership. But they left the cash and annuity in Donald's 401(k) plan.

The new mix proved its mettle during the October 1987 crash. For example, while Standard & Poor's 500-stock index fell 12% in the 12 months that ended July 31, 1988, the Graebs' six stock funds posted an average decline of just 5%—an easily surmountable loss. Thanks to the mutual funds, Donald now spends less than an hour a week managing the portfolio, leaving more time for his job as a designer of industrial exhibits and his avocation as a painter of award-winning watercolors. "I used to feel like we were open to a financial disaster," says Donald. "Now, I don't."

Whether you are starting or unscrambling your retirement nest egg, the key decisions in the years ahead will hinge mainly on how old you are, where your financial assets are concentrated, your outlook for the economy, and—most important—your tolerance for risk. The current moods of the stock and bond markets are but two of the factors you must weigh in deploying your money. You should also make gradual adjustments in your mix of assets to correspond with your changing needs for capital growth, steady income, or a combination of the two as you draw nearer to the day when you finally call it a career.

Youth offers the greatest opportunities for you to start investing toward the distant goal of retirement because you can afford to be more daring than would be the case later in life. To enhance your returns and spread your risks, many advisers recommend that you set aside ample cash for emergencies and diversify the remainder of your funds among different types of growth-oriented investments. Heading the list are domestic and international stocks, real estate, and mutual funds that specialize in these assets. If you believe in gold as an inflation hedge, you might also consider adding some of the heavy metal to your mix.

At 45 to 50, you should begin moving to a middle-of-the-road strategy that stresses growth and income. Thus, you should keep about 50% of your money in stocks (or stock funds), which over time provide the highest inflation-adjusted return of any liquid asset. For additional income, you can put another 30% or so of your holdings into bonds and park the rest in cash equivalents such as a money-market fund. As you approach age 55 and become more concerned with capital preservation, you can reduce stocks to 30% or so of your portfolio and boost bonds to 40% and cash to 30%. Once you retire, conservative in-come-generating investments should dominate your port-folio: 50% in bonds and another 30% or so in money-market funds. To defend against outliving your capital, however, you should still keep about 20% of your funds in stocks for growth.

Since the 1987 crash, many investors have forsaken stocks—and the goal of capital appreciation, a key infla-tion hedge—in favor of seeming strongholds like high-yielding U.S. Treasury securities. Yet few recognize the varied ways in which they are vulnerable to other less-shattering events, such as a sudden rise in interest rates or an unexpected recession. Assessing your own expo-sure to such setbacks requires that you take a long hard look at what you own—and why.

Coming to Terms with Risk

No matter what your age or how well you have diversi-fied your portfolio, the challenge is to find your comfort zone—and to know that it will change as your temples gray and your career progresses. Astute asset allocation begins with a careful analysis of your investments and other aspects of your financial life to determine how each affects your exposure to the following risks:

Inflation. Rising prices will reduce the purchasing power of an investment. An annual inflation rate of only 5% over 15 years will cut the value of $1,000 to $481. Overcautious investors who hoard all of their assets in low-yielding investments such as savings accounts and money funds may not earn enough to outpace rising prices. In addition, rising inflation erodes the value of future income on investments with fixed payments, most notably long-term bonds.

Interest rate increases. Rising interest rates will cause investments to drop in price. For example, higher rates make yields on existing bonds less attractive, so their market values decline. Rising rates also hurt stocks by making their dividend yields look less appealing. Individ-uals who invest borrowed money through margin accounts or who have other floating-rate debt increase their interest-rate risk because higher borrowing costs cut into their net profits.

Changes in the economy. Slower economic growth will cause investments to fall in price. Shares of emerging growth companies may shrink because they require a booming economy to sustain their robust earnings gains. Cyclical companies, such as automakers and chemical producers, cannot easily cut costs during a recession, so their shares may nosedive, too. Economic downturns can also undercut junk bonds issued by financially weak firms that might default.

Market risk. This includes such factors as political developments and Wall Street fads that can batter investment markets. Tax law changes, trade agreements, program trading, and the quirks of investor psychology all contribute to market risk, which has accounted for much of the stock market's day-to-day volatility. Gold also carries considerable market risk because its price moves sharply when political or military upheavals in other countries encourage the flight of capital.

Specific risk. This covers occurrences that may affect only a particular company or industry. For example, the death of a young company's founder could send the business into a tailspin. Individuals often take on a high degree of specific risk when they invest in a real estate partnership run by inexperienced general partners or when they buy stock in a firm with a heavy debt burden. Specific risk also includes the chance that government regulation will harm a particular group of companies, such as banks or savings and loans.

The worksheet on page 102 will help you determine where your own vulnerabilities lie. After uncovering the major risks in your portfolio, you can redeploy assets to reduce your exposure. Don't limit your financial inventory to investments kept in a brokerage account. Your earning power probably is by far your most valuable asset; equity in a home may come next. Many investors also have substantial assets invested in company pension plans or insurance policies with significant cash values.

And entrepreneurs should take a close reading of the risks that could threaten the value of their share of a small business.

Risk has a way of creeping up on even vigilant investors. Your holdings in a retirement plan or insurance policy may grow more quickly than you realize, particularly if you make regular contributions or reinvest your returns. But with this success comes a problem. Growth in one asset can throw a portfolio out of balance if other investments don't keep up. If a prolonged bull market increases the value of your stockholdings, you may need to sell some shares to restore the balance between stocks and other assets. Be particularly wary of buying large amounts of stock in the company you work for through retirement and savings plans. If the company runs into trouble, both your job and your stock could be endangered at the same time. If you live in a one-company town, the value of your home may be tied to the fortunes of that firm.

Keep a close eye on changes in your investment portfolio. A careful inspection of your portfolio may unearth important differences between investments that you thought were similar. For example, a study of mutual fund risk found that Fidelity Magellan and Twentieth Century Growth—two growth-stock funds with similar investment objectives, returns, and overall volatility—have responded quite differently when the economy has slowed. Magellan's stock holdings in large, well-established companies have held up better than Twentieth Century's portfolio of smaller, growth-oriented firms, which are especially sensitive to changes in the level of corporate profits.

To gauge your own situation, you will need to conduct a careful survey of your investments and other aspects of your finances. Here's a rundown of the strengths and weaknesses of various assets:

Stocks. They are vulnerable to the possibility that skittish investors will panic for some reason and drive share prices down en masse—an example of market risk. But risks related to inflation, interest rates, or economic growth may vary considerably from stock to stock. For example, a sharp increase in the inflation rate depresses stock prices because it may reduce the purchasing power

How Risky is Your Portfolio?

Most people shield some of their investments against different types of risk, but few balance all of their important assets so that they are well protected. This quiz can help you identify your points of vulnerability. With each question, you will accumulate points for one or more of the five major investment risks. Write the points in the boxes at right. Then, total the points for each risk and interpret your scores as follows: fewer than five points is low; five to 10 points, moderate; above 10, high. While you may want to vary your exposure to different risks somewhat, depending on your personal circumstances and the outlook for the economy, any score above 10 should set off alarm bells.

Once you have identified vulnerabilities, you can take steps to shore up your defenses. For example, say that you score high for inflation risk and low for market risk. You might balance your portfolio better by switching some money from money funds to real estate, stocks, or gold. While your risk of a temporary decline in the value of your portfolio will increase, you will have a better chance of outpacing inflation over the long term.

In answering the questions, don't forget about IRAs, 401 (k) plans, or any other savings or deferred-compensation plans. It may be difficult to pin down the value of some assets. For instance, you may have a universal life policy with an important investment component. Just make the best estimates that you can. It isn't necessary to be exact. But it is important that your inventory be as complete as possible.

1. Are your assets diversified among fewer than four of these five major categories: stocks, real estate, gold, bonds, and cash? If yes, score one point for each risk.
2. Are more than 35% of your assets invested in any one of the five categories? If yes, score one point for each risk.
3. Is at least 10% of your portfolio in assets such as gold, natural-resource stocks, or high-grade collectibles such as rare stamps? If no, score one point for inflation risk.
4. Is at least 30% of your portfolio in investments such as growth stocks and real estate, which are likely to produce long-term capital gains that can outpace inflation? If no, score two points for inflation risk.
5. Are your real estate and gold investments held primarily in assets such as gold-mining shares, REITs, or real estate mutual funds, which fluctuate with the stock market? If yes, score one point for market risk.
6. Do you generally keep at least 15% of your portfolio in cash equivalents such as Treasury bills or money-market funds? If no, score two points for interest-rate risk.
7. Is more than 30% of your portfolio composed of assets such as long-term bonds, certificates of deposit, or annuities that provide fixed payments over a period of many years? If yes, score three points each for inflation and interest-rate risk.
8. Do highly volatile zero-coupon bonds account for more than 30% of your fixed-income assets? If yes, score two points each for inflation and interest-rate risk.
9. Do emerging growth stocks or junk bonds, which may fall sharply in a recession, account for more than 25% of your portfolio? If yes, score three points for economic risk.
10. Do you switch money among different assets to try and catch the highs and lows of different investment markets? If yes, score two points for market risk.
11. Do you use dollar-cost averaging or a similar plan that involves adding money to your investment portfolio at regular intervals? If no, score two points for market risk.
12. Is more than 20% of your portfolio concentrated in a single industry? If yes, score three points each for economic risk, market risk, and specific risk.
13. Do stocks or bonds issued by one company—including the one you work for—or shares in a single limited partnership account for more than 15% of your assets? If yes, score three points each for economic risk, market risk, and specific risk.
14. Does your share in a privately held business account for more than 30% of your portfolio? If yes, score one point for economic risk and four points for specific risk.
15. Does a rental property account for more than 30% of your portfolio? If yes, score one point for economic risk and three points for specific risk.
16. Do foreign stocks and shares of domestic companies with significant overseas sales account for less than 10% of your portfolio? If yes, score one point each for inflation and economic risk.
17. Will you need access in the next three to five years to principal in volatile assets such as stocks or long-term bonds? If yes, score one point each for inflation, interest-rate, economic, and market risk.
18. Do you own your home? If no, score three points for inflation risk.
19. Do you have variable-rate loans such as mortgages or credit-card debt amounting to 30% or more of the value of your portfolio? If yes, score four points for interest-rate risk.
20. Is 20% or more of your portfolio financed by loans or invested in highly leveraged assets such as options? If yes, score one point each for interest-rate and market risk.
TOTAL

Inflation risk	Interest-rate risk	Economic risk	Market risk	Specific risk

of future dividends to shareholders. Also, inflation generally coincides with higher interest rates, which draw investors from stocks to bonds. Because firms such as retailers, consumer product manufacturers, and service companies can pass cost increases along to customers relatively easily, they are more likely to prosper during periods of high inflation.

Slowing economic growth hurts some firms more than others. Manufacturing companies with high overhead—known as cyclicals—cannot readily cut costs when a recession slices sales, so their earnings quickly tail off. Many emerging growth companies also require an expanding economy to sustain their earnings growth and stock prices. By contrast, firms that sell necessities such as food or clothing can often maintain sales even in a lackluster economy, and their shares tend to hold up relatively well. Since foreign stocks are at least partly immune to changes in the American economy and financial markets, they may post gains while U.S. stocks sink. But unlike domestic issues, shares denominated in foreign currencies carry the risk that a rising dollar will reduce their value.

Stocks also carry specific risks—those that are unique to a single firm or industry. Poor management or bad luck can dampen earnings or even bankrupt a company. And high-flying growth stocks are particularly vulnerable to earnings disappointments. One good way to reduce such risks is to buy shares that appear undervalued because they are selling at comparatively low price/earnings ratios or above-average yields.

Bonds. Their prices generally fall when interest rates rise. But the extent of the drop depends upon a bond's maturity and the amount of its coupon. Short-term bonds fall only slightly when interest rates move upward, and a high coupon also offers some protection against climbing rates. A recession usually brings lower interest rates, which boost bond prices. But some issues react negatively to the threat of an economic slowdown. So-called junk bonds, which are rated less than investment grade by Moody's or Standard & Poor's, may lose ground because investors fear that financially weak firms will default and fail to make payments of interest and principal to bondholders on time. Treasury and high-grade corporate bonds gain the most during hard times because income investors seek them as safe havens.

Real estate investments. Although they tend to beat inflation over the long haul, they present other hazards. For example, if you own a rental property, you run the risk that you won't find a tenant. A real estate partnership that owns several properties in different regions can reduce such risks through diversification, but it may lose value if tax changes or a sluggish economy drive down property values across the country. And real estate investment trusts and real estate mutual funds fluctuate with the stock market as well as with property values. (For more information, see "Arm's-Length Opportunities in Real Estate," page 134.)

Gold and other tangible assets. The price of gold can skyrocket when inflation rises rapidly. Between 1968 and 1988, the consumer price index posted nine annual increases of 6% or more. During those years, gold rewarded investors with an average gain of 34%. (See "The Right Reasons to Buy Gold," page 140.) Gold-mining stocks are more volatile than the metal itself and expose investors to other risks. A South African miners' strike, for example, might boost the price of bullion but cut profits at some mining companies. Gold-related shares also swing with broad stock market moves. In October 1987, mutual funds that invest in gold-mining shares fell 27%, while the price of gold rose 2%. Other tangibles present their own problems. While antique armoires or rare stamps may be able to outpace inflation in the long run, collectibles are often illiquid, and prices of specialized items such as baseball cards are largely subject to collectors' whims.

Once you have identified the risks in your portfolio, you can adjust them to suit your goals and temperament. That might mean reducing your interest-rate risk by selling a few long-term bonds. Then again, you may decide to shoulder new risks in pursuit of higher profits. Even sophisticated investors make mistakes, but common errors you can avoid include:

● Having too much in your company's stock. Investors who concentrate a sizable share of their assets in any single stock are courting trouble. Many people make that mistake—often without even knowing it—because they invest heavily in the shares of the corporation they work for through vehicles such as 401(k), profit-sharing, and other deferred-compensation plans.

● Leaving too much money in cash. Some investors escape the perils of stock market volatility, bond defaults, and real estate slumps by keeping the bulk of their assets in cash. But they often overlook an even more relentless threat—inflation. Cash equivalents such as Treasury bills and money-market accounts offer no chance for capital gains that can outpace rising prices.

● Assembling a portfolio piecemeal. You may be a genius at spotting undervalued stocks or choosing top-performing mutual funds. But a collection of great individual investments does not always provide the balance your portfolio needs. If you have already loaded up on stocks, for example, pass up a promising new stock issue and buy some bonds, CDs, gold, or real estate instead.

● Buying more investments than you can monitor. To diversify fully, you may be tempted to own so many issues that you do not have time to follow them all carefully. Or you may buy investments for which accurate information is difficult to obtain. Remember that less can be more. Choose a mutual fund or two instead of a host of individual issues to fill out the gaps in your diversification plan.

● Overlooking important assets. Many investors focus their diversification efforts narrowly, excluding assets such as their earning power, their home, and their tax-deferred accounts. But such assets may be the most valuable. If your IRA is stashed in long-term bonds and cash, for example, consider tilting your remaining assets toward growth-oriented investments.

Key Indicators to Watch

The economic statistics that regularly spew out of the federal government often seem irrelevant to the everyday lives of most investors and retirees. But ignoring changes in the economy's vital signs could be lethal to your retirement plan's long-term health. By learning how to interpret such data, you gain advance warning of the economic trends that determine the returns you earn on your money and can take action to keep your portfolio profitable. Consider, for example, these unsettling reports on rising inflation and interest rates in April 1989: Many forecasters warned that inflation, which stayed below 4.3% from 1983 to 1988, had moved above 5% and could surpass 6% in the next few years. Resurgent inflation usually fuels higher interest rates, which generally depress prices of stocks and bonds and sometimes presage recession.

At the same time, interest rates on supersecure three-month Treasury bills climbed as high as 9.2%—or 2.7 times the dividend yield on the bellwether Standard & Poor's 500-stock index. That ratio has exceeded 2.5 only four times in the past two decades. In each instance, the stock market fell within eight months, dropping on average a total of 30%.

To make sense of such economic statistics, you must first understand the framework that gives them shape, known as the business cycle. This wavelike pattern of economic activity has undulated from boom to bust for more than a century. The cycle, which normally takes three to four years from start to finish, begins when interest rates and inflation are low or falling. This reduces the price of borrowing, making it easier for consumers to buy homes, cars, and other expensive items. Faced with surging demand for their products and services, businesses also take advantage of the favorable borrowing costs and begin expanding. Pumped-up consumer and business spending leads to higher revenues and profits for businesses and thus nationwide economic growth. When investors expect higher corporate profits, stock prices shoot up.

As demand for credit increases, interest rates rise because more borrowers are competing to get loans. Similarly, when consumers and businesses buy more goods, the inflation rate goes up. Ultimately, inflation and interest rates climb high enough to send stock prices down, stifle business and consumer borrowing, and choke off the expansion. This results in flat economic growth or even a recession—two or more quarters of declining gross national product (the value of all goods and services produced in the country). As this happens, the demand for credit ebbs, interest rates fall, and the cycle starts anew.

As you flip through the newspaper, look for these signs of change in the cycle, key indicators of the five types of investment risk outlined earlier:

Inflation. You can get a reading on this with the consumer price index (CPI). A high rate for this measure of the cost of goods and services is public enemy No. 1 for financial assets such as stocks, bonds, annuities, and certificates of deposit. For example, if you buy a $1,000 five-year U.S. Treasury note or CD that pays 9% annually, you will receive $90 a year in interest. But if consumer prices are bounding ahead by 5%, the real purchasing power of your $90 will be declining by 5% a year. And when you get your principal back in five years, it will have lost 23% of its original value. Inflation usually hurts stock prices as well because higher consumer prices lessen the value of future corporate earnings, which makes shares of those companies less appealing.

You can keep tabs on the pace of inflation during the fourth week of every month, when the Department of Labor announces the consumer price index. An annual inflation rate below 2% is low, 2% to 4% is moderate, and above 4% is high. Check to see, too, whether the inflation rate has been rising—a negative, or bearish, sign for stock and bond investors—or falling, which is bullish.

Interest rates. These give you an idea of what rates you will earn on cash investments such as bank CDs and money-market accounts. Rising interest rates also depress bond prices, and they can send stocks down for two reasons. First, higher rates mean bigger borrowing expenses for companies, which erode corporate profits and, in turn, cut stock prices. Second, share values fall because high rates lure investors away from stocks and into interest-paying bonds and money-market funds.

You can discern broad trends by focusing on two key rates. One is the prime rate, which is what banks charge their best business customers for loans. When the prime rate is climbing, it means companies are borrowing heavily and the economy is still on an upward swing. Since consumer loan rates are also pegged to the prime, you can use this barometer to tell whether your own borrowing costs are likely to rise or fall. During the 12 months that ended April 1, 1989, the prime rate rose steadily from 8.5% to 11.5%. The second rate you should follow is the yields on three-month Treasury bills. When their yields rise sharply—as they did from 5.8% to 8.9% for the year that ended April 1, 1989—this may signal a resurgence of inflation. Subsequently, the economy could slow down.

Key government economic figures. At the very least, you should track three statistics: the nation's gross national product (GNP), the balance of payments, and the index of leading economic indicators. GNP is the nation's broadest gauge of economic health. About three weeks after the close of each quarter, the government announces the annual rate at which GNP has grown in the previous three months. Less than 2% is viewed as low growth, 2% to 5% is respectable, and anything above that is generally considered an unsustainable boom.

The balance of payments figure—reported quarterly as a surplus or a deficit—will help you monitor trends in international trade. It measures the flow of goods, services, and investments between the U.S. and the rest of the world. When deficits persist, this generally reduces the value of the dollar abroad and can boost inflation. Reason: A weak dollar makes foreign goods relatively expensive, often allowing American makers of similar goods to raise prices as well.

For a glimpse at how the U.S. economy could perform in the near future, look to the index of leading economic indicators, which is usually reported during the first week of the month. The indicators represent an average of 11 components of economic growth ranging from stock prices to housing permits. If the index is consistently rising, the economy is still chugging along and a setback is unlikely. But if the indicators fall for three or more consecutive months, look for an economic slowdown and possibly even a recession in the next year or so.

The stock market. Its behavior sometimes gives advance warning of an economic upswing or downturn because investors buy or sell shares based on their expectations of the future. For example, stock prices typically explode midway through a recession, usually a good six to 12 months before the economy itself recovers. Similarly, sharply declining stock prices—a drop of 10% or more over one to three months—may warn of an impending slowdown or recession. The stock market is no guarantee of the economic outlook, though. As Nobel laureate economist Paul Samuelson quipped, "The stock market has predicted nine of the past five recessions."

Monitor basic stock market trends each weekend by reading about the previous week's movement of the Dow Jones industrial average, which averages the stock prices of 30 large industrial companies ranging from IBM to McDonald's. Should you become interested in investing in stocks of small and medium-size companies—or mutual funds that buy such shares—keep tabs weekly on the Nasdaq composite of stocks that trade over the counter.

Industry and company news. If you own shares in a particular company or have a stock mutual fund that is invested heavily in one type of business, be sure to read any news stories on the company or that industry. These articles can alert you to the possible rise or fall in the fortunes of the business. No matter how woeful or wonderful the news, though, never buy or sell an investment solely on the basis of a newspaper story. What may seem like good news to you may be disappointing to professional investors who follow the company. For example, when General Motors announced a quarterly earnings increase of 67% in February 1989, its stock fell $3.12 because most analysts had expected an even larger rise.

Most important, by the time you read about a company in the newspaper, many professional investors have already acted on the information and bought or sold the stock. "As a result, the news is already discounted in the price," says Michael Lehmann, author of *The Dow Jones-Irwin Guide to Using the Wall Street Journal* (Dow Jones-Irwin, $22.50). "So by investing on the story, you're more likely to get burned than make a killing." Such a goof could turn you off the business pages forever, and that would be an even bigger mistake.

Low-Risk Places to Park Cash

Everyone needs to save for that proverbial rainy day—illness, unemployment, or any other financial setback. You should keep this cash reserve where you can get it—all of it—when you want it. Unlike most investments, the ones that you put these funds into must effectively guarantee your principal and give you reasonable access to it. Savers can choose from a smorgasbord of accounts and securities that do just that. They include a variety of bank deposits, money-market mutual funds, and Treasury bills.

If such short-term accounts and securities are mostly for rainy day money, they serve other purposes, too. They are for cloudy day money: You may wish at times to add to them because the outlook for stocks and other alternatives is hazy and you think you may earn more on these so-called savings instruments. And they can be used as long-term investments by people whose circumstances or temperaments demand a high degree of liquidity.

Each of these deposits or securities strikes a different balance of safety, liquidity, and yield. To choose intelligently among them, you need to know what the trade-offs are and which combination of qualities best meets your needs. Just as important is knowing how much to put away. While the emergency-savings component of your cash reserve should equal three to six months of expenses, someone with a secure job—a civil service employee, for example—can shoot toward the low end of that range. You can also maintain a small emergency fund if your rich uncle will help out in a pinch. But a sole breadwinner with three children will want to load up on savings.

The customary place for ready money, of course, is a nearby bank, savings and loan association, or credit union. The chief attraction is safety. Accounts of up to $100,000 are generally insured by the federal government. You can get liquidity and attractive yields at these institutions, too, though not necessarily together.

Say you have less than $1,000 and want a bank account with instant liquidity. Your banker will trot out a federally regulated 5.1% NOW account or a 5½% passbook, both flops in the yield department. The NOW is actually a checking account, and it's costly. Many banks charge $3 to $5 a month and 15 cents to 30 cents a check if balances fall below $1,000. A small saver seeking maximum safety can get the best passbook yields at employer-related credit unions and some state-chartered banks and S&Ls. Credit unions, which are exempt from the federal 5½% rate ceiling, pay about 6¾%. Most require minimum investments of only $5 and, generally, accounts are federally insured.

Some state-chartered institutions in Maryland, North Carolina, Ohio, and Pennsylvania are also exempt from the federal interest-rate ceiling and can pay higher passbook rates, typically 7% to 8½%. Their money is insured by private or state agencies rather than the federal government, making these accounts slightly riskier. Out-of-staters who want to stretch for yield can mail their deposits across state lines. For lists of these institutions' names and addresses, write to state banking agencies.

If you can maintain a $1,000 minimum balance, you've got the price of admission to the best deal at a bank or an S&L: a money-market deposit account. With a federally insured money-market account, you can make unlimited withdrawals at bank branches and automatic teller machines. The accounts permit you to write a limited number per month of so-called third-party checks, but with a phone call you can transfer funds to your regular checking account.

Rates fluctuate, but the accounts tend to pay slightly less than six-month Treasury bills do. If your account drops below $1,000, however, this prince will turn into a frog, paying no more than the 5.1% NOW account rate, usually until the minimum balance is restored. Some banks pay 5¼% interest for the entire month if a customer's balance drops below $1,000 for a single day.

The rates on money-market accounts may vary by nearly a percentage point within the same city, and those institutions with the best rates often keep them consistently high. So shopping for rates pays. S&Ls frequently offer slightly higher rates than banks. If you will be keeping $5,000 or more in a money-market account, ask if the S&L or bank will reward you accordingly. Some institutions pay big savers close to a percentage point more in interest than depositors with modest balances.

A money-market mutual fund is for you if you have less than $1,000 and don't mind sacrificing a little safety. As a rule, you need $1,000 to open a money fund account, although some funds accept initial deposits of $500 or less. Money fund investors are technically shareholders: In most cases, you own one share for every dollar you invest. The funds pool shareholders' cash and invest in Treasury bills, bank certificates of deposit, and commercial paper—that is, corporate IOUs. Yields fluctuate daily, but as a rule share prices do not. Funds tend to yield roughly the same as bank money-market accounts and let you write unlimited checks for $500 or more. You usually invest by mail, though some funds have store-front offices and others sell through stockbrokers. For a list of funds, their toll-free numbers, addresses, and minimum deposits, write to the Investment Company Institute, 1775 K Street NW, Washington, D.C. 20006.

Money funds are not federally insured, but only one of the 348 has gone belly-up during their 12-year history. Shareholders of the First Multifund of New York got back 93 cents on the dollar after trustees liquidated the assets in 1978. Strange as it sounds, there's little reason to invest in the safest money funds. These funds, which hold only Treasury securities in their portfolios, usually yield half a percentage point less than federally insured bank money-market accounts do. But they make sense for people who can't afford the $1,000 bank minimums and demand government security.

To earn the best money fund yields, you must invest in the funds taking the biggest investment risks. They might buy certificates of deposit from foreign branches of U.S. banks or debt from companies without the highest credit ratings. "A money fund has to be investing in something other than certificates of deposit from Chase Manhattan Bank and Citibank to be on the top of the yield scale," says Glen King Parker, publisher of *Money Fund Safety Ratings*, a monthly newsletter (3471 North Federal Highway, Fort Lauderdale, FL 33306). Over the years, Parker says, the funds with the best combination of yield and safety have been: Dreyfus Liquid Assets (phone 800-645-6561; 212-895-1206 in New York City); Fidelity Cash Reserves (800-225-6190; 617-523-1919 in Massachusetts); IDS Cash Management (800-328-8300); and Kemper Money Market (800-621-1048; 312-332-6472 in Chicago).

Tax-free money funds have been outpaced by taxable money funds in most cases. In general, tax-exempt funds

no longer offer fatter after-tax yields for taxpayers in the
28% or 33% federal brackets. The tax-exempt advantage—
worth less than one percentage point for a 33% bracket
investor—remains only for investors in high-tax states,
such as New York and Massachusetts, who buy so-called
triple-tax-free funds whose interest is exempt from state
and local as well as federal taxes.

You will get a higher yield from a bank time deposit
than from a bank money-market account or money-market mutual fund if you're willing to give up some liquidity.
The longer you agree to tie up the money, the higher the
rate. Typically, a three-month account yields half a point
more than a bank money-market account; a one-year
certificate pays a point more and a 2½-year CD pays two
points more. Some banks accept as little as $250 for time
deposits and offer maturities as short as one month.

Banks hit you with penalties if you want to take money
out of time deposits early. By law, a bank must withhold
at least one month's interest on early withdrawals of CDs
with maturities between 31 days and a year. On longer
CDs, the minimum penalty is three months' interest. But
some banks impose tougher penalties than the mini-
mums. Don't put your emergency cash reserve into any
time deposit whose penalty is more than one month's
interest.

Stockbrokers and some mutual fund organizations act
as middlemen, buying and selling bank CDs for their
customers. By purchasing certificates through them, you
can avoid the possibility of interest penalties altogether.
You can, of course, hold on to the CD until maturity and
get back full face value. But if you want out early, rather
than presenting such a certificate to its issuer for redemption, you sell it like a bond. You'll receive whatever a
buyer is willing to pay, which will depend on current
interest rates. If depositors can get a higher rate on new
CDs, they won't want to pay the full face value for your
old one. Unless you think interest rates are going to
decline, you're probably better off buying a certificate
at a bank.

Two little secrets: Suburban banks and S&Ls often pay
higher rates to lure depositors away from their downtown
rivals. Also, there are bargain days for bank CD rates.
Some banks raise their rates by a percentage point or so
at Christmas. That's the time when banks are especially in

need of cash because many of their customers are drawing down their accounts.

If you have $10,000 that you can commit for three months to a year, your savings choice should be a Treasury bill. Government-guaranteed T-bills are unbeatable for safety. And their after-tax yields usually best those of CDs with similar maturities. That's because interest on Treasury securities is free of state and local taxes.

Plan on holding your T-bill until it matures. A banker or broker could charge ¼% to 3% of the bill's price to sell it; and if rates have gone up, you probably won't get what you paid for it.

Figuring out a T-bill yield is a little tricky. Bills are sold at discount and redeemed at face value on maturity, making their actual yield more than their stated interest rate. Say you hand over $10,000 for a one-year Treasury bill whose rate is 10%. A week later, you will get back a $1,000 check from the government—the amount of the discount. When the year is up, you get the full $10,000 back. Since you received $1,000 on a $9,000 investment, your annualized yield is $1,000 divided by $9,000, or 11.1%.

Treasury notes and bonds, which have longer maturities than T-bills, may be fine as income-producing investments, but they're not liquid enough for your cash reserve. You're more likely to lose principal by selling one of these securities than you are with T-bills.

You buy Treasury securities through banks or brokers, who will charge $25 to $50. Or you can buy them directly, at no charge, from one of the Federal Reserve's 37 banks and offices or at the Treasury Building in Washington, D.C. Three-month and six-month bills are issued weekly; one-year bills and two-year notes are brought out monthly; and other notes and bonds, irregularly. Many daily newpapers publish announcements of upcoming sales. For more information, send for the free booklet *Buying Treasury Securities at Federal Reserve Banks,* Federal Reserve Bank of Richmond, Public Services Department, Box 27622, Richmond, VA 23261.

U.S. savings bonds are fine for long-term savers with small amounts to invest. You can purchase them for as little as $25 through banks, stockbrokers, and company payroll plans. Savings bonds pay a rate equal to 85% of that paid by five-year Treasury securities—but just if you hang on to them for five years. Redeem the bonds early and you may get a 4.2% yield.

Wherever you end up putting your rainy day money, be sure it's a spot that makes you comfortable. "If you are happy only when your money is in a 5½% passbook account, there's no reason to feel guilty about it," says Robin Oegerle, president of Financial Strategies, a Washington, D.C. planning firm. Peace of mind is, after all, what savings are all about.

Yields Too Good to Be True

If you decide security is important to you and turn to so-called "safe" investments—CDs and money-market funds—a note of caution: In today's fierce competition for investors' dollars, many financial institutions are using misleading ads and gimmicks to puff up the yields they claim and disguise the true risks involved. To avoid a wipeout when riding for awesome income, watch out for these common ploys:

Teaser CDs. Some banks and savings and loans promote certificates of deposit paying teaser rates—initial yields as high as 20% that expire within a few weeks. For example, in 1989, AmSouth Bank of Alabama offered a three-year CD with a 19.89% teaser rate; after 30 days it declined to 8.35%. The combined rates return only $260.12 on a $1,000 investment, compared with $304.09 that an investor could earn on a three-year CD paying a fixed rate of 9.25%.

Other teaser CDs switch to variable rates after a short time, making it impossible to predict their actual return. But it is likely to be lower than the initial rate—and also lower than that of fixed-rate CDs of similar maturity. "Why lock up your money to earn a variable rate?" asks Frank Diekmann, editor of *Bank Advertising News* (P. O. Box 088888, North Palm Beach, FL 33408; weekly, $298 a year). Instead, Diekmann suggests buying six-month, fixed-rate CDs, which currently yield as much as 10%. When the CDs mature, investors can reinvest the money in new six-month certificates—or switch to longer-term certificates if yields seem likely to fall.

Phantom yields. A number of institutions quote annual

yields on three- and six-month CDs without disclosing that the yields are strictly hypothetical. Reason: There is no guarantee you will be able to reinvest at an equally attractive rate for the rest of the year when the CD matures. In 1989, Massachusetts state regulators cited six savings institutions in the Boston area for an even worse variant of this practice—showing compound annual yields for CDs that pay simple interest. The culprits included Bank of New England, which advertised a 9.58% compound yield on a three-month CD along with its actual 9.25% simple interest rate.

Tiered rates. Many institutions advertise high yields on savings accounts and other investments, but you have to deposit big bucks to earn them. For example, First Federal Savings & Loan of Rochester, New York advertised an 8.5% yield on a savings account, compared with an average yield of 6.42% for similar accounts at other banks, but paid that high rate only on deposits of $25,000 or more. Small savers who deposited less than $10,000 earned a piddling 5.25%.

Pseudo-CDs. Consumer lending companies, banks, and S&Ls sell certificates yielding up to 13% that resemble bank CDs but actually are nothing more than IOUs. While the government guarantees deposits of up to $100,000 at federally insured banks and thrifts, pseudo-CDs have no federal protection.

Advanta Corporation, a finance company in Horsham, Pennsylvania recently sold one-year subordinated notes yielding 10%. That topped the average 8.93% rate on one-year CDs but was well below the 12.5% yields on corporate debt issues with similar risk.

Waived fund fees. About 20% of the 540 or so money-market funds available to investors waive all or part of their annual management fees to boost yields. Among them: Alger Money Market Portfolio, the top-performing money fund during the past year according to *Donoghue's MoneyLetter* (P. O. Box 6640, Holliston, MA 01746; bi-weekly, $87 a year). But, typically, when such a fund's high yield has lured enough investors, management increases fees and the yield may decline by as much as three-quarters of a percentage point.

Excessive distribution rates. The SEC issued regulations in 1988 that prevent income funds from advertising yields inflated by options trading and other speculative activities. But some government bond funds—which often carry names like "Government Plus" or "Government High-Income"—still quote unusually high "distribution rates" in sales literature. Some of these funds sell call options on the bonds in their portfolio and pay out the profits to shareholders. But that options strategy reduces the funds' potential for capital appreciation. Worse, high distributions may eat up gains that a fund could use to offset losses in its portfolio. Result: Over time, the fund's share value may fall as such losses accumulate.

Prudential-Bache Government Plus Fund, for example, recently had a distribution rate of 10.57% even though its yield was actually only 8.15%. The fund's share price has declined by 12% since 1985. "Investors probably don't realize that fat distribution checks can come at the expense of total return," says Catherine Gillis, a securities analyst with *Mutual Fund Values* (53 West Jackson, Chicago, IL 60604; $325 a year). "They would be better off investing in a conventional Treasury fund."

Taking an Interest in Bonds

Prudent investors should move at least some of their retirement savings into bonds. Although the most tempting—and difficult—strategy is to buy long-term bonds as rates peak, most investors fare poorly at such precision timing. Thus, you probably should take a buy-and-hold approach to bonds. If you do, you won't be too disappointed should interest rates rise and bond prices fall; you'll receive the interest payments that led you to bonds in the first place, and you'll get your money back in the end. To play it safest, you probably want to emphasize high-quality, intermediate-term (five- to 15-year maturity) bonds, thereby reducing the time you might be stuck with a bond whose yield is no longer attractive.

While buying and holding is best as a rule, it doesn't insulate you entirely from interest-rate storms, for a couple of reasons. First, rising rates are usually accompanied by higher inflation—and inflation is a bondholder's biggest worry. While stocks can keep up with moderate

inflation through rising earnings, bonds can't because
they are fixed-dollar investments. If inflation consistently
runs higher than the rate you lock in, the interest and
principal you receive will be worth less in purchasing
power than what you paid for the bond.

The other reason that buy-and-holders aren't immune
to rate fluctuations is that most corporate and municipal
bonds are sold with call provisions. These allow issuers
to buy back the debt before it is due if interest rates fall.
The bondholder receives a premium, usually equal to a
year's interest or less. The effect is to cap the amount you
can earn from your bond, by both limiting your potential
price gain and depriving you of high interest income. Why
would issuers do such a thing? Because they want to be
free to refinance their debt at a lower rate. U.S. Treasury
securities are not callable, except for 30-year Treasury
bonds, which can be called after 25 years.

Most investors are better off catching the wave of high
yields by buying shares of bond funds rather than individual issues. One advantage that funds offer is diversification. By spreading their portfolios over 50 or more
separate issues, corporate and municipal funds protect
investors' capital from being ravaged by one or two
defaults. And as long as you avoid load funds—those that
levy a front-end sales charge—as well as those with
expense ratios greater than 1%, investing in funds is
usually cheaper than buying individual bonds. You side-
step a broker's commission, typically 2%, and also avoid
the undisclosed dealer markup that can add 1% to 4% to
the bond's price.

Investors, however, must understand a crucial difference in the way rising interest rates affect bond funds
versus bonds. If rates go up one percentage point, the net
asset value of a fund with an average weighted maturity
of 10 years drops about the same as the price of a 10-year
bond. The similarity ends there. With a bond, no matter
what interest rates do, you know that you will receive full
face value at maturity, assuming there is not a default. But
a bond fund never matures; it continually buys and sells
bonds. Thus, there is no date when you are certain to
recoup your original investment.

The following overview of bonds and bond funds available can help you to put together a portfolio that provides
the highest returns without undue risk:

U.S. Treasury bonds. Whether you are interested primarily in high yields or capital gains, funds that invest solely in bonds backed by the U.S. government or federal agencies can help you reach your goal with the greatest degree of safety. The government guarantee, of course, protects you only against loss through default. You still run the risk that your Treasury bonds will drop in value if interest rates rise. As a result, you must find a fund whose sensitivity to interest-rate movements matches your tolerance for risk.

First, check the fund's average weighted maturity with the fund's telephone representative. Conservative investors interested in earning high yields but avoiding hits to principal should stick to no-load funds that usually keep their average maturity between five and seven years. If you want a better shot at capital gains, and are willing to take slightly more risk, opt for funds that have average maturities of 10 or so years.

Investors hunting for big capital-gains, however, are better off to bypass funds and buy long-term Treasury bonds through their brokers or directly from the Federal Reserve, which charges no commission. The problem is that many long-term government funds invest up to 85% of their portfolios in mortgage-backed securities issued by the Government National Mortgage Association (nicknamed Ginnie Mae) and other agencies. These issues add to the fund's current yield but limit potential capital gains. Reason: When rates drop, homeowners often refinance their mortgages. This results in early repayment of mortgage-backed securities, which robs investors of capital gains. There is one drawback to buying individual Treasuries: While a bond fund lets you reinvest your interest, however small, in additional fund shares, Treasury bonds are sold in $1,000 minimums. At yields of between 9% and 9.5%, then, it would take roughly $11,000 in Treasury bonds to throw off enough interest to buy another $1,000 bond each year.

Municipals. Individuals' voracious appetite for tax-free income has inflated prices of muni bonds, which are usually sold in $5,000 denominations, and kept their yields from rising in tandem with those of Treasury bonds. Even though munis' rate advantage over taxables has slipped, investors can still get an edge by going to

funds that invest in tax-exempt bonds with maturities of
15 years or longer. High-quality, 15-year munis recently
yielded around 7.3%, equivalent to a 10.1% taxable yield
for a married couple in the 28% tax bracket—joint 1989
taxable income of $29,750 to $71,900. That is about one
percentage point higher than taxable issues with comparable maturities.

For investors looking for top tax-equivalent yields,
some advisers suggest long-term, high-yield muni funds,
which recently paid at least a half a percentage point
more than their high-grade counterparts. Unlike high-
yield corporate bonds (a.k.a. junk bonds), the credit quality of many high-yield muni funds is quite high because
managers often keep 85% or more of their portfolio in
investment-grade bonds. A spike in interest rates, of
course, would zap the value of long-term funds. If you
are inclined to bail out during such a free-fall, opt
instead for the lower yields and greater security of
intermediate-term funds.

If you live in a high-tax state, such as New York or
California, you can grab an effective half-percentage
point of extra yield by investing in a fund that buys only
bonds of your state. One caveat: Restricting your portfolio to one state increases your credit risk. In addition, if
you live in a state with a puny supply of munis—Ohio or
Minnesota, for example—high demand can depress
yields.

High-grade corporates. Investment grade corporate
bonds, typically sold in $1,000 denominations, are those
issued by companies sound enough to earn a BBB rating
or higher from Standard & Poor's. But in an era of
mergermania, the term high-grade corporates is rapidly
becoming an oxymoron. The mountain of debt heaped
onto a company to finance a takeover can turn investment-grade bonds into junk faster than you can say
leveraged buy-out. Standard & Poor's lowered its ratings
on 284 issues in 1987 and a record 386 in 1988, representing $356 billion in debt for the two years. Then, too,
corporate bonds lately were yielding only from one-half
to one percentage point more than lower-risk Treasury
bonds. As a result, analysts recommend that most investors shun high-grade corporates and opt instead for the
safer returns in U.S. Treasuries.

Junk bonds. In 1988, daredevils who seized the ultra-high yields in corporate bonds rated below BBB by Standard & Poor's came away winners. Funds that invest in such junk bonds topped all other fixed-income funds with a 12.4% total return, compared with 11.3% for second-place, high-yield munis. But some experts believe a smashup in the junk market is inevitable. One reason is that the craze for leveraged buy-outs has spawned a more default-prone strain of high-yield debt. In a recession, according to estimates from Standard & Poor's, $15 billion of the roughly $186 billion in junk bonds outstanding could default—more than three times the volume of defaults in 1988. So many strategists suggest that investors cut back their exposure in junk funds to no more than 15% of their assets. Better yet, avoid junk altogether until after the next recession hits.

Closed-end bond funds. Hybrid closed-end funds hold securities like conventional mutual funds do, but trade on an exchange like stocks. Shares are issued to the public through brokers at the fund's initial public offering, or IPO. After that, you buy shares at the current market price—which, depending on investor demand, may be higher or lower than the fund's underlying net asset value.

Be wary if a broker calls touting the IPO of a new closed-end bond fund. For each $1,000 you invest, $70 is usually siphoned off in underwriting fees—which means you are, in effect, paying $1,000 for $930 worth of bonds. Instead, look for a closed-end fund that already trades on an exchange and is currently selling at a discount to its net asset value. As with an open-end fund, turn to the fund's prospectus and annual report to assess the overall riskiness of the fund by examining the credit quality and average weighted maturity of its portfolio. And steer clear of *leveraged* closed-end bond funds that tout tantalizing yields by borrowing at short-term rates and investing the proceeds in long-term bonds. This strategy can backfire when short-term rates rise above those on long-term bonds, as was the case in 1989. Rising rates can also trigger defaults in leveraged, corporate bond funds, which will magnify losses of principal.

Zero-coupon bonds. These issues sell at a deep discount to face value rather than pay interest regularly and are redeemed for face value at maturity. As a result, zeros make sense for two opposite types of investors: risk-takers seeking hefty gains and conservative savers hoping to lock in a given rate of return.

If you are convinced that interest rates are at or near a peak and are poised to slide as low as 7.5%, then 10- to 30-year, zero-coupon Treasuries are your best bet for spectacular capital appreciation. The price of a zero is more volatile than that of a conventional bond because all interest is paid in a lump sum at maturity. For instance, if interest rates drop two percentage points, the price of a 30-year zero yielding 9.1% will jump 78%. On the other hand, if interest rates rise two percentage points, you will get mauled with a 45% loss.

If you must be sure your investments will grow to a specific sum at some future date, like retirement, zeros are ideal. For example, 20-year zeros yielding 9.1% would turn a $5,000 investment into $30,000 at maturity two decades later. One disadvantage: Even though you receive no income until your zero matures, you are taxed as if you were paid interest each year. Thus, unless you plan to sell your zeros as soon as possible for capital gains, invest in taxable zeros only in a tax-exempt account, such as an Individual Retirement Account or Keogh, or your kids' Uniform Gifts to Minors Act accounts. Or you can avoid the tax complications altogether by investing in tax-exempt, municipal zeros. There are no zero muni funds, so you must buy the actual bonds.

Only two investment companies offer taxable, zero-coupon bond funds: Scudder Stevens & Clark and Benham Management. But if you intend to hold the zeros more than a few years, buy individual bonds instead of the funds. Reason: The longer you hold, the better off you will be because you won't get hit with the fund's expense ratio year after year.

Go for Growth in Stocks and Mutual Funds

In recent years, more and more retirement-minded investors have come to regard the stock market as a financial safari that is exciting but fraught with too many dangers. Yet many seasoned strategists warn that those who stay too close to camp will likely forgo the superior

returns—and higher standards of living in retirement—
that stocks' long-term growth historically delivers.

Despite periodic setbacks such as Black Monday,
stocks have outperformed fixed-income investments by
an average of around six percentage points a year since
the early 1920s. Moreover, a study by the investment firm
Sanford C. Bernstein & Company notes that people who
remained fully invested in stocks between 1975 and 1984
earned an impressive 15% compound annual return. But
had an investor missed the five months when the market
scored its largest gains—three of which were at the
beginning of the two major market upturns in this 10-year
period—the annual return would have dropped to less
than 9%. That is the same return earned during the period
on risk-free Treasury bills.

The moral: Since no one knows when the market will
make its next great charge, investors who want to ride the
bull market of the 1990s should look for prudent ways to
position themselves before stocks bolt from the gate.
There are strategies—and mutual fund surrogates—that
allow skittish shareholders to go for growth and still
sleep at night.

One time-honored method is to buy defensive stocks—
growing but glamourless firms whose bargain share
prices help to cushion you against losses during market
squalls. Such stocks include issues selling at price/earn-
ings ratios 25% or more under the market average, lately
12; those with ratios or price-to-book value (or net worth
per share) 20% or more below the recent 2.1 average; and
ones with above-average dividend yields of more than
3.6%. To find these yardsticks of value, consult the *Value
Line Investment Survey*, available at large public libraries. It also lists stocks with the highest yields, lowest
price-to-book ratios, and lowest P/Es.

Also favor high-yielding stocks of electric utilities, regional phone companies, and commercial banks with a
penchant for raising their dividends. They have the potential to reward retirees with higher payouts each year—
which is more than you can say for bonds—plus capital
appreciation if interest rates decline in reponse to an
economic slowdown. As rates fall, investors are willing to
pay more for the income provided by such stocks. Although prices of these shares will slump during a recession, they typically will drop only about half as far as

the market overall for the following reasons.

In the case of electric utilities, the demand for power is fairly steady. In addition, utility yields are comparatively high and generally secure. Managements know that investors buy the stocks for income, so they try to maintain dividends at almost any cost. For best results, look for well-managed companies with steadily increasing dividends that operate in areas where power demand could grow. But be wary of utilities that rely almost exclusively on coal. The dividends could go up in smoke if proposed legislation is enacted to curb acid-rain by requiring plants to be overhauled or replaced.

Regional phone companies have attractive yields and also provide a measure of protection in economic downturns—people don't pull the plug on their phone during a recession. Increased competition in the Baby Bell's basic telephone franchises could squeeze future profit margins. But many analysts believe that the firms' forays into new areas such as cellular-phone and radio paging services give them solid growth prospects.

Home in on banking stocks that excel in a deregulated environment. Most analysts expect banks to keep moving into the securities industry even if Congress doesn't, as anticipated, repeal the Glass-Steagall Act, which prohibits banks from underwriting stocks and bonds. But stay clear of institutions whose portfolios are stuffed with risky oil-patch real estate and energy loans. Concentrate instead on banks with a broad range of consumer and commercial lending and a history of raising their cash payouts.

To further dampen your portfolio's volatility, you should generally own at least 10 different stocks in as many industries. And, ideally, these companies should not be in industries whose fortunes are tied to the same economic trends. For example, to prevent your portfolio from being devastated by skidding auto sales, avoid owning a large number of shares of General Motors and Simpson Industries, which manufactures auto parts.

Also consider a tactic called dollar-cost averaging, in which you systematically invest a set amount at regular intervals—every three or six months, for example. On average, you will buy fewer shares when prices are high than when they are low. Thus, over time you are likely to pay less than the average price per share and to be in a position to sell at a decent profit. The tactic obviously won't work if you choose an investment that falls ill and never recovers. To reduce this risk, pick a diversified stock fund rather than a single stock. Or select among the many blue-chip companies that let you buy their shares directly at no fee through a dividend-reinvestment plan.

If your vision of retirement is closer to pouring piña coladas at poolside than poring over stock tables in your home office, then you are an ideal candidate for stock funds. The most obvious advantage of investing in funds is that you can buy the services of a professional money manager at a low cost. The average stock fund's annual expenses run between 1% and 1.5%. That compares with the 3% or so you would pay to hire a first-class money manager, few of whom take on a portfolio of less than $500,000. And since funds typically hold the securities of dozens of companies, you get far greater diversification than you could ever achieve on your own. Funds also offer liquidity and flexibility—key features for anyone who might need to dip into capital to pay for regular or unexpected expenses. You can often redeem your shares by simply writing a check or making a telephone call. If you buy into a family of funds, you can switch among various types of funds as market conditions or your own needs change.

But hyperproliferation—there were more than a thousand stock funds at last count—has made choosing promising funds almost as daunting as picking winning stocks. Yet it need not be. The best way to start is by weeding out less-desirable funds. Those sold by brokers and financial planners usually carry a load, or sales commission, which can be as high as 8.5%. Since this fee does not help the fund's performance and erodes your initial investment, you are generally better off sticking to no-load or low-load funds—those that charge no sales fee at all or a modest one of 4% or less. Other poor choices for a retirement portfolio are aggressive growth funds, which buy speculative stocks, and so-called sector funds, which limit themselves to stocks of a single industry.

Concentrate instead on acquiring not just individual funds but an all-star team. (For leads, see *Money*'s risk-adjusted fund recommendations beginning on page 128.) Then, your portfolio can better withstand threats, from rising interest rates to stock market stumbles, while attending to your income demands as well. You can build such a portfolio with a combination of funds spread, according to your own needs, across the following categories:

Growth funds. Investors who are a decade or more from retirement should tilt the mix of their portfolios toward long-term growth funds, which invest primarily in brand-name stocks renowned for their consistent growth in earnings and share price over time. Such funds can produce superior gains over periods of five years or more. So, too, can their younger siblings that specialize in small-company growth stocks. Though relatively risky, small but adaptable companies typically respond quickly to change and zoom ahead in the early stages of a bull market. In addition, after being largely ignored in the last major market advance, shares in small and medium-size firms are comparatively cheap. Both types of funds, however, are vulnerable to short-term risk: if recession wrecks the market, their net asset values will plunge.

Total return funds. This group—which includes balanced, growth and income, and equity income funds—is ideal for investors approaching or in retirement. The funds' strategy is to buy dividend-paying stocks, often buttressed with some bonds, that produce an annual yield between 3% and 6% and also give you some capital appreciation. The yields, in turn, help prop up the prices of these funds in times of market turbulence.

Favor growth and income funds if you are looking more for capital gains than for income. These funds pitch their mix toward stocks that pay modest dividends but also have growth potential. For a bit more income, and moderate long-term gains, you are better off in equity income funds, which are distinguished by high-yielding stocks such as utilities. Extremely conservative investors who want more income and less volatility may prefer balanced funds, which divide their portfolios roughly equally between stocks and bonds.

International funds. You needn't be a polyglot to interpret the fetching profits that have been made in foreign stocks in recent years. Falling oil prices accounted for part of this hot performance abroad; European and Asian economies tend to be more heavily dependent on imported crude than is the U.S. Even greater impetus was provided by the declining dollar. The rise of a foreign currency against the greenback amplifies the dollar value of that country's stocks and their profits. But shareholders in international funds are unlikely to see the same magnitude of gains now that the dollar's value abroad appears to have stabilized, and they could suffer currency-related losses if the dollar rebounds strongly. Still, investing in funds with extensive foreign holdings helps you balance the downside risk of a stock or fund portfolio that responds primarily to the U.S. economy.

Twenty Top Funds to Buy and Hold

Faced with the multiplicity of mutual funds, how do you choose the ones that are best suited to your retirement portfolio? To help you narrow the field, *Money*'s research has uncovered 20 exemplars—10 stock and 10 bond funds—that have historically delivered extraordinary returns for the risks they take. As a group, they should appeal to longer-term investors who want such assurance—at least as great as past performance can provide.

Readers of the magazine may note that seven of the funds were members of *Money*'s most recent roster of All-Weather Funds. That is because the methodology used to winnow out this solid score is in the main the same as that behind the All-Weathers. Both rely on a risk-adjustment formula developed by Stanford University finance professor William Sharpe. The method rewards funds for high total returns and docks them for nail-gnawing volatility (in this case defined as the amount by which their month-to-month returns deviate from their average monthly returns).

This trusty 20, however, not only had to post a top risk-adjusted score for the five years to January 1, 1989, but also had to rank near the top of their classes on a risk-adjusted basis for the preceding five years—that is, from January 1, 1979 to January 1, 1984. (Because several fund categories—namely, small-company growth and international on the stock side and U.S. Government and mortgage-backed securities on the bond side—have so

few entries with 10-year records, they were graded only
for the five years through 1988.)

These two extra stock categories were added to help
investors who want to broaden their portfolios—or perhaps go after higher returns, albeit at higher risk. Indeed,
some investment pros think that after several years of
taking a back seat to blue chips, small-company stocks
are overdue for big gains, and almost no one these days
questions the desirability of keeping a portion of your
holdings in international shares. To qualify for consideration, a fund had to have assets of $25 million or more,
accept initial investments of $10,000 or less, and be open
to new investors in a majority of states as of the first
of 1989.

You should be able to find at least one fund whose
investing style matches yours. But also pay attention to
the funds' widely varying front-end sales charges and
total expenses. Unless you are convinced that a higher-
cost fund is absolutely right for you because of its record
or investment strategy, stick with the no-loads on the
lists. And don't assume that these funds are immune to
risk just because they have admirable risk-adjusted rank-
ings. Consult the tables on page 132 to get an idea of how
much you might be chilled if a fund encounters three
months of rough sledding. Here are thumbnail sketches of
these risk-adjusted champs:

The stock funds. The six diversified stock funds com-
bine an estimable record of smooth performance with an
ability to earn returns well above the 66% gain posted by
the average stock fund over the five-year period studied.
In most cases, their portfolio managers hold a mix of
cash, bonds, or high-dividend stocks to boost yields and
thus dampen the effect of market downturns.

This buttoned-down bias can be a little bit misleading.
Mutual Shares manager Michael Price, for instance, led
his no-load to the top spot on *Money*'s list partly by
putting a substantial portion of his $2.8 billion portfolio in
potential takeover targets, bankrupt firms, and other can-
didates for financial restructuring. But Price tries to
protect his investors from the risks of these notoriously
undependable deal stocks by periodically keeping as
much as 30% of his assets in safe, secure cash.

The No. 2 diversified fund, the $6.5 billion no-load

Vanguard Windsor, is piloted by 25-year veteran John Neff, who is known for buying stocks with low price/earnings ratios and usually keeping his fund close to fully invested. His average P/E was about 6, compared with 11 for Standard & Poor's 500-stock index. The managers of the no-load *Lindner Fund* share Neff's nose for low P/E stocks. But fund founder Kurt Lindner and his associates Robert Lange and Eric Ryback are more willing than the Windsor helmsman to switch to cash when stocks seem overpriced.

Phoenix Balanced manager Patricia Bannan, who keeps at least 25% of her 8.5% load fund in fixed-income securities, favors blue-chip stocks of companies with steady earnings growth. At *Fidelity Puritan* (2% load), manager Richard Fentin buys high-yield shares in out-of-favor industries and keeps a fifth or more of fund assets in fixed-income securities. *Merrill Lynch Basic Value* gives investors the option of either paying a 6.5% front-end load or ponying up an annual marketing fee and being subject to an exit charge upon redemption. Manager Paul Hoffmann gravitates toward stocks that have little or no current earnings but that sell at bargain prices well below the per-share value of the company's assets.

Investors should be prepared for a bumpier ride in the small-company and international categories. Although small-company stocks trailed the market averages during the five-year period, no-load *Nicholas II* has outgained 96% of stock funds during the period. Manager Albert Nicholas buys shares of emerging companies with strong balance sheets, above-average growth potential, and P/Es that are high when compared with the S&P 500's multiple of 11 but low for small stocks. *Acorn Fund,* the other small-cap entry, also shuns the priciest growth issues. Manager Ralph Wanger has spared his no-load shareholders big losses by avoiding inherently flighty high-technology issues.

The Japanese stock market rose 525% during the five-year period, so it's no surprise that one of the international picks—the no-load *Japan Fund*—usually puts at least 80% of its portfolio in that market. Manager Laura Luckyn-Malone reduces risk by purchasing shares that trade at P/E ratios about 20% below the market average. Unfortunately, the Japanese market's P/E is a nosebleed-high 62, which suggests to many analysts that Japan's bull market is riding for a fall. If you share their fears, consider the other choice in this category, *Vanguard Trustees' Commingled International*, a no-load that invests less than 30% of its holdings in the Land of the Rising Stock.

The bond funds. The risk-adjusted winners among bond funds easily whipped their five-year category averages (67% for taxable funds and 59% for tax-exempts) but are not always the steadiest in their classes. Instead, they earned top honors by converting the risks they took into returns that more than compensated investors.

The two U.S. Government funds on the list can put up to 100% of their assets in Treasury issues, but they are free to range among other forms of government-backed debt. For example, 4.75% load *Lord Abbett U.S. Government Securities* goes for U.S. Treasury obligations and higher-yielding Ginnie Maes, which are mortgage-backed securities issued by the Government National Mortgage Association. Portfolio manager Carroll Coward frequently adjusts maturities to take advantage of interest-rate moves. She rarely misfires, but the fund will suffer setbacks when she does. By contrast, Milton Schlein, who manages the no-load *Value Line U.S. Government Securities*, follows a buy-and-hold strategy in an effort to avoid sharp swings in share values.

Mortgage-backed securities funds, the second fixed-income category, are required to invest at least 65% of assets in GNMAs and similar issues. Patrick Beimford, manager of *Kemper U.S. Government Securities*, maintains an average portfolio maturity of five to 12 years and diversifies into Treasury notes and cash. "We are for conservative, income-oriented investors," he says of his 4.5% load fund. "If you want to gamble on interest-rate moves, look elsewhere." Jack Lemein's 4% load *Franklin U.S. Government Securities* is among the few that hold close to 100% of assets in GNMAs. He cuts shareholders' risk by investing in securities with relatively short, three- to 10-year maturities, and chops expenses by reducing turnover.

Among high-grade corporate funds, *Bond Fund of America* (4.75% load) is unusual in that it is run by six portfolio managers. The fund is usually widely diversified among a core holding of high-grade corporates, junk

Top Ten Stock Funds

These funds are ranked within categories according to their five-year risk-adjusted returns to January 1, 1989. For steady gains, choose the diversified stock funds. The small-company growth and international funds offer diversification but are more volatile, as detailed in the accompanying article.

Ranked by five-year risk-adjusted return	Type	% gain (or loss) to 1/1/89			
		1988	Three years	Five years	10 years
DIVERSIFIED STOCK FUNDS					
Mutual Shares	G&I	30.9	62.7	135.9	581.0
Vanguard Windsor	G&I	28.7	56.7	139.7	565.7
Lindner Fund	Gro	20.4	49.4	101.4	634.1
Phoenix Balanced	Bal	2.9	35.4	100.5	376.6
Fidelity Puritan	Eql	18.9	41.0	100.7	398.9
Merrill Lynch Basic Value	G&I	22.7	51.0	113.7	488.2
SMALL-COMPANY GROWTH					
Nicholas II	SCG	17.2	39.4	118.2	—
Acorn Fund	SCG	24.7	52.1	108.7	460.9
INTERNATIONAL					
Japan Fund	Intl	19.5	166.5	266.5	431.4
Vanguard Trustees' Com.-Intl	Intl	18.8	121.8	208.8	—

Top Ten Bond Funds

These 10 selections include two choices from five major categories of fixed-income funds. The tax-exempt funds provide relatively low total returns before taxes, but their after-tax payoffs make them worth considering for investors in the 28% and 33% federal tax brackets.

Ranked by five-year risk-adjusted return	% gain (or loss) to 1/1/89			
	1988	Three years	Five years	10 years
U.S. GOVERNMENT BONDS				
Lord Abbett U.S. Government Securities	8.4	26.4	75.7	201.5
Value Line U.S. Government Securities	8.0	23.7	71.0	—
MORTGAGE-BACKED SECURITIES				
Kemper U.S. Government Securities	6.4	26.9	74.3	145.3
Franklin U.S. Government Securities	7.5	24.1	68.2	131.8
HIGH-GRADE CORPORATES				
Bond Fund of America	10.7	30.0	84.4	205.6
Axe-Houghton Income	8.7	28.4	87.8	207.9
HIGH-YIELD CORPORATES				
Kemper High-Yield	14.4	47.5	100.0	262.1
Fidelity High Income Bond	12.6	34.5	86.5	250.0
TAX-EXEMPT BONDS				
SteinRoe Managed Muni	10.9	37.7	89.2	142.7
Kemper Muni Bond	8.7	33.4	78.3	122.0

% gain (or loss) in worst quarter since 1/1/84	Minimum initial investment	Five-year expense projection*	Telephone	
			Toll-free (800)	In state
(16.3)	$5,000	$38	553-3014 —	
(18.6)	10,000	24	662-7447 —	
(16.3)	2,000	59	—	314-727-5305
(8.8)	500	127	243-4361 —	
(14.7)	1,000	59	544-6666 —	
(18.2)	250	95	637-7455 —	
(16.8)	1,000	43	—	414-272-6133
(20.8)	4,000	46	—	312-621-0630
(16.8)	1,000	50	535-2726 —	
(12.0)	10,000	27	662-7447 —	

*Figure represents the total an investment would pay on a $1,000 investment that compounds at a 5% annual rate and is sold after five years. Source for data and test calculations: Lipper Analytical Services, Summit, N.J.

% gain (or loss) in worst quarter since 1/1/84	% 12-month yield to 1/1/89	Five-year expense projection*	Telephone	
			Toll-free (800)	In state
(3.8)	11.9	N.A.†	223-4224	212-848-1800 (N.Y.)
(4.1)	8.7	$37	223-0818 —	
(3.0)	10.5	N.A.†	621-1048 —	
(3.5)	10.2	68	342-5236 —	
(3.8)	9.6	86	421-9900	714-671-7000 (Calif.)
(4.1)	10.0	86	366-0444 —	
(2.2)	12.6	83	621-1048 —	
(3.7)	11.7	49	544-6666 —	
(4.6)	6.9	36	338-2550 —	
(3.7)	7.6	72	621-1048 —	

Source for data and test calculations: Lipper Analytical Services, Summit, N.J.

bonds, Treasuries, and other government-backed issues. Manager Robert Manning of the no-load *Axe-Houghton Income* concentrates on high-grade corporates with relatively steep average maturities of about 12 years. Those issues provide higher income than shorter-term bonds but suffer greater losses when rates rise.

Although funds that hold junk bonds are rightly branded as risky investments, *Kemper High Yield* (4.5% load) delivered a smoother ride during the five-year period than 70% of bond portfolios. Managers Kenneth Urbaszewski and William Buecking avoid the lowest-rated corporates and diversify among different industries to reduce risk. In addition, they occasionally shift up to half of the fund's assets into higher-quality issues. By contrast, no-load *Fidelity High Income* stays close to fully invested in junk bonds. Manager William Pike relies upon yield to buoy shareholders during the market's ups and downs. But investors must recognize that there is no lifesaver for junk holders if a recession leads to credit jitters or defaults.

Among tax-exempt funds, no-load *SteinRoe Managed Municipal* sported a 6.9% tax-free yield that was equivalent to a 10.3% taxable payout for an investor in the 33% federal tax bracket. The riskiest of the 10 bond fund selections, it was more volatile than 90% of all bond funds during the five-year period. One reason: Manager Dave Snowbeck concentrates on municipals with maturities of 10 years or longer, regardless of the interest-rate outlook. Patrick Beimford's *Kemper Municipal Bond* (4.5% load) had an even higher average maturity (15 years) than did Snowbeck's fund. But Beimford has reduced his fund's volatility by hedging his portfolio with futures contracts. Like the rest of *Money*'s top 20, it passes the long-term investor's ultimate test: make my gain worth the pain.

Arm's-Length Opportunities in Real Estate

The case for investing a portion of your retirement money in real estate rests mainly on diversification. Even though other investments are likely to produce greater returns over the next several years, real estate will help keep your nest egg from shrinking if inflation unexpectedly soars to double digits. Like most tangible assets, bricks and mortar tend to grow in value when prices surge, while financial assets such as stocks and bonds usually slump.

Besides inflation protection, the right real estate investment can offer you steady income and a chance for capital gains. Moreover, you don't have to be landed gentry to get in. For $5,000 or less, you can choose among five types of investments that leave property management to the pros: real estate investment trusts (REITs), master limited partnerships (MLPs), mutual funds, variable annuities, and limited partnerships. If you invest directly in real estate, you can probably earn greater profits and tax benefits by buying and managing a rental property on your own. But the money, time, and expertise required are beyond the means of most investors.

The best real estate investments now for small investors are ones that pay regular dividends from rental income. For safety's sake, advisers suggest that you invest mainly in economically strong areas in the Northeast, Mid-Atlantic states, and on the West Coast. Rental apartments in those regions look promising because of strong housing demand. Strategies for investing in each form of real estate follow, from the types most favored by analysts to the ones they like least:

Real estate investment trusts. Known as REITs, these investments can wrap the attractions of real estate into one package. Well-run REITs provide reliable yields, potential for appreciation, professional management, tax benefits, and—because REIT shares trade on major stock exchanges—instant liquidity. A REIT pools investors' money to purchase as many as 20 commercial or residential buildings. Then it hires an independent company to manage the properties. A REIT can offer an appealing yield—lately 6% to 13%—because it does not pay corporate taxes and is required by law to pass on 95% of its net income to investors. Up to 40% of a REIT's dividend may be treated as a return of your capital, which lets you defer taxes on that part of the dividend until you sell your shares.

Investors probably should plan to hold REITs for at least three to five years to take advantage of property appreciation, which will be reflected in rising share prices. If you want to limit your risk, buy only REITs with yields below 10%. The reason is that double-digit yields could reflect a highly volatile type of real estate or a REIT with heavy leverage—one that borrows more than 60% of the purchase price of its buildings. Also look for REITs specializing in areas with strong, diversified economies and those whose executives own at least 5% of the shares. This information can be obtained from a REIT's latest annual report or—if it's a new issue—its prospectus.

Master limited partnerships. Call MLPs the Comeback Kids of the real estate world. Shares of these partnerships, which own or build properties, trade on major stock exchanges. (They are known as *master* limited partnerships because the deals are often consolidations of smaller, nontraded partnerships.) Real estate MLP prices skidded 23% in 1987, largely because Congress debated whether to tax MLP earnings twice, like those of regular companies—first as corporate profits and again as dividends—or only once, at the shareholder level. Congress finally decided that real estate MLPs could keep their favorable tax status indefinitely, and the share prices rebounded in response. Congress also left intact a law allowing up to 100% of MLP dividends to be considered a return of capital, making them, in effect, tax deferred until you sell your shares.

Yields lately have averaged 11%. Investment advisers say MLPs are best for aggressive investors who can stand some risk, because MLPs have short performance records—most are no more than three years old. Furthermore, those high yields could indirectly increase your tax-preparation bill. MLP shareholders, like other partnership investors, must deal with complex calculations and fill out an extra tax form known as a Schedule E. That can add $100 to $150 per MLP to an accountant's fee.

Real estate mutual funds. Anyone who has never invested in real estate and is bewildered by the alphabet soup of REITs and MLPs might consider one of the fairly new real estate mutual funds. The funds primarily hold shares of REITs and other real-estate-related companies, such as builders. Like other mutual funds, these portfolios offer liquidity, professional management, diversification, relatively low sales fees, and small minimum investments. They do not, however, provide tax benefits.

Yields recently hovered around 7.5%. The major funds are National Real Estate Stock Fund, Fidelity Real Estate Fund, and U.S. Real Estate Fund.

Real estate variable annuities. When you are setting cash aside for retirement, you might consider putting some of it in a real estate variable annuity. All income and capital gains in an annuity grow tax deferred until you withdraw the money. Sold by financial planners, stock brokers, and insurance agents for a minimum of $1,000, a real estate annuity invests in one of two ways. Either it resembles a mutual fund that buys REITs or it purchases property outright. A real estate annuity may give you the option of switching from its portfolio to stocks, bonds, and money-market funds offered by the sponsor. You can withdraw your money whenever you wish, but the insurance company will levy surrender fees as high as 9%. And if you are under 59½, the Internal Revenue Service will charge a 10% penalty as well as income taxes on your withdrawal. Such costs make a variable annuity appropriate only if you plan to hold it until you retire or until the surrender fees phase out in five to eight years.

Real estate limited partnerships. Sponsors of public real estate partnerships—those registered with the Securities and Exchange Commission—pool money from hundreds of investors and typically buy up to a dozen or so properties, planning to sell them in seven to 10 years. Until that time, investors collect income—typically 5% to 8% a year—mostly from rents.

Yet real estate partnerships are problem-prone investments. Investors who sell their units before a partnership disbands will usually get back only 50% to 70% of the value of the properties. Up-front fees and sales charges often run to 25%. What's more, most public programs are blind pools, meaning that general partners decide which properties to buy only after investors put up the money. The topper: Many partnerships formed in the early 1980s have delivered little or no income to investors because they bet so heavily on buildings in the overbuilt Sunbelt.

For years, limited partners were willing to accept such drawbacks in exchange for tax write-offs often worth as much as their investments. Then came tax reform, which threatened to do for partnerships what the ice age did for brontosauruses. Investors in programs bought after October 22, 1986 can now deduct losses only against income from so-called passive investments, chiefly other partnerships and rental real estate. The tax changes drove many hucksters out of business, but attractive deals are still scarce.

Financial planners and brokers who specialize in partnerships now frequently prefer moderately leveraged concerns that borrow 30% to 60% of the purchase price of their properties. Annual yields are rarely higher than 6% during the early years of a leveraged program because much of the income from properties must be used for loan payments. In the first few years of a partnership, as much as 100% of an investor's income is tax sheltered by the program's depreciation and mortgage deductions. Then, as the size of the cash distributions grows, the tax shelter diminishes. If the properties appreciate steadily, the deal might produce an annual after-tax yield of 8% to 12% before any capital gains.

Do not invest in a partnership until you have studied the sponsor's record, which is set forth in the prospectus. Look for a company that has been buying similar types of properties for at least three years. Also check the results of a sponsor's past partnerships that have sold buildings. A handy yardstick: The average annual return on those deals, including capital gains, should be at least five to seven percentage points higher than that of medium- or long-term Treasury bonds during the same period. Your adviser should be able to supply you with these comparison returns. If not, perhaps you should look for another adviser and a better deal.

The Scherers: The Lifelong Payoff from Property

Rich and Karol Scherer, both 36, devised their early-retirement strategy almost a decade ago when they bought the first of eight single-family houses they rent out in or near Sacramento, 15 miles from their Rancho Cordova home. The Scherers figure they will own the houses free and clear starting in their early fifties and will build steady rental income. Although rental expenses have generally offset their rents, about $650 a month per house, the Scherers expect positive cash flows in 1989.

They will bank the surplus and perhaps prepay their mortgages. Moreover, their plan will also help cover college costs for their son, Korey, 13, and daughter, Erin, 6. When the children reach college age, each will get one of their parents' rental properties. Rich expects that the kids will sell the houses and use the profits to finance college or else exchange the properties for houses where they attend school, renting out spare rooms to other students.

Give the Scherers high marks for foresight, ingenuity, and discipline. But Rich, a $65,000-a-year commercial real estate broker, jokes that laziness was also an impetus for his early-retirement blueprint. "I don't like working 11-hour days, but I do it now because I can see somewhere down the line when I won't have to," he says. Karol, who earns $17,000 as a secretary for the Cordova parks district, looks forward to globetrotting in retirement. "We'd like to see a lot of the world," she says. The couple have not chosen a precise retirement age. "One day we'll wake up and decide it's time," predicts Rich.

The Scherers believe you don't need to be a real estate professional to follow their example. Here are six tips that worked for them:

● Buy in a blue-collar area for its dependable, long-term renters. "Constant turnover is aggravation," moans Rich. The Scherers take only tenants planning to stay at least a year. Two current occupants have rented for six years.

● Look for a rental vacancy rate below the U.S. average, around 8% at year-end 1988. A local commercial real estate office should be able to estimate the rate in your area.

● Don't count on wild appreciation. The Scherers paid about $60,000 a house and estimated their properties were worth about $80,000 each—up roughly 5% a year.

● Borrow with 30-year, fixed-rate mortgages, to help lock in investment expenses.

● Take advantage of all tax breaks. If your adjusted gross income is $100,000 or less, you can deduct rental losses of up to $25,000 from your regular income provided you actively manage the property.

● Expect to spend one day a month managing any property—handling tenant problems, making repairs, and collecting rent checks. You can hire a professional manager, but that will cost 3% to 7% of your gross rent.

The Scherers will undoubtedly refine their retirement tactics as they watch two role models: Rich's mother and stepfather, who have been buying rental properties since 1978. In 1987, Rich's 59-year-old mother retired from her own real estate business. His stepfather, 57, an aerospace foreman, expects to retire within a few years. Then the couple will tour the country in a motor home, using their rental income to supplement their savings. "We're on exactly the same program as Rich's parents," says Karol. "And we started even sooner."

The Right Reasons to Buy Gold

Ask any financial planner to outline a diversified retirement portfolio and odds are that he or she will recommend that 5% to 10% of it be in gold. Good advice? Only if you have realistic expectations about what gold can—and can't—deliver. Too many people remember only that gold went from $35 an ounce in 1970 to $825 an ounce in 1980, and they expect it to shoot up $50 each time there's the slightest hint of inflation or bad news. Yet consider this: In 1988, the average price of an ounce of gold fell 2.4% to $437 while inflation climbed 4.1% for the year. And as consumer prices generally rose through April 1989, an ounce of the heavy metal sank to around $380.

The key to investing in gold, precious-metals experts say, is to understand that it is not an investment in the conventional sense of something you buy hoping it will pay dividends or grow in value. Instead, gold is insurance against economic or political disaster—its price tends to rise on fears of calamity, as the dizzying price appreciation of the 1970s showed. Gold was then a relatively new investment for Americans. Only in 1971 had its price been freed to float on the market, rather than be fixed—as it had been—by the world's central banks. And not until

1975 could Americans legally purchase it in bullion form—coins and bars. But the upward spiral really took off in 1979 when the U.S. inflation rate topped 13%, the unending oil crisis seemed to threaten limitless price hikes, and the Soviets invaded Afghanistan. Gold shot to an all-time high of $825 an ounce on January 21, 1980, then it sagged back to $635 just five days later as people began to realize that the world wasn't coming to an end.

That surge actually set the stage for lower prices this decade. When gold topped $800, a lot more companies were encouraged to mine for the metal and they found it, increasing supply dramatically and driving down prices. Though South Africa, the world's leading producer, is actually mining slightly less gold than it did in 1979, worldwide production is up over 40%. As a result, the future prospects for gold are not particularly bullish, although some analysts predict that the metal's recent price of around $380 an ounce will rise to $600 some time in the next three years. Other forecasters, however, say slack demand will undercut prices during the 1990s—perhaps to $250 an ounce.

Proponents of gold most often tout it as the ultimate hedge against inflation. They like to point out that an ounce of it bought a handsome suit of men's clothes in 1600—and it still would today. But gold's reputation as an inflation-buster has been tarnished in recent years. A survey of 14 categories of investments by Salomon Bros. shows that while gold's compound annual rate of return beat the rise in the consumer price index by 6.5 percentage points over a recent 20-year period, it actually lagged 1.1 points behind the CPI during the last five years. Super-secure bank certificates of deposit or Treasury bills would have been a better hedge against inflation during that time.

What about the argument that gold reduces your portfolio's risk because it performs well when paper assets, such as stocks and bonds, are falling? On that score, gold lives up to its billing so long as you expect it only to hold its value—not rack up stupendous gains—and are prepared for it to drop again when paper assets recover. Gold was at $461 when the stock market crashed in October 1987, for example, and rose to almost $500 by mid-December 1987. But then it headed southward again as investors regained some confidence in the market and the economy.

The bottom line? If you can hold gold for more than 10 years, a modest investment—say 5% or so of your assets—could help you raise cash in a hurry to take advantage of good buys in a bear market or offer a money cache should the U.S. financial system collapse or some other disaster occur. On the other hand, like all forms of insurance, gold entails an opportunity cost: the income you forgo by not holding some revenue-producing asset. If that opportunity cost is less disturbing to your peace of mind than visions of doomsday, then here are some tips on buying gold:

Bullion. The metal comes in a variety of sizes ranging from thin wafers up to 32-ounce bars. The most convenient form is probably coins, since they are easiest to store, price, and sell. If you buy through a bank or broker, you may want the firm to store and insure your coins at a fee of about one-half of 1% of their value.

Gold accounts and certificates. Several banks, brokerages, and coin dealers will sell you a fractional interest in gold bars or coins that they hold. Some give you a certificate of ownership; others just send a monthly statement. When comparing services, ask for a total of all fees, including application or storage charges (one-half of 1% to 1% is standard).

Gold-mining stocks and mutual funds. These stocks, and the funds that invest in them, are probably the worst way to buy gold, since you are buying not the metal but simply a piece of the company that mines it. Mining share prices tend to swing more widely than the price of gold. Funds are slightly less vulnerable to this last danger since they usually invest in 50 or 60 companies at once.

How to Retire on the House

*I*n the past two decades, the fourfold rise in single-family house prices has become the cornerstone of American affluence. Indeed, for most middle-income people, the process of trading up or improving on their homes now represents the foundation of family wealth and retirement planning. They began the housing sweepstakes deep in debt and—thanks to inflation—ended up with a tidy treasure that often can be tapped absolutely tax-free to buttress retirement income from other sources.

Yet the demographic trends that produced homeowners' double-digit annual appreciation in the 1970s and early 1980s are history, albeit one that may not repeat itself soon. Longer term, the number of new household formations per annum—a key determinant of single-family housing demand—is expected to decline by as much as 37% by 1995. More recently, rising mortgage rates and fears of recession have created soft housing markets in many regions of the country. House-price deflation, once written off as a quirk of overbuilding in Texas and other oil-patch states, is quietly eroding the net worths of millions of Americans nationwide. Among the most vulnerable are empty-nesters who have planned to trade down or tap their home equity to help finance their retirement dreams. They could end up with less of a cash cushion than they had anticipated for their golden years.

About 75% of Americans over 65 own their own homes, with an average of more than $50,000 in equity, or the market price minus one's outstanding mortgage. Most retirees living on fixed incomes, however, don't earn enough to qualify for conventional home-equity loans, the simplest way to exploit this burgeoning asset. But selling out and buying or renting a smaller place—trading down—is usually the smartest move anyway. On balance, it also outperforms such alternatives as taking a reverse mortgage, which is a loan against home equity that allows the borrower to defer repayment, or just staying put (see the table on page 146).

What's best for you depends greatly on whether you

need to raise money from your home—and how much. If your expected income from investments, Social Security, pensions, and other sources falls well short of your requirements, you may have little choice but to tap your prime asset. But executing a trade-down calls for careful planning. Financial planners and housing specialists advise you to:

Estimate your profit in advance. Before you sell your old house, try to find out what you will need to spend for a suitable replacement. If your potential profit is small, trading down might not be worth the trouble and expense. Be sure to take into account any savings you will realize from reduced maintenance and property taxes on a smaller home. Lower costs and taxes might make it worthwhile to move even if your profit from the trade-down is slim.

Time your sale to take advantage of tax benefits. If you or your spouse are 55 or older, you may be able to exclude from taxes up to $125,000 of the capital gain on the sale of your home. Should your gain exceed $125,000, you can defer tax on the excess by reinvesting the money in a new residence. If you have lived in your home for less than three of the five years preceding the sale, however, you do not qualify for the exclusion. In that case, it's probably worth delaying the sale until you can take the tax break.

Consider lending the buyer part of the purchase price. Interest payments on the loan will provide more income than you would receive if you sold for cash and invested the proceeds conservatively, such as in five-year Treasury notes, recently paying 9.3%. The reason is that fixed-rate mortgages lately have been about two percentage points higher. Insist on a down payment of at least 20%. That will protect your principal if the buyer defaults on the loan and, in fact, is an incentive for him *not* to default.

Pay cash for your new home. You could take out a mortgage and invest your house profits elsewhere, but the returns on conservative investments would not cover the loan payments. Just be sure that you leave yourself

Why Trade-Downs Work

The tables show three options available to a 65-year-old couple with a mortgage-free house worth $250,000.

The couple get the biggest payoff if they sell the house and buy a smaller one for $100,000. Then they can invest their $150,000 gain in a diversified portfolio of investments, in this case yielding 9%. The income will more than cover their housing costs.

The couple can take out an Individual Reverse Mortgage Account, which provides payments of $5,676 a year for life. If they live for at least 15 years, their estate will owe the lender an amount equal to the home's value.

If they stay put and leave their equity intact, the couple will retain the full value of their property, which increases by 4% a year in our example. But they will need income from other sources to meet rising costs, including maintenance, insurance, and property taxes.

TRADE-DOWN

Year	Additional income	Annual housing costs	Home equity and principal
1	$13,500	$3,200	$254,000
5	13,500	3,744	271,665
10	13,500	4,555	298,024
15	13,500	5,541	330,094
20	13,500	6,742	369,112
25	13,500	8,203	416,584

REVERSE MORTGAGE

Year	Additional income	Annual housing costs	Home equity
1	$5,676	$8,000	$223,312
5	5,676	9,359	185,293
10	5,676	11,386	106,979
15	5,676	13,853	0
20	5,676	16,855	0
25	5,676	20,506	0

DO NOTHING

Year	Additional income	Annual housing costs	Home equity
1	0	$8,000	$260,000
5	0	9,359	304,164
10	0	11,386	370,061
15	0	13,853	450,236
20	0	16,855	547,781
25	0	20,506	666,459

SOURCES: HOUSTON ASSET MANAGEMENT; AMERICAN HOMESTEAD

enough cash to meet emergencies and that you have other investments to offset the risk that your house might lose value. When you tie up all of your cash in a house, you lose the protection of a diversified portfolio. If you must borrow to pay for your new home, get a mortgage with a fixed rate so that you never have to worry about payments rising sharply.

One alternative to trading down is selling and renting permanently. In the long run, selling your house and becoming a tenant might be less financially rewarding than trading down. But it might well provide enough cash to defray your housing costs and free considerable cash for travel and other expenses. And if you decide to move again, you won't be pinned down by the task of selling a home, which could prove difficult if the real estate market in your area goes soft.

Of course, you may be among the homeowners who, like impoverished nobility in an English novel, wouldn't think of abandoning their castle even if they have to sell all the silver to pay the upkeep. In that case, you may want to consider one of the following techniques to hold on to the old place. Some of them are limited to certain regions, and others require the cooperation of relatives or outside investors:

Reverse mortgages. They pay the borrower a fixed monthly amount and defer repayment. Reverse mortgages come in several forms, with closing costs of typically 2.5% of the total loan. The most attractive type offered is the Individual Reverse Mortgage Account (IRMA), whereby the lender receives part or all of the value of your home, including its appreciation during the term of the loan, in return for deferring repayment until you move or die. (In the latter case, your estate pays off the loan.) American Homestead, a Mount Laurel, New Jersey mortgage bank, has made about 2,300 such loans since 1983 in California, Connecticut, Delaware, Maryland, Massachusetts, New Jersey, New York, Ohio, Pennsylvania, and Virginia.

For example, Janet Roscoe, a 67-year-old widow in Fallbrook, California, signed up for an American Homestead reverse mortgage that will pay her $400 a month for life. Terms: 11.5% interest on her borrowings, and she or her heirs will forfeit 80% of the future appreciation—

starting when the contract was signed—of her five-room attached house, recently worth about $153,000. "For a long time, I've had a desire to learn to fly," she says. "This additional income will make it possible."

Your income from an IRMA depends on the size of the mortgage and the life expectancies of you and your spouse. If you live beyond your life expectancy at the time you signed the mortgage agreement, your lifetime payments from an IRMA may exceed the value of your home. But if you die soon after you enter the program, your estate must repay the lender all of the monthly checks you received, with interest, plus all of the appreciation in the house since the mortgage was signed.

One variant on this type of loan, called a term reverse mortgage, is downright dangerous for most homeowners. With a term reverse mortgage, the lender makes monthly payments to a homeowner for a given period of time, typically seven years. At the end of that term, the homeowner must repay the loan, which often means selling the house. But occasionally, the loans do make sense. For example, an elderly person who is on a waiting list for a nursing home might take out a term reverse mortgage to meet his expenses in the interim.

In a pilot program begun in 1989 and continuing until September 30, 1991, the Federal Housing Administration will insure up to 2,500 reverse mortgages written by banks, mortgage banks, and thrifts. Generally, borrowers, who must be over 62, will be assured of staying in their homes as long as they wish. If all goes well with the tryout, Congress will probably greatly expand FHA insurance. The new FHA-insured loans will not have to be repaid until a borrower dies or decides to sell, even if the amount due eventually exceeds the property's worth. When the mortgage comes due, the lender recovers what is owed from the borrower or his or her heirs. If the total exceeds what the house fetches on the market, FHA insurance makes up the difference.

Borrowers pay a two-part premium for this insurance: an annual fee of one-half of 1% on the loan's principal balance and 2% of the lesser of the home's value or the maximum FHA loan amount, which varies by county from $67,500 to $101,250. A borrower whose house is worth more than the FHA loan limit and who wants a higher monthly payment would have to do business with a lender, like American Homestead, that doesn't offer FHA insurance.

To find out which lenders in your area, if any, will offer FHA-backed reverse mortgages, call the agency at 800-245-2691. For a list of publications about converting the equity in your home into cash, send a stamped, self-addressed envelope to the National Center for Home Equity Conversion, 110 East Main Street, Room 605, Madison, WI 53703. If you have questions about insured or uninsured reverse mortgages, address them to the AARP's Home Equity Information Center, 1909 K Street N.W., Washington, D.C. 20049.

Sale-leasebacks. Here is how this type of arrangement worked for a 79-year-old California widow who sold her home in 1984 to an investor for $92,400. She received a down payment of $25,000 and granted the investor a 13-year mortgage that pays her $825 a month. Just over $400 goes for the rent she pays to the investor, who qualifies for tax benefits because of the house's status as a rental property. The rest supplements her income from Social Security and the violin lessons she gives to local children. The mortgage payments will stop in 1997, when she turns 89. To ensure that her income continues indefinitely, she took the precaution of investing $6,800 from the down payment in a single-premium deferred annuity, which will begin paying her $825 a month when the mortgage payments stop. Meanwhile, the lease limits her annual rent increases to 2%, and she has managed to set aside some money for her heirs.

With a sale-leaseback, the buyer generally agrees to a 10% to 20% down payment and 15-year mortgage. The buyer also covers the cost of property taxes, insurance, and maintenance. For example, a typical sale-leaseback with a 10% down payment and a 15-year mortgage on a $250,000 house might generate $32,000 in income to the seller, who would pay about $21,000 in rent during the first year. The income would remain constant, but the rent might climb to about $36,000 by the end of the mortgage term. As an added precaution, you probably should invest part of the down payment in a deferred annuity so that you will continue to receive income should you outlive the mortgage.

Finding an investor to take part in a sale-leaseback may

be difficult, unless your children or other family members can afford to make the investment. Either way, you should enlist the help of an experienced attorney. Local bar associations and real estate boards will probably recommend professionals who can help you structure a typical deal for approximately $1,500 to $2,000. And for $45, the National Center for Home Equity Conversion (110 East Main Street, Room 605, Madison, WI 53703) will send you its booklet, *Sale Leaseback Guide and Model Documents*.

Charitable donations. If you can't find an investor to do a sale-leaseback and you have no children, you might try an institution such as a school, hospital, or charity. They will sometimes grant you a lifetime annuity in exchange for a remainder interest in your property. You continue to own it but, when you die, it's all theirs.

Accessory apartments. If you have rooms to spare in your home, you might consider turning them into an apartment that you can rent. Before you do anything, find out if zoning regulations in your community permit such an arrangement. If so, ask a contractor to estimate the cost and real estate agents how much rent you will be able to charge. Also, ask your local agency on aging if your area has a household matching service, which helps bring people with extra rooms together with prospective tenants. The service might help you find a suitable tenant; otherwise, try real estate agents. The book, *Creating an Accessory Apartment* (McGraw-Hill, $16.95) by Patrick H. Hare and Jolene N. Ostler, includes a sample lease and other useful information.

While you're weighing these options, give careful consideration to the emotional impact each will have on you as well. Anything that makes you uncomfortable is not worth doing, no matter how smart it may be in dollars and cents.

Questions to Ask about an IRMA

Before deciding whether an Individual Reverse Mortgage Account is for you, consider:

● What are the monthly payments? Will they adequately add to your income? If not, look to a more lucrative strategy, such as trading down.

● How long do you intend to live in the house? If you plan to move within five years, the costs of an IRMA will be exorbitant.

● Do you have children or other heirs to consider? Discuss your plans with them, since any repayment of your loan will come out of your assets.

● How much is your house likely to appreciate? If you are in a hot housing market, remember that you will give up part or all of the profits to the lender.

● Do you plan to make major improvements to the house? They will increase its value, all or part of which will go to the lender.

The Best Places to Live in Retirement

Another important housing consideration is *where* you want to live. Only one in four retirees is as yet daring enough to follow the sun or some other long-harbored fantasy. But migration analysts say the likelihood of you making such a major move increases each year.

One reason is financial: Retirees are receiving fatter pensions and higher prices for their houses than ever before, even adjusted for inflation. Another is the trend among affluent retired people to sojourn—that is, to live in one home half the year and in another the rest. Furthermore, as families grow farther apart geographically, retirees have less reason to stick close to the old homestead.

Choosing where to live in retirement could be the most critical housing decision of your life. You may be less flexible financially than when you were younger, and the new place could be your home for the next 25 years. If grandchildren are nearby, a big move may only show you just how indispensable that proximity has been. Start your search by determining why you might want to move. The most popular reason, according to one survey, is to reduce expenses, followed by the desire for a smaller home or to eliminate maintenance chores.

Your reasons could be quite different. You might seek a warmer climate, a smaller city, an area suited to your hobbies, or a place where your friends live. To help you better assess your options, *Money* identified six top retirement locations, selected on the basis of geographical diversity, climate, cultural and recreational activities, and the cost of living in 1988. They were culled from interviews with retirees and authors of books about retirement locations, as well as U.S. Census migration statistics and reporters' visits to the areas. (A table on page 154 estimates living costs in the six locations as well as 14 other popular retirement spots.)

Prescott, Arizona. No one researches retirement places as exhaustively as does Peter Dickinson, author of *Sunbelt Retirement* (American Association of Retired Persons), *Retirement Edens Outside the Sunbelt* (AARP), and a monthly newsletter on retirement places (*The Retirement Letter*, 44 Wildwood Drive, Prescott, AZ 86301). Dickinson has appraised more than 800 such spots from Aberdeen, SD ("great pheasant hunting") to Zurich, Switzerland ("excellent quality of life—if you can afford it"). So when Dickinson bought *his* future retirement house in Prescott in 1987, that was about the most towering testament a town could get.

Dickinson had been falling in love with Prescott's mountainous beauty and moseying pace since he first passed through in 1949. But once he figured out how inexpensive retirement there is today, he was sold. "I paid $117,000 for a three-bedroom house on a third of an acre with a spectacular view of the Thumb Butte ridge of the Bradshaw Mountains," he says. "The house and land are comparable to what I owned in Larchmont, New York worth $500,000. My property taxes will be $900 a year versus $6,000 in New York. I can live on 50% to 70% of my New York income and have the same life-style. I just had to give up the New York ballet. But Phoenix is only 102 miles away, and it is home to Ballet Arizona, an up-and-coming troupe."

He is hardly the only retiree to fall for little Prescott (pop. 25,000). The past decade has seen a steady stream of retired people settling into this tidied-up throwback to the Old West whose nostalgic downtown strip, known as Whiskey Row, draws its character from a sprinkling of 19th-century saloons that are now bars and boutiques and equally antique hotels that have been lovingly restored. The crisp, clean air is another strong lure. Credit belongs partly to Prescott's position one mile high. The altitude makes Prescott far cooler in the summer than Phoenix (average daytime temperature of 70° versus 88°) and permits year-round golfing at the two local public courses. On winter mornings, you may need to scrape frost off your car's windshield, then drive with the top down by 2 p.m.

Prescott is a mostly white, middle-class town. But the lack of diversity is balanced somewhat by the happy contrast between its two major demographic blocs: A third of the population are retired and a third are students at three colleges—Yavapai, Prescott, and Embry-Riddle. Yavapai welcomes retirees the most. Retirees pay $12 to $35 a course there while full-time students pay roughly $400 a semester.

Chapel Hill, North Carolina. Of all U.S. college towns, Chapel Hill (pop. 35,000) is home to the most retired people—about 11,000. The University of North Carolina is here, Duke is a 10-minute drive away in Durham, and North Carolina State in Raleigh is a half-hour drive. The 20 square miles of rolling countryside that surround the three cities is called the Research Triangle or sometimes simply the Triangle. Durham, a former tobacco town, is transforming itself into a regional medical center, and Raleigh, like many other state capitals, is pushing for more commercial growth. Chapel Hill is the most courtly city in the Triangle, partly because of the predominance of campus life, partly because it is the smallest of the three.

Many of its retirees are well-to-do Northerners who settled in Chapel Hill to enjoy the cultural comforts of home without the hectic pace and harsh winters (February's temperature averages 42°). The campus setting has proved fertile ground for educational innovation. For example, more than 300 retirees both teach and attend classes held at local churches in programs known as Shared Learning and Peer Learning.

Bibliophilia notwithstanding, the fun begins at the drop of a divot. North Carolina has 400 golf courses, including 60 in the renowned Pinehurst area, a 1½ hour drive south of Chapel Hill. Both the Atlantic Ocean and the Blue Ridge Mountains are three hours away and provide blessed relief from the hot, sticky summers (average temperature: 77°; average humidity: 71%). The hottest

How Costs Compare In 20 Popular Towns

As this table shows, the cost of living varies enormously in 20 popular retirement locations. In Honolulu, a condominium sells on average for more than four times a house price in Provo, Utah. Even Seattle and Tacoma, while only 25 miles apart, are distinct in many ways, not least of all the 22% difference in the price of a house. A pattern is hard to find. For example, Honolulu has the highest rents and steak and egg prices, but its greens fees and energy bills are among the lowest. The house-price figures represent what a retired person would pay for a house or condominium—typically two bedrooms—whichever is most common in the area. Greens fees are for 18 holes of golf on a public course (private in Palm Springs, where the cart is also included).

	House price	Property taxes
ALBUQUERQUE, NEW MEXICO	$85,000	$400
AMHERST, MASSACHUSETTS	190,000	2,300
BLOOMINGTON, INDIANA	80,000	850
CHAPEL HILL, NORTH CAROLINA	135,000	1,500
FORT LAUDERDALE, FLORIDA	62,500	400
HONOLULU, HAWAII	190,000	980
KERRVILLE, TEXAS	80,000	850
MYRTLE BEACH, SOUTH CAROLINA	80,000	640
PALM SPRINGS, CALIFORNIA	85,000	950
POINT PLEASANT, NEW JERSEY	150,000	1,600
PORTLAND, OREGON	85,000	2,500
PRESCOTT, ARIZONA	68,500	655
PROVO, UTAH	45,000	405
ST. PAUL, MINNESOTA	90,000	1,600
SAN ANTONIO, TEXAS	88,000	1,350
SAN DIEGO, CALIFORNIA	150,000	1,500
SARASOTA, FLORIDA	77,500	850
SEATTLE, WASHINGTON	98,000	1,000
TACOMA, WASHINGTON	80,000	700
TUCSON, ARIZONA	100,000	825

tickets during the fall and winter seasons are college football and basketball; Tar Heels and Blue Devils games are typically sold out.

The medical care is exceptional. The doctor-patient ratio in the area far surpasses the national average. For example, in Durham there are seven doctors per 1,000 residents—nearly quadruple the national average. Nearby Duke University Medical Center has one of the largest cardiac rehabilitation programs in the United States. Its doctors perform about 1,500 open-heart operations a year.

Rent	Monthly energy bill	Top state income tax rate	Sales taxes	Hospital room	Doctor's visit	One pound of steak	One dozen eggs	Greens fees
$395	$99	8.50%	5.25%	$238	$25	$3.79	$0.69	$8.00
520	125	5.00	5.00	337	30	4.99	1.10	5.50
360	124	3.40	5.00	215	20	4.42	0.77	10.00
440	105	7.00	5.00	197	30	5.22	0.68	7.00
540	130	—	6.00	249	30	4.44	0.78	10.00
1,550	53	10.00	4.00	241	40	5.69	1.55	6.00
410	97	—	7.50	118	25	3.92	0.81	6.50
390	72	7.00	5.00	200	25	5.23	0.72	30.00
590	117	9.30	6.00	296	40	4.05	1.32	70.00
850	65	3.50	6.00	200	40	4.99	1.09	10.00
355	75	9.00	—	307	25	4.24	0.76	10.00
340	65	15.00	7.00	205	40	3.98	0.89	7.50
310	85	7.70	6.25	236	20	3.05	0.69	9.00
500	125	8.00	6.00	312	25	3.86	0.58	5.25
325	117	—	7.50	175	30	4.43	0.78	6.50
850	86	9.30	6.00	300	30	3.33	1.31	9.00
390	35	—	6.00	227	30	3.78	0.71	11.00
430	59	—	8.10	266	40	4.86	0.70	8.50
415	70	—	7.80	295	25	4.49	0.85	12.75
455	83	15.00	7.00	248	30	4.13	0.77	12.50

Sarasota, Florida. Welcome to the retirement capital of America. Almost a third of Sarasotans (pop. 244,364) are 65 and older, and most have migrated from outside Florida. What attracted them and kept them loyal is a report card of attributes that gives this city straight A's in climate, cultural and recreational activities, and services.

Start with soft Gulf Coast winters in which the temperature averages 62°. In the summer, the thermometer can jump to a sticky 86°, but even that is mitigated by cooling bay breezes in the evening and omnipresent air conditioning. Golf, tennis, and boating abound, and local beaches—particularly Lido Beach—are said to have the whitest, finest sand in the state. Sarasota's streets sparkle, a matter of civic pride. The city maintains some Spanish flavor in older buildings, but that is being gradually upstaged by modern residential communities in lush green settings, often with their own golf courses and tennis courts.

What sets Sarasota apart from so many other Florida cities is its cultural life. Art and theater lovers, in fact, have nearly as much to choose from here as they do in Baltimore, more than three times the size. The Ringling Museum of Art has one of the largest Rubens collections in the world. The Van Wezel Performing Arts Hall, Asolo State Theater, and Florida West Coast Music Inc. are just some of the distinguished arts presences in the area.

Spring in Sarasota has a special sweetness. So many people watch the Chicago White Sox at spring training that a new stadium with seating for 7,800 and expanded parking will replace smaller Payne Park. The Pittsburgh Pirates play at McKechnie Field in Bradenton, just a 15-minute drive north.

Classes in subjects from fitness to religion to architecture are offered at the Longboat Key Adult Education Center for about $50 a course. The Sarasota Institute of Lifetime Learning holds 35 lecture series just for retirees on literature, politics, religion, and history. For $20, you can attend an unlimited number of lectures.

Amherst, Massachusetts. Calling Amherst (pop. 36,000) a college town is an understatement. Perhaps that's poetic justice for a place whose personality is as elegantly understated as if it never forgot that Emily Dickinson lived her entire life here. Amherst and the surrounding

Pioneer Valley in western Massachusetts are home to Amherst College, Hampshire College, Mount Holyoke College, Smith College, and the University of Massachusetts. Yet this place also manages to deliver cosmopolitan living, the amenities of a first-class suburb, a ravishing rural setting, many services designed specifically for retirees, and a friendliness for which New England towns are definitely not renowned.

As you might have guessed, the price of such a package of superlatives comes high. Housing costs are a shock, as in much of economically vibrant Massachusetts. The median house price in the area is around $200,000, compared with $93,100 nationwide. Apartments are hard to find (typical monthly rent for a two-bedroom apartment: $520), but they come with a special tax break. Tenants may deduct half their annual rent, up to $2,500, from their state income taxes.

Downtown, serious browsers will find a bookstore practically every 50 yards. Dozens of retirees take classes at UMass, where day and evening courses providing college credits are tuition-free for anyone 60 or older. Roughly a third of the area's 3,000 retirees have ties to one of the valley's colleges, according to John Clobridge, executive director of the local council on aging. In the summer, groups of retired residents often take a scenic 1½-hour drive west through the Berkshires to concerts at Tanglewood or dance performances at Jacob's Pillow.

Although only about 8% of Amherst's population are retirees, the town makes special efforts to reach out to them. Amherst's cable-television channel lists activities at the local senior center. Free vans take retirees to any personal appointments upon request. The 90,000-volume public library is known throughout the region for its collection of 1,850 large-print books. With both town and campus police, Amherst is notably safe, too. Its crime rate is half that of a typical U.S. metropolitan area.

Bloomington, Indiana. If you are one of those Renaissance folks who relish Bob Knight, grand opera, Kurt Vonnegut, and ice fishing, this lively university town (pop. 53,045) is made for you. Bloomington caught its worst case of Hoosier fever in decades in 1987, when the Indiana University basketball team, flogged to a frenzy by Coach Knight, won the national collegiate championship.

Even if you are not much of a fan, you could turn to the university for a feast of cultural opportunities. The school of music, one of the best in the country, mounts professional and student opera, jazz, ballet, theater, and musical productions almost every evening. Many are free. A season's subscription to the opera costs as little as $36—less than the price of a single ticket in some cities. IU also offers a noncredit, adult education program with 37 courses from Greek to computer programming.

Recreational activities tend to be vigorous. The city operates 35-acre Riddle Point Park at Lake Lemon, which is 15 miles northeast of Bloomington and has camping and beach facilities. And at Lake Monroe, the state's largest park with nearly 26,000 acres of land and water, activities span the seasons from ice fishing for large mouth bass and bluegill to some of the finest sailing in the Midwest.

Seattle/Sequim, Washington. Seattle's setting is extravagant, with gleaming Puget Sound to the west and two mountain ranges—the Olympics and the Cascades—towering to the west and north. Downtown is dotted with parks. The waterfront bustles with stylish shops and restaurants. Pioneer Square has lovingly restored buildings dating from before the Gold Rush. Seattle (pop. 493,000) is also the cultural center of the entire Northwest, with its Seattle Symphony, Gilbert & Sullivan Society, and a professional ballet company, Pacific Northwest Ballet. There are about a dozen professional and semiprofessional theaters.

Yet, what if you are picky enough to object to two drawbacks: the weather (156 rainy days a year) and Seattle's fairly fast pace? Then head 70 miles northwest, via a scenic half-hour ferry ride over Puget Sound and an hour's drive. There you will find what some airplane pilots call "the blue sky of the Northwest." Sequim (pronounced *squim*) has a population of 3,300, and nestles in a valley protected by the Olympic Mountains. So it gets only 16 inches of rain annually, compared with Seattle's 50. Summer temperatures in Sequim rarely exceed 80°, and the winter average is 32°.

Sequim transplants claim to have seen 100-pound halibut and 40-pound salmon landed in the vicinity. Clamming and crabbing are cherished pastimes. When residents tire of Sequim's lone moviehouse, two 18-hole golf courses, and four seafood restaurants, they can always retreat to Seattle. They may not even have to do that much longer for specialized medical care: the Olympic Memorial Hospital in Port Angeles, 15 miles away, will soon open a cardiac and radiation center in Sequim.

Sojourners: Have Two Homes, Will Travel

There is a small but growing flock of mostly retired people—call them sojourners—who split their time between two places. Most keep a house back where they worked and raised children and buy a second dwelling where they can escape from winter's frost or summer's steam. Many of them have discovered they can sojourn on less than mammoth money. By shuffling their real estate holdings creatively, some people run two households and two cars on an unprincely retirement income of as little as $22,000 a year.

Managing double lives, however, takes planning, coordination, and endless energy. The joys of seasonal migration can fade if housing budgets are strained, summer clothing consistently turns up in the wrong place, two states weigh in with tax bills, or the unoccupied house is invaded by burglars. Resourcefully, most sojourners have scoped out ways to cope with the problems and enhance the advantages of their interstate existence.

While retirees have been commuting semiannually for generations, the new sojourners represent an economic vanguard, says Robert Atchley, director of the Scripps Gerontology Center at Miami University of Ohio. There are simply greater numbers of retired people whose incomes can support the back-and-forth life. Many can afford to own two dwellings now because of the tremendous appreciation they realized on the houses they bought 30 or 40 years ago. Commuting also lets people live in a retirement community long enough to enjoy its benefits—people of the same age with similar interests, endless opportunities for golf and recreation, and early-bird restaurant specials. Yet, they need not commit themselves to full-time residence in what they view as a ghettoized Wrinkle City. One example of successful sojourning is Harry Holtz, 70, former chief executive officer of First Trust Company of St. Paul, and his wife Pat, 68. The Holtzes began escaping Minnesota winters by vacationing in Arizona. Pat, who competes in swimming meets, came to love the dry heat and winter days around the pool. When Harry retired, however, he was reluctant to give up business entirely. He also wanted to keep his hand in the civic affairs of the Twin Cities, where he sits on the boards of several charitable foundations and does fund raising for Children's Hospital and the Minnesota Orchestra.

To accommodate their diverse needs, the Holtzes decided to stay in Minnesota more than half the year and spend the rest of their time in Arizona. They sold the big house in which they had raised their three children and bought two $200,000 condominiums. One overlooks the Minnesota River in Mendota Heights and the other fronts on a man-made lake in northeast Scottsdale. Pat usually stays south for the whole winter, while Harry hops north once or twice to attend to business and philanthropic obligations. But when he is in Arizona, he says, "I'm less hyper. There's less tension. In Arizona, the phone rings all morning. In Minnesota, it rings all day."

It took years for fellow Minnesotans Phyllis and Robert Prigge to put a somewhat similar plan into effect. Phyllis, 58, a real estate agent, and Robert, 67, a former schoolteacher, figured that when they retired, they could afford to commute to Texas by selling their house in suburban St. Paul, buying a place down south, where prices are lower, and using a vacation cabin for summer sojourns in Minnesota and visits to their children. They had begun making regular visits to Harlingen, Texas when Phyllis' parents retired there in 1963. The Prigges came to value Harlingen, which is near Brownsville, not only as a low-cost winter escape from frozen Minnesota but also as a base for exploring Mexico, one of their hobbies.

In 1980, four years before Robert was due to retire, the Prigges bought their cabin, on Leaf Lake near Henning in the northwestern part of the state. They paid that off in 1983 and began looking for property in Harlingen. That same year, a friend's three-bedroom ranch house came on the market, and they bought it for $32,000 at "a very low interest rate," says Phyllis. Then they sold the St. Paul house and stashed the money in income-producing investments. The earnings pay the mortgage on the

Harlingen house, about $300 a month, with plenty left over. Their total tab for two houses, including taxes and utilities, is $527 a month, which they can easily swing on their $1,800 monthly income.

Shallower-rooted retirees are finding creative ways to re-establish themselves in two altogether new and appealing locations. Don and Pat Woods, both 67, now spend about nine months of the year in Anacortes, a pleasure port on Puget Sound near Seattle, and the rest of the year in the balmy breezes of Kauai, one of Hawaii's most unspoiled islands. Woods, a former regional manager for manufacturing with Texaco in the Midwest, wound up his career in Chicago. When he retired in 1981, he and his wife sold their house and built a bi-level in Anacortes, near where their three daughters lived. "The house is really too big, but it has views of the water from both floors," notes Don.

A year later, a friend approached him with a novel idea. He had just bought a $120,000 one-bedroom condominium on Kauai and wanted to form a partnership with five other couples who would share the expenses. The Woodses signed on. Each couple is entitled to two months in the condo, part of a development that sits high on a cliff overlooking the crashing surf. From their living room window, they gaze at a garden of hibiscus and oleander. They spend their days golfing, swimming in the ocean, and hot-tubbing at the condo pool.

The Woodses sound like stars from a segment of TV's *Lifestyles of the Rich and Famous*, but "on a budget," adds Don. "We're not rich—we don't have that much surplus." One-week time shares on Kauai cost $10,000 to $15,000, while the condo owners paid $20,000 each for their two-month shares and chip in only about $100 a month for maintenance. The one real hitch in the Woodses' arrangement and others like it is air fare. There are no direct flights from Seattle to Kauai. The Woodses have to fly to Honolulu and take an inter-island plane from there. They pay $350 to $400 each for a round trip, depending on the season.

Commuting to a foreign country need not be much more expensive. Jean Blum, 78, a retired lawyer, and his wife Gloria, 48, lay out $450 for each round trip to Acapulco, 2,200 miles from their other home in Los Gatos, California. They spend about nine months a year in

Acapulco, where decades ago Blum bought a three-story, Mexican-style townhouse up a hill three blocks from the bay. He paid about $40,000. Now, he says, even small condos on the beach cost about $150,000. Otherwise, food, clothing, and almost everything else is cheap because the dollar buys a lot of pesos and a lot of labor. The Blums employ three live-in servants for a total of $300 a month.

Alas, few retirees happen on such existences without enduring a fair amount of muss and fuss—not to mention thoughtful planning. Those who contemplate sojourning should ponder this sampler of complications and the solutions some trailblazers say work for them:

Double furnishings. Those who live in two places find that they own not just two dwellings but also two of everything else. Some try to cut costs by buying a furnished apartment or decorating from the attic. For the first years, they lug blenders and TV sets with them, but that can be a pain in the neck, shoulders, and arms. The most successful sojourners seem to be those with a knack for turning any place into a nest, which may explain why so many commuters say their chief hobby is decorating.

Two sets of wheels. For many, a car journey is often too long and arduous. They commute instead by airplane and buy two cars. To cut costs, some sojourners buy a used car for one locale. Don and Pat Woods can't drive to Hawaii, but they have worked out a cooperative arrangement for a car as well as their condo. "Five of us who own the apartment also went in on a car—a 1982 Mercury Cougar purchased from a rental car company," says Woods. Their share cost only about $1,000.

Deciding where home really is. Sojourners should make up their minds soon which of their two homes will be their official residence. Charles Longino, director of the Center for Social Research on Aging at the University of Miami in Florida, points out that double domiciling doesn't always last forever. One spouse may fall ill or get tired of making the twice-yearly journey. A couple may then have to settle down in one of the two places. You are well advised to figure out which of the two is most inviting as your eventual stopping place. Deciding in advance will save worry later.

Barring burglars. The security of the unoccupied house is a major worry. Condo owners are least threatened because the development's management usually provides security. Those with freestanding homes hire house-sitters or have relatives check in. But if your hideaway is out-of-the-way, you may want to install an alarm system and insure your possessions to the hilt.

Catching up with the mail. Harry Holtz, the former bank chairman, found that one of the biggest hassles was mail. Bills and letters invariably piled up at the wrong address, provoking the ire of creditors and correspondents. Now, his daughter picks up mail in St. Paul, sorts it, and forwards urgent items by Express Mail. He also leaves a supply of signed checks made out to the telephone company, the power company, and others. His daughter fills in the amounts when she gets the bills.

Doubling up on doctors. Another problem is coordination of medical care. Holtz still relies on his Minnesota physician, but he has also recruited a Scottsdale doctor to examine him, order lab tests, and confer with his Minnesota doctor by telephone before prescribing treatment. Both doctors maintain his medical records.

Making friends. Social adjustment is necessary. One sojourning woman felt that every time she commuted, she had to break the ice anew with her friends in the other place. It sometimes took weeks to get back in sync with her crowd. Some people avoid the problem by moving back and forth as a group. Gang sojourning? Isabel Johnson, 68, and her husband Henry, 72, a onetime salesman for Du Pont, own a condo on Great Egg Harbor Bay in Ocean City, New Jersey. They and their circle of friends belong to the local yacht club and get together for dining, dancing, concerts, and bridge. They also hold twice-a-month "tea" parties in dry Ocean City. Every winter, says Isabel, "Everybody heads south to Delray Beach in Florida together." They don't travel in a caravan—"We all drive or fly down separately"—but they continue the party, including "tea," down south. Some might find such

relentless groupiness oppressive, but Johnson firmly declares, "This is the way we want to live."

The Taxing Double Life

One potential pitfall for sojourners is that those with
dual residences could wind up with dual income tax
bills—one from each state in which they have a home.
Back home in Indiana may be where your heart and your
main address are. But be careful about investing money
where you winter, because a few states—particularly
California—may try to claim you as a resident so that
they can tax the income you earn within their borders.
Worse, they may attempt to stick you with their top-
bracket rate.

The right choice of an official residence can save a
bundle. That, for example, would probably not be New
York, which has a graduated income tax that tops out at
8.4% for joint incomes over $34,000 in 1989. Texas, on the
other hand, has no income tax at all, while Florida levies
only an intangibles tax on a couple's investment assets
over $40,000, and its $1-per-$1,000 bite is more like a
gentle nip.

Once the choice of an official residence is made, you
can nail it down by registering to vote, obtaining a driver's
license from that address and using it on passports,
deeds, and contracts. Tax lawyers recommend that you
notify your employer and insurance companies paying
pensions and annuities of your official residence. If the
companies that will pay these benefits are located in the
state of former domicile, they may not release the funds
unless they receive a waiver from that state's tax author-
ities. Also, keep most of your securities and savings
accounts in that state. Most important, when you file your
federal tax returns, use your primary address. In addition
to all this, some states—Florida, for example—require
that a declaration of change of domicile be filed with a
local court.

Finally, your estate could wind up with death-tax bills
from two states as well as the federal government. This
threat is unlikely to arise in the many states that impose
taxes only on estates subject to federal taxation—those
over $600,000. Above that level, your estate gets a

dollar-for-dollar federal credit for any state tax up to a certain limit, which depends on the size of the tax. The state merely collects an amount equal to the credit that would otherwise go to the IRS. In a few states, however, the death tax could exceed the allowable federal credit. Further, the laws of many other states could trigger a death tax even if your taxable estate is less than $600,000. So anyone who occupies homes in two states should really consult an estate lawyer.

Spotting Bargains in Vacation Condos

Would-be retirees in search of smaller and easier-to-maintain places in the sun should consider vacation-area condominiums, currently a buyer's market. In recent years, the effects of tax reform have forced out many investors who previously bought residential properties more for tax than for human shelter. The stock market's Black Monday simply hastened the exodus. The result is that prices in mid-1989 were off 10% to 40% or more from their early 1980s highs in places where the skies are bright (Palm Springs, California), the powder is deep (Vail, Colorado), and the surf is close at hand (Kiawah Island, South Carolina). Even in many spots where second-home prices continue to bubble, condos often lag behind.

Most of the blame goes to tax reform. Before 1987, if you bought a second home primarily for investment and restricted your personal use to fewer than 14 days a year, you could write off tax losses on the place—depreciation, mortgage interest, real estate taxes, and operating expenses exceeding rental income—against your ordinary income. Under the new rules, such losses can usually be deducted only against "passive" income from limited partnerships or other rental properties. There is one major loophole: If your adjusted gross income is $100,000 or less and you actively manage your holdings, you can still claim up to $25,000 in passive losses against your salary. With the top marginal income tax rate slashed from 50% to 33%, however, the value of write-offs is vastly diminished.

As a result, most real estate analysts agree that any decision should ultimately be based on how and where you plan to spend your retirement days. What follows is a regional roundup of the most intriguing possibilities, plus some tips on how to get the bargain of your choice:

The Northeast. Second-home prices remain generally firm in this densely populated and economically overachieving area. Some of the best condo deals lie in New Hampshire's Lake Winnipesaukee region and in Ocean and Monmouth counties along New Jersey's coast. For instance, prices of two-bedroom, nonwaterfront condos near Weirs Beach and Laconia, New Hampshire started at around $100,000 in mid-1989, or roughly 8% less than the asking prices 12 months earlier. And a block or so from the Atlantic Ocean in Point Pleasant Beach, New Jersey, neat, traditional-style one-bedrooms were selling for $95,000—a 5% to 15% markdown from the year before.

The South. Dixie resort condos suffer from energy price woes, overbuilding, and sputtering local economies. On Hilton Head Island, South Carolina, prices have dropped 15% on average since 1985. Typical cost of a two-bedroom-and-bath condo a 10-minute walk from the beach: $110,000. On tony Kiawah Island off Charleston, gracefully-designed luxury condos nestle among cypresses or perch atop bluffs. One-bedrooms, a minute's stroll from the Atlantic, fetched $110,000, versus $160,000 the year before.

More bargains line the Gulf Coast, where many condominiums at popular retreats such as Gulf Shores, Alabama and Destin, Florida sell for 20% to 30% less than in 1985. Farther south in Florida, prices are nearly as flabby. Brokers say East Coast units in Dade and Broward counties harbor particularly good deals. In Clearwater, for example, the asking price of a two-bedroom unit on the Gulf of Mexico was $209,000, down from $250,000 in 1983.

The Midwest. You can fish, golf, swim, or cool off with an icy six-pack at Missouri's languid Lake of the Ozarks, where prices have dropped 5% to 25% since 1986 because of overbuilding. Attractive two-bedroom waterfront units were selling for $70,000 there.

The Rockies. For most of this decade, the real estate market in Colorado's ski country has been painfully flat or headed downhill. The oil price collapse is the chief leveler. The choicest deals are in Vail and in Park City, Utah, which are less prestigious and more overbuilt than top-of-the-line Aspen. At Park City, two-bedroom units a few blocks from the lifts were offered at $125,000, all the way down from $225,000 in 1985. More reasonable still are the buys in northwestern Montana, where the depressed agriculture and lumber industries sent the region reeling. At unspoiled retreats such as Whitefish Lake, Flathead Lake, and Big Mountain, a fire sale is in progress. At Big Mountain, for instance, a four-bedroom condo was priced at $86,000, down from $125,000 in 1985.

The Far West. Oregon's majestic Mount Hood caps a vacation culture that thrives on winter skiing, summer hiking, and white-water rafting in the Deschutes River. Yet, condo prices in the region have come down 30% since 1980 as a consequence of rising interest rates, tax reform, and a depressed timber economy. Two thousand miles south, on the floor of the Coachella Valley, lies Palm Springs, California. Mayor Sonny Bono's bailiwick, which boasts 107 area golf courses, has been widely overbuilt. Real estate prices have fallen as much as 30% since 1980, and desirable two-bedrooms were selling for as little as $112,500.

Before you buy anywhere, keep in mind that a condo bargain is not always a good value. Here is how to ensure that you get both:

● Go for the best location you can afford. The closer to the lake, for instance, the easier the sell.

● Check out the developer's reputation. A thoughtfully planned, well-maintained complex will hold its value better.

● Haggle. Some experts suggest offering a miserly 60% of a condo's asking price as a starting figure.

● Also consider buying at auction. Most big-city newspapers carry an auction page in their Sunday editions. Look among the classified ads for such major auction houses as Hudson & Marshall, Sheldon Good & Company, and JBS

Associates. The biggest markets are Florida's Gold Coast, Texas' Padre Island, and coastal South Carolina. Always be sure to check out the building, the developer, and the location first. Usually, auctioneers set a predetermined time for inspecting condos—for example, a couple of days in advance. In addition, scrutinize the closing records (available at the local courthouse) to see how much any similar units sold for a year ago, then bid no more than that.

Housing Terms You Should Know

If you do decide to sell or buy a house for retirement, you will face a complicated array of financing options. Terms you should be familiar with include:

Adjustable-rate mortgage (ARM). A loan with an interest rate that fluctuates according to movements in whatever index it is tied to.

Assumable loan. An existing mortgage that can be taken over by a buyer, usually on the same terms as those given to the original borrower.

Balloon mortgage. A loan with monthly payments that are too small to retire the debt within the specified term, typically three to five years. The balance must be paid in full when the term expires.

Bridge loan. A 30- to 120-day loan secured by equity in your house. The proceeds are used to make the down payment on a new house when you haven't sold the old one.

FHA mortgage. A loan insured by the Federal Housing Administration that requires only a 5% down payment.

Fixed-rate mortgage. A loan with an interest rate and monthly payments that do not vary during its life.

VA mortgage. A loan guaranteed by the Veterans Administration that allows an eligible veteran to buy a house without making a down payment.

Bridging Gaps in Your Medical Coverage

Chapter Seven

*I*f a fortune-teller were to scan your pre-retirement palm, chances are that she would have mixed portents to report. The good news: You are likely to lead a long life. The bad news: Your wealth line may weaken along the way as the cost of health care in your later years rises steeply. If you are nearing retirement, you should make sure—before you stop working—that your leisure years hold no unpleasant surprises from medical bills. That's mostly a matter of understanding what insurance you have and what you will need. If you are a decade or more from retirement, count only on the fact that responsibility for assuming more medical costs is shifting slowly but steadily toward you.

Should you be planning to retire in the next couple of years, pay a visit to your company's benefits department to find out what kind of health insurance you'll be entitled to. Most large corporations offer some coverage to their retirees. Because Medicare is generally available only to persons 65 and over, coverage for those taking company-sanctioned early retirement is often the same as for active employees. A 1986 law, known by its acronym of COBRA, requires that your employer at the very least continue your health plan, at your expense, for up to 18 months after retirement. Once you retire at 65, however, coverage usually shifts to Medicare-integrated insurance. This means, typically, that you'll lose some or all of your company coverage for expenses eligible for Medicare reimbursement, even though Medicare may pay only a portion of the actual bills. Corporate post-retirement benefits differ widely, and many small employers offer no health coverage at all. Consequently, it's necessary to understand in advance what you will or won't be getting so you can look around for extra insurance if you need it.

You should begin your search for insurance as early as you can so you'll have time to examine several policies and reflect on what's best for you. Also, think about attending to medical needs you've neglected that are covered under your present policy, particularly if you

determine that you'll have little or no employer coverage
after retirement. If you need dental work, new glasses,
even minor surgery, get them before you call it quits. A
general checkup—which might also be covered—could
reveal other needs.

If you're under 65 and not eligible for Medicare, you'll
probably want what is known as a comprehensive policy.
As its name suggests, it offers coverage on a broad range
of services, both in and out of the hospital. The high
premiums on individual comprehensive insurance are a
heart-stopper, though its cost varies widely based on your
age, where you live, and your health. In New York City,
Aetna's Comprehensive Medical Plan policy, which has
an unlimited maximum benefit, would cost a healthy
55-year-old couple—who choose a deductible of $1,500
each—about $2,667 yearly. In Los Angeles, they could pay
between $4,188 and $6,159, depending on where they live.

You can lower overall costs by assuming more risk
yourself. One way to do this is to buy a policy with a fixed
benefit limit, meaning the insurer stops paying at a certain—usually fairly low—amount. A better way is to buy a
policy that has high deductibles but also a high benefit
limit. This is often referred to as the catastrophic provision. While you'll have to pay a lot of the initial expenses,
such as the first day or so in the hospital, you'll be
protected from extremely high final bills. Consequently,
you might put several thousand dollars in a money-market fund or bank account earmarked for upfront medical
expenses and buy insurance with an annual deductible of
at least $1,000 and a catastrophic provision of $250,000
or more.

Complicated though your insurance choices may be
before you reach 65, moving to Medicare at that age won't
make them much easier. You'll need to fill in for Medicare's shortfalls with additional insurance. In 1989, the
medical bills of people 65 and over are estimated to reach
an average of more than $6,600 a person, of which Medi-
care will pay about $4,700. The details of Medicare are
complex, but your Social Security office will give you
several clearly written guides to explain your coverage.

Armed with these booklets, which contain charts item-
izing your benefits limitations in each category of care,
you may well conclude that you need so-called Medigap
insurance: supplementary policies that—to varying

extents—pay the deductibles and uncovered percentages of your doctor and hospital bills. (For details, see page 176.) What most Medigap policies don't cover is what Medicare doesn't cover either—and that's a lot. Dental work, long-term nursing-home care, most types of prescription drugs, and eyeglasses are all items that older folks have greater-than-average need of and less-than-average chance of getting coverage for. Medicare doesn't cover such needs, and private insurers are reluctant to provide individual policies that include these vital health aids to people over 65 who are likely to be heavy users.

One attempted solution to this dilemma is for retirees to enroll in health maintenance organizations. For a prepaid fee, HMOs provide a wide range of medical services to their members, including doctor and hospital care, laboratory testing, drugs, therapy, and other items. Two aspects of HMOs make them attractive to older people. One is their emphasis on preventive medicine. Since an HMO accepts a fixed fee for your medical services, it has a large incentive to keep you well. The other is that an HMO is, in effect, an insurer that provides the actual services you need instead of just reimbursing you for them. This enables the HMO to keep a grip on its—and your—costs. But there are mounting concerns about the calibre of care provided by some HMOs. So, take a hard look before you sign on.

Is an HMO Right for You?

In 1988, some 75 doctors, disgruntled over their fees, pulled out of North Carolina's largest HMO, the Raleigh Blue Cross Personal Care Plan. The increasing incidence of such service brownouts has dimmed the once bright promise of HMOs—most of which are operating at a loss—and prompted punishing rate increases levied to staunch the flow of red ink. Insurance experts and state regulators also see more mergers and closures of ailing HMOs in cities such as Denver, Minneapolis, New Orleans, Raleigh/Durham, and St. Louis, where competition for HMO subscribers has suppressed premiums to below the cost of care.

Although only 13% of Americans hold memberships, the consequences of the HMOs' problems are more insidious than you might think. Employers, goaded by insurers who are worried about exploding health-care costs, have been turning more and more to HMOs and similar restricted-service options and away from traditional free-choice plans that let you pick your own doctor. Between 1984 and 1987, for instance, free-choice plans dropped from 96% to 40% of insurers' group business, according to Health Insurance Association of America, a trade group of health insurers. Over the next year or so, according to analysts, total HMO enrollment of about 30 million people will rise by 10% while the number of plans shrinks by an equal 10%.

With all the drawbacks, are HMOs still worth the trouble? The answer is, ultimately, yes; at the moment, maybe. The concept is undeniably attractive. By paying hospitals and doctors under yearly contracts, rather than by fees per patient, HMOs can provide economical health care. In return for this service, you agree to give up only one thing—your unlimited choice of doctors. And HMOs can save you money—up to 28%, in fact—compared with traditional health insurance. The difference is that HMOs cover virtually all medical costs. Insurance almost always has deductibles and requires you to pay a percentage, generally 20%, of most bills.

These cost comparisons, however, gloss over certain complications. In order to contain costs, HMOs may make you wait longer for an appointment with a doctor, discourage you from entering a hospital, and limit the number of tests and other services you receive. Not everyone is happy with a system of medicine with limits. If you object to anything less than top-drawer health service, an HMO isn't for you.

Yet, it is far from an all-or-nothing choice. The original HMOs, and those that still tend to be the most successful, employ only salaried staff doctors who work together under one roof. Later came the independent practice association, which is now the format of the majority of plans. In this type of HMO, doctors in private practice agree to treat some HMO members in their offices along with their regular fee-paying patients. The catch is that doctors in private practice have less incentive to control costs, since their reimbursement from HMOs is usually a small portion of their income. Until the mid-1980s, failures to contain costs and control doctors were covered

by rising revenues from new members. Then, as the
market became saturated, the losses began to mount with
no prospect of subsiding soon. At worst, this means that
subscribers lose insurance coverage when their HMO
goes bankrupt. Federal law provides the subscribers with
the slimmest protection: Newly defunct HMOs must continue to provide coverage for one month (six months for
Medicare recipients). After that, patients must transfer to
other insurance. And coverage can be interrupted for
months before a switch is completed.

Government supervision hasn't been much help either.
About half of all HMOs have qualified with the Health
Care Financing Administration, which administers Medicare, to take Medicare patients. Such an HMO is expected
to follow a list of rules. For instance, it must carry
insurance in case of insolvency to cover subscribers'
outstanding medical bills and the cost of completing
treatment that is already in progress. The HMO must also
include clauses in its contracts with doctors and hospitals
proscribing them from seeking payments directly from
patients if the HMO cannot pay its bills.

No one knows how many federally qualified HMOs live
up even to these standards because the number of government auditors is too small to guarantee compliance.
Indeed, stories abound of impatient doctors and hospitals
dunning patients for money owed by their HMOs. And the
biggest HMO failure of all time—that of the International
Medical Centers in Florida in 1987—involved a federally
qualified chain. The 170,000 members of the bankrupt
HMO went back on Medicare or, with government help,
found new HMOs to join. Though no subscriber is immune to trouble when an HMO gets into financial diffi-
culty, the elderly are particularly vulnerable. Some 18% of
the 161 HMOs that accepted Medicare subscribers in 1986
decided that government reimbursement was inadequate
and refused to sign up these older members again in 1987.
That forced 53,000 of them to find new prepaid plans or
return to their more expensive and less comprehensive
regular Medicare coverage. Since HMOs can vary in quality, here are some key questions to ask:

How can I be sure this HMO is financially sound?
Call the state office that regulates HMOs and get an
opinion. Your risk of joining a potentially ailing HMO is

less if the plan has been operating for at least three to five years, or if it has the financial support of a big insurance company. If you're tempted by a brand-new HMO, you should ask who its founders, backers, and board members are. If the executive mix doesn't include physicians, your health probably would be better served by going elsewhere.

How can I be sure I'll get topnotch care at this HMO? The most reliable sign of quality is a satisfied membership. Consult enrolled friends or co-workers about how they rate the plan. Also, group-practice HMOs frequently hold open houses, where you can see for yourself whether the facilities are clean and orderly. Ask for a roster of the HMO's staff, with specialties and credentials. A majority of the doctors should be certified by national boards in their medical specialties, and the rest should be eligible to become so. Federally qualified HMOs are required to set up a way for members to complain or make suggestions. Ask the HMO what some typical gripes are and how they're being resolved. Also ask for the percentage of subscriber turnovers each year. Anything higher than 30% suggests trouble. If you are told that the HMO doesn't keep turnover statistics, be wary.

Where do I go if I need to be hospitalized? It's reason enough to reconsider an HMO altogether if the plan's affiliated hospital has a poor reputation or is too far from your home. You should also have the HMO spell out its procedures in the event of an emergency. Can you get prompt nighttime help at an HMO office or over the telephone?

How long must I wait to get an appointment or to see a doctor once I've arrived in the waiting room? HMOs have a vested interest in saving patients' time, and punctuality is a sign of a well-run group. You shouldn't patronize any HMO that can't guarantee a doctor will see you the same day you call in sick. Find out whether patients can expect less than 30 minutes in the waiting room and less than two months' advance scheduling for a checkup or some other non-urgent care.

Medicare versus Medigap Coverage

If you are 65 or over, at least a portion of your medical expenses are covered by Medicare. Since the first of 1989, however, Medicare premiums have increased in exchange for more comprehensive medical benefits. Under the Medicare Catastrophic Care Act passed in 1988, Medicare now picks up the bill for unlimited hospital stays after you pay an annual deductible—$560 in 1989. The length of time that Medicare will pay for acute care in a skilled nursing home has been increased from 100 days a year for each illness to 150 days for one or more illnesses. And terminally ill patients may now collect unlimited hospice-care benefits. Even more changes are effective in 1990, when the maximum amount you pay for Medicare-approved outpatient doctors' services (once unlimited) are capped at $1,370. That year Medicare also starts paying up to 80% of limited prescription drug expenses, expanding in 1991 to 50% of nearly all prescription drugs.

Despite those improvements, there are still gaps in your Medicare coverage. But since they are far narrower than they used to be, you might want to bridge them yourself rather than paying $400 to $1,200 a year for a private Medigap insurance policy to supplement Medicare. Consumer insurance experts warn that going without a policy in 1989 could leave you exposed to potentially unlimited out-of-pocket expenses. But in 1990 there is a ceiling of some $2,700 on them. As a result, Robert Hunter, president of the National Insurance Consumer Organization in Alexandria, Virginia, maintains that one shouldn't pay more than $500 a year in 1990 for a Medigap policy that fills the basic gaps in your Medicare coverage.

If you already own such a policy, it has been rewritten to conform to these new provisions. But many insurers did not slash prices even though they eliminated or reduced benefits. The annual premium paid by a married couple in Chicago, both of whom are 65, for a group health plan marketed by the nonprofit American Association of Retired Persons (AARP) and underwritten by Prudential increased as much as 42% in 1989 to $36.95 a month. (For more on the insurance and other services sold by the AARP, see Chapter 9.) Should you keep your old Medigap policy, buy a new one, or go bare in 1990?

Here's a look at Medicare's remaining gaps and the extent to which you can fill them with private insurance:

Hospital stays. Medicare covers all costs after you pay the 1989 deductible of $560. By law, companies offering Medigap policies have a Hobson's choice: they must pick up either none or all of this deductible, and most do cover it. Medicare still doesn't pay for private-duty nursing, but Medigap policies such as AARP's Medicare Supplement Plus from Prudential ($443 for the Chicago couple) does to this extent: up to $30 per eight-hour shift for a registered nurse; as many as three shifts per day, 60 shifts per hospital stay.

Nursing-home care. Most people who enter nursing homes need custodial care, which Medicare doesn't cover. Medigap policies don't either, but John Hancock's ProtectCare and other policies do for $1,692 to $4,316 a year for a 65-year-old couple, depending on the comprehensiveness of the coverage. To collect Medicare benefits for skilled care in a nursing home, you must be confined to a Medicare-certified facility. Medicare will then pay for a maximum of 150 days a year, but you must contribute $25.50 daily for the first eight days in each year. Medigap policies are required by law to pick up this $25.50-a-day co-payment. Most policies also provide some benefits after you have been institutionalized for more than 150 days.

Home health care. You can collect unlimited Medicare benefits only if you are homebound and your doctor certifies that you need part-time skilled nursing care or physical or speech therapy. Starting in 1990, benefits continue for an unlimited period, if you need care for up to six days a week. Also in 1990, if you need help daily, Medicare will stop after 38 days unless it is extended by your doctor. Neither Medicare nor Medigap policies cover round-the-clock skilled nursing care, custodial care, homemaker services, or home-delivered meals. (See "Coping with the Cruel Cost of Long-Term Care," on page 180.)

Physicians and other outpatient services. After you pay an annual deductible ($75 in 1989), Medicare covers

80% of approved charges. Starting in 1990, your liability will be limited to a deductible of $1,370 a year. Most Medigap policies cover your share of Medicare-approved expenses but not the deductible. An exception is Blue Cross/Blue Shield of Maryland's 65 Choice plan, $1,347 for the 65-year-old Chicago couple. You must still make up the difference between Medicare's approved rates and what your doctor actually charges, however. Only a few Medigap policies, such as Blue Cross/Blue Shield of Iowa's Protection Plus ($1,300 a year for a 65-year-old couple in Iowa), pay a portion of the difference.

Outpatient prescription drugs. You foot the bills now, and most Medigap policies do not pay for prescription drugs. But starting in 1990, federal law requires Medigap policies to cover your 20% share of approved expenses for home intravenous therapy and 50% of the cost of immuno-suppressive drugs after you pay a $550 deductible. In 1990, an increasing number of policies are expected to take care of $100 to $200 of that deductible.

In shopping for a Medigap policy, look only at ones that are guaranteed renewable for life. That way, your coverage cannot be canceled as long as you pay the premiums. Further, don't buy more than one policy. A single comprehensive plan is always better than several with overlapping benefits. To learn more about Medigap coverage, send for these free booklets:

● *Medicare Catastrophic Protection and Other New Benefits*, Consumer Information Center, Department 65, Pueblo, CO 81009

● *Catastrophic Coverage Under Medicare: New Health-care Protection for Older Americans*, D13299 AARP Fulfillment, 1909 K Street N.W., Washington, D.C. 20049

The New Medicare Surtax Explained

While the Medicare Catastrophic Care Act filled critical gaps in the federal health insurance program, it also required Medicare beneficiaries—Social Security recipients over 65, plus some disabled people—to foot the cost by a small increase in their premium and an income tax surcharge. As a result, many on Medicare may want to rethink their investment strategy.

The surtax, effective January 1, 1989, adds $22.50 to every $150 in federal income taxes that a person on Medicare owes in that year. There's a cap of $800 for taxpayers filing individually ($1,600 for couples). But in subsequent years that cap rises, reaching $1,050 for individuals ($2,100 for couples) by 1993. The surtax, which cannot be deducted as a medical expense, amounts to a new tax on the elderly middle class, says John Goodman, president of the National Center for Policy Analysis, a research institute in Dallas. "Once you reach the cap, the tax doesn't go any higher, so it doesn't hit wealthy people as hard." Indeed, a single person earning as little as $16,000 in 1989 could be socked with a $360 surtax.

To lessen its bite, your best move is to reduce taxable income. You can do so by boosting your deductible expenses or by investing in tax-free municipal bonds or muni funds and tax-deferred annuities. Since the surtax makes your effective tax rate higher—those in the 15% bracket pay 17% in 1989; those in the 28% bracket, but below the cap, 32%—lower-yielding, nontaxable investments may be more attractive than they once were. For someone in the 28% bracket, for example, a municipal bond paying 7.6% used to be the equivalent of a taxable bond paying 10.6%. With the surtax, that rate is now comparable to a taxable payout of 11.2%.

Another way to reduce income for those who can control what they earn is to bunch taxable income into a year during which you know your surtax will reach the cap. This applies in 1989 to single people with more than $27,573 in taxable income and to couples with more than $52,384. Past those points, you can make more money without paying added tax.

If you have further questions about the changes in Medicare coverage, call the Department of Health and Human Services at 800-888-1770.

Coping with the Cruel Cost of Long-Term Care

In addition to the routine medical costs associated with growing old, what *should* rank as the No. 1 financial fear for people planning retirement is the cost of long-term care if they become too feeble to look after themselves—a nonstop expense that can quickly deplete resources built up over a lifetime. Now this problem too can be alleviated. Growing numbers of insurance companies are offering long-term-care policies that are more comprehensive and affordable than you might think.

The longer we live, the more likely it is that we will have to pay others to dress and groom us, feed us, and move us around. Americans' life expectancy at age 65 is increasing dramatically. Since 1940, the chances of living another 20 years have doubled, from one in five to two in five, and they are expected to rise to three in five by the year 2030.

With longevity comes a new set of medical problems. Where once disability came largely from strokes, cancer, or other acute diseases for the over-85 generation, it is more likely to come as a gradual loss of the ability to take care of oneself. Elderly people live for years with chronic ailments, such as Alzheimer's disease, that seldom require long hospital stays but render the victims more and more helpless. In the past, the duty of caring for them fell to their children or other family members. Now, with the generations dispersed geographically, the givers of care tend to be paid strangers. While only 8% of people 65 to 84 years old are in nursing homes, 32% of the 85-plus group are institutionalized. Of the rest, an estimated 23% stay at home with regular assistance from nurses, housekeepers, or other types of assistance.

The cost can be crushing. At average rates, nursing homes charge $24,000 a year, and the fees are escalating in step with inflation. Expect to pay on average $30 to $50 a day for home-care services, which include physical therapy, administration of drugs, and food preparation. Few people are up to the costs. In 1987, a congressional subcommittee on aging found that 70% to 80% of nursing-home residents used up all of their capital in a year or so and were forced onto welfare. Once impoverished, nursing-home patients usually have to move to less desirable accommodations in the same facility or to a less costly institution.

Most Americans have done little or nothing to prepare for the high risk of needing long-term care—or its rising cost. One reason is that they assume incorrectly Medicare will pick up their nursing-home bills. Medicare pays only for stays in skilled nursing homes—ones staffed with doctors and nurses—and then only if admission follows a hospital stay. Furthermore, this coverage is limited to 150 days. Supplemental Medigap plans also exclude long-term care. So does the catastrophic coverage that Congress added to Medicare. This new plan, which is being phased in between 1989 and 1991, is aimed at expenses resulting from acute illnesses such as heart attacks, and injuries such as bone fractures.

Long-term care necessitated by the gradual enfeeblement of aging rather than acute illness is uncovered except by Medicaid, the medical welfare program for the indigent. Worse yet, many of the most desirable nursing homes discourage—or refuse outright—applicants who are on Medicaid.

What to do? The best protection against long-term care's financial wipeout is a comprehensive, solidly funded life-care community, a retirement residence that provides medical and personal care to the elderly in or out of a nursing home. But you have to pay an entrance fee of at least $20,000—and usually much more. Another alternative, so far open to only a few, is a specialized HMO that includes long-term care among its prepaid services. The third choice, and the only one for most people, is to buy their own long-term-care insurance policy. The premium is likely to be more than $1,000 a year if you put off the purchase until you are past 70. Fortunately, the coverage is becoming more comprehensive and some insurers are abandoning escape clauses that marred earlier policies.

Whether you should sign up for long-term-care insurance depends largely on your age. People under 50 are best advised to do nothing because broader and better solutions, public or private, probably lie ahead. But those past 50, or the children who might someday have to support them, can't afford to wait. Since purchase of long-term-care policies is limited to those in good health and few companies sell insurance to anyone over 80, it is prudent to insure yourself by age 60 or so.

Comparing Six Long-Term Policies

Because long-term-care insurance is expensive, you should be able to customize your coverage. Some policies offer a few flexible options. Others allow you to pick nearly every feature. Ideally, you want to pay for only the types of care you think you will require and to keep benefits flowing for as long as you are likely to need them. The policies dissected here pay benefits primarily for nursing-home care. They share these four strong points:

● All are guaranteed renewable; your coverage cannot be canceled if you pay the premiums on time.

● All will cover you for Alzheimer's disease.

● All can be written to pay benefits for at least four years.

● And all are available in most states.

The rates shown here apply if you are in good health; certain ailments may be insurable at a higher rate. Where inflation protection is optional, we include the cost of one year's increased coverage. After that, the premium rises when the benefit is hiked.

Company	Policy (number of states where it is sold)	
Aetna Life & Casualty Hartford 203-273-4510	**Long-term care** (35)	Plan A
		Plan B
AIG Life Wilmington 302-594-2000	**Nursing-home insurance** (28)	
American Republic Insurance Co. Des Moines 800-247-2190 Ext. 2175	**Americare** (all but Alaska and Minnesota)	Low Option
		High Option
CNA Insurance Chicago 800-262-1919 In Illinois, 800-325-1843	**Long-term care** (all but Kansas and Minnesota)	Low Option
		High Option
John Hancock Mutual Life Boston 617-421-3517	**ProtectCare** (35)	Basic
		Comprehensive
The Travelers Hartford 203-277-9101	**Group long-term-care plan** (29)	

* 60-day wait
† Three days in the hospital required before benefits are paid to new buyers 80 or older, and benefits last only one year

Covers custodial nursing homes, home care, and day care, except as noted	No prior hospital stay required, unless otherwise noted	Inflation protection available	Annual premiums for $50 per day of benefits, after a 90-day wait, at ages 60 to 79	Comments
	Three days	Optional at extra cost	$299 to $1,918	Inflation protection boosts benefits 5% a year for 15 years and adds 5% a year to the premium.
		Optional at extra cost	$393 to $3,514	
Home-care benefit requires 30 days in a nursing home; no day care	Three days	No	$272 to $1,616	Primarily nursing-home coverage
Covers only skilled and intermediate-care homes		No	$367 to $1,037*; $1,563 at age 85	One of the few plans available to people who sign up at age 85 or older
Home care only		No	$419 to $1,171*; $1,781 at age 85	
Home care costs extra; no day care	Three days	Optional at extra cost	$299 to $1,608; $556 at age 80†	Plan can be tailored to several levels of coverage. High-option premium includes home care.
No day care		Optional at extra cost	$447 to $3,094; $668 at age 80†	
	14 days in a skilled nursing home	Optional at extra cost	$277 to $1,550	Extra coverage is offered every three years to keep pace with inflation.
		Optional at extra cost	$367 to $2,733	
		No	$600 to $2,292	Available only to large, employer-sponsored groups

Many commercial insurers and Blue Cross plans offer coverage for long-term care—generally meaning up to six years—in either a nursing home or the patient's own dwelling. Because the coverage is fairly new, insurers are wary of assuming too much risk, and the few plans offering affordable protection are not available in every state. (For the names of companies selling long-term-care insurance in your state, write to the Health Insurance Association of America, 1025 Connecticut Avenue N.W., Washington, D.C. 20036.) Take a close look at the following characteristics of any policy you might consider:

Costs and benefits. Annual premiums for long-term-care insurance range from $100 or so for those in their thirties to more than $3,000 for the broadest coverage on people nearing 80. Almost all policies have one major drawback: They indemnify you for a fixed dollar amount per day, no matter how much you are paying for services or how much their cost may rise over the years. An antidote provided optionally in a few policies is an inflation provision at extra charge, typically 1% more a year for each 1% of additional benefits. In contrast, hospital and major-medical insurance pays all or a high percentage of each bill.

On average, U.S. nursing homes charge $65 a day, and top rates are more than twice that. The daily amount reimbursed by most nursing-home policies is up to you. The higher the premium you pay, the higher the benefit, with twice the coverage generally doubling your cost. For instance, American Republic Insurance in Des Moines would charge a 70-year-old $837 annually for a $50 daily benefit lasting 1,500 days and $1,674 for $100 a day. Once you become insured, however, your premium should remain constant unless it includes inflation protection.

Deductibles and duration of benefits. How many days of care come out of your pocket before your benefits begin and how long they continue will greatly influence the premium you pay. Most insurers offer at least two choices of waiting periods, typically 20 or 100 days. Selecting a 100-day waiting period can reduce your premium by as much as 30%. So choose as long a waiting period as you can afford. At the other end, though, more coverage is worth paying for. Since the majority of policyholders will need care for less than a year, benefits that quit after 12 months or so may cost only half as much as those continuing for the six-year maximum many policies currently offer. The extra coverage, however, can mean the difference between solvency and bankruptcy for the minority of policyholders whose confinement continues for years.

Benefit prerequisites. Many policies require hospitalization for three days or so before benefits begin. Yet the need for paid care is often the result of a deteriorating condition such as arthritis, which may not put you in the hospital at all. The most worthwhile policies require only that a doctor certify the need for care.

Types of services covered. Some people require medical services; others just need personal care. Some people can get along in their own home; others have to be in a nursing home. Ideally, a long-term-care policy should offer the widest possible options, including nursing homes in three categories of medical care: skilled homes; intermediate homes, which provide rehabilitative therapy; and custodial homes, which offer little more than practical nursing. The best policies also pay for care at home, adult day-care centers, and brief intermittent care at a nursing home, also known as respite care. The policy should offer those benefits in nearly equal amounts so as not to bias your choice. A policy that covers nursing-home care for years but home care for only a month or so forces you to opt for institutionalization or to skip benefits. The fewer the types of care covered and the more heavily the choice is skewed toward one type of care, the less useful the policy is.

Exclusions. Alzheimer's disease can leave victims helpless for 15 years or longer. That's why some insurers exclude "organic brain disease" from the conditions their policies cover and why you shouldn't buy any such policy. (All of the policies in the table, "Comparing Six Long-Term Policies," on pages 182-183 cover organic brain disease.) Most policies have a six-month or so waiting period before they start paying benefits for diseases you had before paying the insurance. This pre-existing illness clause is standard, and you can't avoid it.

Renewability. Be sure your coverage will continue for as long as you want it to and that your premiums can't be hiked unless everybody's are raised in your area. In the language of insurance, such a policy is guaranteed renewable. An examination of premiums indicates that you pay little or no more for this highly desirable feature. If you live in Arizona, Hawaii, Indiana, Iowa, Kansas, Nebraska, North Carolina, North Dakota, Oklahoma, or Virginia, you are protected by law against cancellation of a long-term-care policy because of age or deteriorating health. Any policy that can cut you off just as liability begins to increase is a bad deal.

Choosing a Life-Care Community

Just a couple of years ago, you might have been scared off from life-care communities as possible places to live in retirement. They were bright on promise: A stiff entrance fee of, say, $30,000 guaranteed you food, housing, and, if necessary, nursing-home care until the day you died. But the industry was marred by financially incompetent and sometimes unscrupulous operators. In the decade to 1985, 40 communities ran into financial difficulties—in a few cases leaving residents bereft of both money and services.

Since then, the life-care industry has undergone a thorough housecleaning. New state laws require communities to have substantial reserves and more fully disclose the condition of their finances to prospective residents. The industry itself has sponsored an accrediting commission to help screen out inept operators. As a result, you stand a better chance than ever of finding financially sound, well-managed life-care communities, also known as continuing-care retirement communities. Specifically geared to the comfort and physical limitations of older people, usually 75 and up, they typically offer studio, one- and two-bedroom units, plus facilities for long-term care. The communities also provide physical therapy and home care, and usually feature extra help for housekeeping. One of their most attractive aspects to many older people and their families is that providing needed care and services falls to the communities' social workers, not to inexperienced family members.

Average entrance fees at all-inclusive communities—those that provide shelter plus all medical and support services—range from $37,000 for a studio to more than $100,000 for large apartments. Monthly fees are $700 to $1,100 a person. A majority of these communities fully or partly refund entrance fees to residents if they leave, or to their estates when they die. A continuing-care community with refunds, however, may charge entrance fees that are twice those of a nonrefunding facility. At somewhat lower cost—$27,000 to $85,000 entrance fees and $650 to $750 monthly fees—some communities offer modified continuing-care contracts. They provide all residential and some medical and support services. Typically, 50 or 60 days of nursing-home care might be included in the community's fee or a discount of 15% to 20% on daily, weekly, or monthly rates at the nursing home.

A third type of continuing-care community is the fee-for-service contract. For entrance fees ranging from $21,000 to $56,000 and monthly fees of $570 to $690, you can buy residential apartment space and pay for medical and personal services as you use them. A fee-for-service community can then be combined with a long-term-care insurance policy.

Whatever type of community you find attractive, make sure that you thoroughly understand exactly what expenses are covered and what you will be paying for them over and above the cost of your living unit. Since both your living arrangements and your medical care will be provided by the community, be sure it's capable of doing the job. Check the performance record of the community itself or, if it's brand new, of its sponsors, owners, and managers. Ask your state attorney general's office whether there are regulations governing reserves and other financial obligations and whether the community meets them. At last count, some 23 states had such regulations, and one industry trade group, the American Association of Homes for the Aging, has been sponsoring accreditation reviews for the past four years. Accreditation assures that the community is financially sound and maintains a high standard of service to residents.

For a list of accredited communities and a useful consumer guide to choosing one, send $2 to American Association of Homes for the Aging, 1129 20th Street N.W., Suite 400, Washington, D.C. 20036 (202-296-5960).

Keeping It All in the Family

Chapter Eight

*W*hile planning for your retirement, there is one unpleasant contingency you might not have considered—your death. But by organizing your estate to the best advantage, you can ensure that your hard-earned wealth stays in the family.

If you die without a will, in most states you partially disinherit your spouse and condemn your estate to an unnecessarily prolonged and expensive wait in probate. Similarly, if you fail to prepare for estate taxes, your legacy could be clipped by federal transfer taxes at rates as high as 55%. With proper planning, most estates could reach their intended heirs without losing a penny to federal taxes.

A good estate plan has two aims: To make sure your wealth reaches your intended heirs in the manner you choose, and to minimize your estate's erosion by federal and state taxes. To accomplish both, you must manipulate the forbidding tangle of ancient common-law traditions and modern tax regulations that govern estate transfers. Do not attempt it without the help of a practiced estate attorney; if you go it alone, you risk having the orderly transfer of your wealth disintegrate into an ugly court battle among your heirs. Even with a lawyer, though, you need to understand the process in order to pass on your wealth. The more you know about the fundamentals of estate planning—wills, trusts, joint ownership, lifetime gifts, the marital deduction, and the $600,000 exemption—the better you will understand what the obstacles are and what you must do to succeed.

Preparing a Will

You need a will whether you are single or married, old or young, healthy or ill. This document not only instructs your survivors about how to distribute your property but also enables you to nominate a guardian to care for your children if they become orphaned. Another crucial function is to designate someone as your estate's executor, the person who will be responsible for taking inventory of all your property, paying your estate's creditors and taxes, and ultimately splitting your estate among your heirs.

If you die without a will—intestate, in legal jargon—the courts take control of your estate and, in effect, write a will for you in accordance with your state's intestacy laws. It is unlikely that the result will match your wishes. For example, in most states your mate does not automatically inherit all your property if you have children. New York's intestacy law would award your spouse $4,000 plus one-third of the balance of the estate. The rest would be evenly divided among your children, regardless of their ages or special needs.

In the absence of a will, the court must also appoint an administrator for your estate and a guardian for your children. Normally the courts prefer a relative as administrator, but if one is not available or willing to serve, your estate could end up in the hands of a professional administrator. This official generally takes 3% to 5% of your estate in fees a year, an arrangement that gives him little incentive to settle your estate quickly or to minimize your estate for tax purposes. The court would also select a relative as guardian if the children were orphaned, but there is no guarantee the court would choose the one you prefer. And since the court's appointment does not carry the moral weight of your last wishes in your will, your children could become the object of a bitter custody battle.

Considering the anguish it prevents, a will is a bargain. If your estate is simple—less than $600,000 with no out-of-state real estate—you can expect to pay between $50 and $200 for a will. You could draft one even more cheaply on your own by using a do-it-yourself form. But the savings are hardly worth the risk that your homemade testament could founder on a technicality.

The Pitfalls of Probate

Whether you write a will or not, your worldly effects will generally be subject to the ponderous process known as probate. At this time your executor (or the court-appointed administrator) values your assets, pays off your creditors, files the estate's taxes, and finally awards what is left to your heirs. Probate occurs under the supervision of a local court known in various states as probate, surrogate, or orphan's court. In addition to approving your will—or writing one for you if you failed to—the probate court rules on the legitimacy of any creditors' claims against your estate and supervises the actions of your executor until your affairs are completely settled. If your minor children inherit any property directly, the court also oversees the guardian's use of that property until the children reach legal adulthood. All guardians—even the children's surviving parent—must keep records of their routine use of the children's inheritances and must petition the court for any unusual expenditures on the children's behalf. To spare your offspring this red tape, do not leave property directly to them. Instead, bequeath it to a trust established for their benefit and name their guardian as trustee.

Other than that, the major drawback to probate is that even with a fairly efficient court and executor, the process takes a minimum of four to eight months. If disgruntled relatives contest the will or if you owned property in another state, your heirs might have to wait years. Administrative and legal expenses during probate normally run between 5% and 10% of the estate, and naturally, the longer your estate lingers in probate, the more these costs grow.

Minimizing delays. A properly drafted will holds probate delays and expenses to a minimum. In most cases, you should give your executor broad powers to settle disputes or sell property as he or she sees fit without having to ask the court for permission. You should also avoid provisions likely to be invalidated by the probate court or to spark a challenge from disappointed heirs. For example, in most states you cannot leave your spouse less than the portion he or she would receive under intestacy laws. Disinheriting a child, on the other hand, is permissible everywhere but Louisiana. If total disinheritance is your aim, be sure to specify in your will that you know you are doing it. Otherwise, the child might claim to have been overlooked by mistake.

Also be careful about bequests, no matter how well intentioned, that could be interpreted as favoritism or slights by disgruntled heirs. For example, do not cut off the daughter who married the millionaire without explaining that her struggling siblings need your legacy more than she does. Her hurt feelings could spur a contest over the will or at least cause a lasting rift in your family. You can also avoid probate problems by keeping your will up to date. You need to have it reviewed whenever your circumstances change significantly—if, for example, you divorce or move to another state. In any event, have a lawyer look over your will every five years.

In addition, keep your affairs in order. Maintain an inventory of all your assets and make sure your executor knows where that inventory is. Your estate should have enough cash on hand to meet your cash bequests and to pay off your estate's creditors, including the state and federal tax collectors. If your wealth consists largely of illiquid assets such as real estate or stock in a family business, you can provide liquidity by purchasing additional life insurance. You might, for example, have your business purchase insurance on your life in an amount roughly equal to the value of your stock in the company. When you die, the firm could use the proceeds to buy back the shares from your estate. Otherwise, your executor might have to unload the stock at fire-sale prices to raise cash.

Avoiding probate. The surest way to avoid probate is to keep your property beyond the probate court's jurisdiction. In fact, a surprisingly large amount of your estate is likely to pass outside probate without any effort on your part. For example, the proceeds of a life insurance policy and the balances in your employee retirement plan, Individual Retirement Account, or Keogh account will pass directly to your beneficiaries. Any property you own jointly with rights of survivorship will pass automatically to the co-owner at your death. If you live in one of the eight community property states—Arizona, California, Idaho, Louisiana, Nevada, New Mexico, Texas, and

Washington—half of any possessions you acquired during your marriage (except gifts or inheritances) belongs to your spouse; the other half passes under your will.

If you live in one of the more numerous common-law states, holding some—but not all—assets jointly with your spouse is smart estate planning. By putting at least your home and checking account in joint title, you will ensure that your surviving spouse at least owns the roof over his or her head and can get some cash immediately after your death. Owning everything jointly with your spouse, however, is no substitute for a will. If the two of you were to perish at the same time, your children's inheritance would be left to the rough justice of your state's intestacy laws.

The most practical mechanism for skipping probate altogether is probably the so-called revocable living trust or *inter vivos* trust. A revocable living trust is one that you set up while you are alive, in which you have the power to change or revoke the terms of the trust. (A trust that you establish in your will, called a testamentary trust, does not keep you out of probate.) You may designate yourself as trustee of a revocable living trust; you may prefer to have a bank or trust company as co-trustee if you want to have your assets managed professionally. (For more information on the relative advantages of wills and revocable living trusts, see "The Lowdown on Living Trusts," on page 199.)

Trusts and Other Tax-Saving Devices

Keeping your estate out of probate, for all its advantages, does not protect your wealth against taxation. Probate concerns itself only with property that you own in your own name when you die. By contrast, the federal transfer tax, known as the Unified Gift and Estate Tax, potentially counts as fair game every piece of property that you transfer to someone else, regardless of whether you give it while you are alive or have it transferred on your death. Your taxable estate at your death includes not only the property you own in your own name but also half your jointly held property; the face value of any life insurance you own, regardless of the beneficiary; and any property you do not directly own but over which you have general power of appointment, that is, the right to take it yourself or give it away. (This includes all the principal held in a revocable living trust.) This all-encompassing tax base is accompanied by a particularly voracious bite: in 1989, the maximum estate tax is 55% on taxable estates of more than $2.5 million.

Lowering the tax bill. Fortunately, the estate-tax law leaves enough escape routes so that you can avoid federal estate and gift taxes altogether, provided you plan ahead. To begin with, your estate can deduct all its administrative costs, the value of any debts you leave behind, and any bequests to charity. But the most valuable deduction by far is the so-called marital deduction, which lets you leave any amount of property to a spouse tax-free.

The trouble is, if you leave everything to your spouse, some of your wealth will end up in the tax man's hands when your spouse dies and your property passes to your children. To minimize the tax liability on that second estate, you can make use of a second crucial sheltering provision of the estate-tax law: a credit that allows you to give away during your life or leave at your death a total of $600,000 free of federal gift or estate taxes. Moreover, you can also give away as much as $10,000 per person per year—$20,000 if you are married—without using up any of the $600,000 exemption. As long as you give away less than those amounts, your executor will be able to apply the full $600,000 exemption against your estate taxes.

Together, the $600,000 exemption and the marital deduction enable parents to pass an estate of up to $1.2 million to their children without federal estate tax. For example, consider a husband who has assets of $1.2 million. In his will, he bequeaths half the property to a testamentary trust called a bypass, or family, trust. He directs that the income from the trust go to his wife for the rest of her life and that the principal pass to their children at her death. The husband's estate owes no tax on this bequest, thanks to the $600,000 exemption. And, because the wife does not control the property in the trust, the tax code excludes it from her estate as well. The husband leaves the remaining $600,000 to his wife. This property escapes taxation at his death because of the marital deduction. Though the assets are now in the wife's estate, she can use her $600,000 exemption to bequeath them tax-free to the children, ensuring that more of the estate remains intact.

Marital and QTIP trusts. Tax-skirting trusts allow some variation on this basic strategy. Suppose, for example, that the husband does not want to leave property directly to his wife, perhaps because she is infirm. He can instead put the money in a so-called marital trust with, say, an adult child as trustee and his wife as sole beneficiary with general power of appointment. The contents of the trust would be considered part of her taxable estate; so even though the husband has not left the property to her directly, his bequest qualifies for the marital deduction.

Giving the wife general power of appointment allows her to leave the trust property to whomever she chooses—including a new husband. Thus, the first husband has no guarantee under this arrangement that the property he leaves in the marital trust will ever reach his children. To allay that concern, he could leave the property in a qualified terminable interest property, or QTIP, trust. In this arrangement, the trust agreement, not the spouse, controls who gets the property at the spouse's death. Such a trust would still qualify for the marital deduction provided it meets two requirements: All the trust's income must go to the wife during her lifetime and be paid at least annually, and the principal must be considered part of her estate.

Charitable bequests. To avoid taxes on an estate larger than $1.2 million, you first need to reduce the estate by charitable bequests or, better yet, by giving away assets while you are alive. If you leave property to a charity in your will, you get a deduction against your estate taxes. But if you donate property to a charity while you are alive, you not only reduce your eventual estate but also get a deduction on your income taxes. You need not make all your gifts to charity, of course. You can also give property to your family. As long as you and your spouse keep the gifts below $20,000 annually per heir, you do not use up any of your $600,000 exemption.

The best assets to give away are those you expect to appreciate rapidly. Suppose you intend to bequeath your $300,000 portfolio of stocks, currently appreciating 15% a year, in trust to your grandchildren. If you give the stocks

Estimating Your Estate Tax

It's useful to make a list of your assets and their values. That way you can determine how much of your property can be easily converted to cash. First, add up your assets in lines 1-8.

Don't despair if your gross estate exceeds the federal estate-tax exemption. A trio of deductions can erase or reduce your tax liability. Next, add up your outstanding debts *(line 10),* including mortgages, liens, income and property taxes, credit-card balances and loans. Then, estimate funeral expenses and the cost of settling your estate *(line 11).* Court costs, executor's, attorney's, accountant's, broker's, and appraiser's fees can easily devour 5% to 10% of your gross estate. Find your adjusted gross estate *(line 12)* by subtracting debts and expenses from your gross estate.

The unlimited marital deduction *(line 13)* allows you to leave your entire estate to your spouse tax-free. Of course, you needn't bequeath everything to your mate. But if you choose to do so, your spouse should also fill out the worksheet in order to determine the federal tax on his or her estate. Subtract charitable bequests *(line 14)* from your adjusted gross estate as well to find your taxable estate *(line 16).*

If you've made taxable gifts after 1976 *(line 15)*—when gift and estate taxes were unified—add them to your taxable estate. Remember, only gifts that exceed the annual exclusion are taxable.

The table will tell you how much, if any, federal estate tax you owe. For example, before credits are taken into account, the federal tax *(line 17)* on a $1 million taxable estate is

1. Investments

    Stocks $_____

    Bonds   _____

    Real estate   _____

    Other   _____

    Cash   _____

2. Personal belongings

    Household furnishings   _____

    Automobiles   _____

    Jewelry   _____

    Works of art   _____

    Other   _____

3. Share of jointly held property   _____

4. Life insurance policies and annuities   _____

5. Retirement benefits   _____

6. Gifts with strings attached   _____

7. Assets over which you own general power of appointment   _____

8. Other   _____

9. Total gross estate (lines 1-8) $_____

10. Outstanding debts   _____

11. Administrative and funeral expenses   _____

12. Adjusted gross estate
[line 9 - (line 10 + line 11)]   _____

13. Marital deduction (unlimited)   _____

14. Charitable bequests   _____

15. Taxable gifts made after 1976 minus gift taxes paid   _____

16. Taxable estate
(line 12 + line 15) - (line 13 + line 14)   _____

17. Federal estate tax before credits
(refer to Table, column B)   _____

18. Maximum credit for state death taxes   _____
    (refer to Table, column C)

19. Federal estate taxes less state
    death tax (line 17 - line 18)   _____

20. Federal credit for gift and estate taxes: $192,800 _____
    (same for everyone)

21. **Total federal estate tax due** $_____
    (line 19 - line 20)

$345,800. You're entitled to a credit against that amount for paying state death taxes *(line 18)*. In this case, you can subtract $33,200 from $345,800 to get $312,600. Deduct the credit *(line 20)* for gift and estate taxes from $312,600 to determine the IRS' share of your estate *(line 21)*. In 1989 the credit is $192,800.

FEDERAL ESTATE TAXES AND CREDITS			
A Taxable Estate	**B** Federal Estate Tax before Credits	**C** Maximum Credit for State Death Taxes	**D** Federal Estate Tax Less State Death Tax
$ 50,000	$ 10,600	—	$ 10,600
100,000	23,800	—	23,800
200,000	54,800	$ 1,200	53,600
300,000	87,800	3,600	84,200
400,000	121,800	6,800	115,000
500,000	155,800	10,000	145,800
600,000	192,800	14,000	178,800
700,000	229,800	18,000	211,800
800,000	267,800	22,800	245,000
900,000	306,800	27,600	279,200
1,000,000	345,800	33,200	312,600
1,200,000	427,800	45,200	382,600
1,500,000	555,800	64,400	491,400
2,000,000	780,800	99,600	681,200
3,000,000	1,290,800	182,000	1,108,800
	$1,275,800 in 1988 and thereafter		$1,093,800 in 1988 and thereafter

away now, you will still have roughly half of your
$600,000 exemption to apply against your estate taxes.
But if you keep the stocks and live another five years,
your portfolio will have grown to more than $600,000.
Leaving that amount to the grandchildren will absorb
your estate's entire exemption.

You can get an asset out of your estate without making
an outright gift by transferring ownership to what is
known as an irrevocable living trust. In this arrangement,
you give up any right to trust income and principal as well
as the power to change the trust agreement. Because you
have, in effect, renounced the benefits of owning the
property, it is not considered part of your taxable estate.
When you draw up the trust, however, you are free to give
the income to any beneficiary and to specify who inherits
the principal. Note, though, that property transfers to an
irrevocable living trust are considered gifts to the trust.
So you may owe gift taxes if you put in more than $10,000
a year.

Obviously, the realm of QTIP trusts and irrevocable
living trusts is no place for a layman—or even a lawyer
who is not skilled in estate planning. Ask your accountant
or financial planner for names of estate attorneys. They
deal with such lawyers regularly and ought to know
which ones are best in your area. In fact, it makes sense
to coordinate all your estate planning with your accountant and financial planner since they are the experts most
intimately familiar with your finances.

In selecting your attorney, interview at least three,
telling them as much about your estate as you can. While
you may lack the expertise to judge the legal merits of
their proposals, you can gauge how well they listen and
judge how comfortable you feel discussing family and
financial matters with them. Avoid lawyers who seem
inclined to dictate an estate plan rather than to hear you
out. A good attorney will tell you what you may do and
the best way to do it. But it is for you to decide what you
really want for your family after you are gone.

The Lowdown on Living Trusts

Who would actually want to die without a will? Your financial plan, no matter how carefully crafted, would be forgotten, your assets would be disposed of according to a rigid legal formula, and your estate might be diminished needlessly by taxes.

The problem with a will is that it must be proved valid in probate court. Your heirs may have to wait four months to two years for their inheritances, depending upon the efficiency of your executor and the local court. The procedure can drag on even longer if your survivors squabble over who gets what. If you own property in more than one state, your heirs may have to deal with two or more probate proceedings. Worse yet, 5% to 10% of your legacy will be lost to court costs and attorney's and executor's fees.

Though probate procedures and fees are less onerous in some states than others, you can spare your heirs those nightmares by establishing a living—sometimes called an *inter vivos*—trust. (A living trust should not be confused with a living will, a document in which you formally, and in some states legally, express your wish to forgo extraordinary medical treatment when you become terminally ill.) Property placed in a living trust bypasses probate, as does your share of assets that are jointly owned or have named beneficiaries, such as pension and profit-sharing plans, Individual Retirement Accounts, and life insurance policies.

Even if you establish a living trust, you will still need a simple will. The chief reason is that you cannot use a trust to name a guardian for your minor children. In addition, your will should include a "pour-over" clause stipulating that any property that you forgot to place in your trust should go there after your death. These assets will be subject to probate, but the process should not be lengthy or expensive for small estates, assuming you shifted most of your property to your trust before your demise. That is because most states have simplified probate procedures for small estates that can take as little as a day or two to complete and may not even require the services of a lawyer. The definition of a small estate varies by state, with limits ranging from $500 in New Hampshire to $60,000 in California. To find out what the ceiling is in your state, ask an attorney who specializes in estate planning or call your local probate court. And the price of a living trust should not break the bank. For a modest and uncomplicated estate, a living trust and a will with a pour-over clause cost about $400 to $1,000. A simple will runs $50 to $200.

Living trusts may be either revocable or irrevocable. But revocable ones are preferable because of their greater flexibility. For instance, you can keep any or all income a revocable trust produces, change its provisions, or terminate it. Many people even act as their own trustees. As a result, trust income is taxed at your rate (and reported on your tax return if you or your spouse serves as trustee). In addition, property in a revocable living trust is included in your taxable estate.

If you create an irrevocable living trust, on the other hand, you cannot control property in it. If you serve as trustee you can act only as an administrator; you cannot change the trust's provisions. Since you part with your assets forever when you place them in an irrevocable trust, they are not included in your taxable estate unless you receive income from the trust. But there are better ways to avoid or reduce estate tax that do not require you to relinquish control of your assets during your lifetime (see "Trusts and Other Tax-Saving Devices," page 193).

After your death, a revocable living trust can remain intact for the benefit of your heirs, or it can terminate with assets distributed to those same survivors. Your wishes, which you set down in your trust document, are carried out by a successor trustee of your choice. A relative, friend, or one of your beneficiaries may agree to perform this service free; banks and trust companies generally charge a fee equal to 2% of the assets distributed. There are no fees associated with living trusts during your lifetime unless you hire an institution, attorney, or a professional money manager to act as your co-trustee.

Even those fees seem reasonable compared with the expense of probate. Traditionally, attorneys' fees have been based on the size of an estate or dictated by local custom. Only a dozen or so states have set fee schedules, usually 1% to 11% of an estate's gross value. Generally, fees consume greater percentages of smaller estates. In California, for example, a lawyer handling a $100,000 estate would earn at least $3,150, or 3%; for probating a $3 million estate, he would earn $61,150, or 2%. The attorney could charge additional fees for selling assets, preparing an estate tax return, or defending the estate against claims by creditors or dissatisfied survivors. You can obtain a fee schedule from your county's probate court.

Unlike a will, a living trust can also shield your estate from creditors. With a will, your executor is required to notify your creditors of your demise by mail and newspaper advertisement so they can submit their claims against your estate. If you placed your assets in a living trust, however, no such publicity is necessary. But you cannot escape your creditors during your lifetime by transferring your assets to a revocable living trust. (They would be safe in an irrevocable living trust that you do not benefit from, though.) Say you cause an automobile accident and are liable for damages that exceed your insurance coverage. In most states, assets in your revocable living trust could be attached to satisfy court judgments against you.

Privacy is another advantage of living trusts. Nosy neighbors cannot find out how you apportioned your assets. In fact, the terms of your trust may become public only if someone objects to your provisions or lack of provisions for him or her. That is unlikely, however, because it is more difficult to contest a living trust than a will. Instead of filing a challenge against your estate in probate court, an unhappy survivor must sue your successor trustee as well as your beneficiaries.

Another benefit is that you can serve as trustee while you are in good health, but your successor trustee can take over if your physician certifies that you are no longer mentally or physically capable of managing your money. This arrangement is less costly and time consuming than a court-appointed conservatorship. A conservator must make an annual accounting to the court and may have to get its approval to make major expenditures or investments. Your successor trustee, on the other hand, simply follows the wishes you have set down in your trust document.

Once you decide to set up a living trust, you must transfer title to all your assets to it. Your attorney should handle the paperwork required to shift your house and other real estate into your trust. He or she should also prepare a document called an assignment of personal property to transfer personal possessions to a living trust. Standard legalese covers appliances, furniture, and other household goods, but you should list valuable antiques, art, and jewelry separately.

It is ordinarily up to you to put the rest of your assets in your trust unless you want to pay for the time it takes for your lawyer to do this. To transfer bank accounts to your trust, for example, you must either have your banker retitle your existing accounts or you must open new ones. The easiest way to transfer stocks, bonds, and other intangible investments is to have your broker open a new account in your trust's name and place your securities in it. If you intend to trade on margin or buy and sell options, say so in your trust document. You can transfer motor vehicles by applying for new titles at your state's motor vehicles bureau.

Special rules apply if you live or have lived in Wisconsin or a community property state. In those states, all income earned and assets acquired during marriage, except for individual gifts and inheritances, is considered community property. Each spouse shares equally in this property, so half of it is included in each spouse's estate. There is no problem if spouses agree to transfer community property to a trust created for their mutual benefit. But if you want to put community property in a trust that benefits only you, your partner must agree to give up his or her rights to the property.

Taking Care of Your Children

One of your primary considerations in planning your estate will be protecting your children's future. Unfortunately, tax reform cut out a loophole that allowed assets to be easily shifted from high-bracket parents to low-bracket children through gifts and trusts. The device was the most cost-effective way to fund a child's college education, launch him or her in a business, or provide the down payment on a first house.

With the new tax law came a provision dubbed the kiddie tax. Now any interest, dividends, or other investment income over $1,000 earned by a child under 14 is taxed at his or her parents' rate—as much as 33% this year. In the year in which a child turns 14, he or she goes through an economic rite of passage, and such investment income above $500 is taxed at his or her own rate, which presumably will be lower than the parents'.

Grim as the changes are, they have not knocked the life out of asset shifting. You can continue to give a child up to $10,000 a year ($20,000 if giving with your spouse) without paying a gift tax. And most financial advisers believe there are sizable tax advantages to be reaped from doing so. Assuming a hefty return of 10%, a child under 14 could still have assets of $10,000 and not be taxed at his or her parents' rate. At age 14 or older, the child could have assets of $178,500 before being pushed above the 15% bracket. Of the shifting techniques still available, the one for you depends on how old your child is, when you want your child to make use of the money, and how much money is involved. Here are the choices:

Custodial accounts. The easiest way to give money to a child under 18 is to set up a custodial account under the Uniform Gifts to Minors Act (UGMA) or its newer sibling, the Uniform Transfer to Minors Act (UTMA). These accounts, which cost nothing to set up through a banker or broker, are administered by a custodian—preferably someone other than yourself. The reason: If the assets are in your control, they are considered part of the donor's estate and would be taxed as such if you die.

UGMAs and UTMAs are essentially the same, except for two key provisions. In an UGMA, parents are limited to gifts of cash or securities. Another drawback: In most of the 23 states that permit UGMAs, the assets automatically come under your child's control when he or she turns 18. If the child would rather have a BMW than a B.A., that is his or her choice. With UTMAs, which have been adopted in 27 states and the District of Columbia, distribution of the assets can be deferred until the child reaches age 21—or 25, in the case of California. Also, the law allows you to place a wider range of property in an UTMA, including real estate, royalties, patents, and paintings.

If you set up a custodial account, you should take your child's age into consideration when making gifts. Richard Coppage and Sidney Baxendale, accounting professors at the University of Louisville, have computed the ideal amounts and timing of parental gifts in custodial accounts. Say the parents of a newborn wanted the child's UGMA to total $100,000 by the time he or she turns 18. (That, incredibly, is how much four years at a top private college may cost by 2006.) Assuming a yield of 8% annually, Coppage has calculated that parents in the 28% bracket who time their gifts properly (see table on page 205) would have $9,458 more for their child's education than parents who ignore timing.

Tailor UGMA investments to your child's age, too. If he or she is well under 14, financial advisers suggest that you go for long-term growth by investing in growth-stock mutual funds. If your child will not reach 14 for five years, you could give him or her supersafe Series EE U.S. savings bonds, which, if held for a minimum of five years, have a guaranteed yield of 6% (recent yield: 9.3%). They are only federally taxable and not until the bonds are cashed in—by which time the child will be taxed at his or her own rate. When the child reaches 14, parents should shift into more conservative fixed-rate instruments such as certificates of deposit or corporate bonds with maturities matched to the time of need.

Minors' trusts. You need a lawyer to set up a minors' trust, also known as a 2503(c) trust (which will cost about $500), and you must file annual trust tax returns. For those reasons, a minors' trust usually makes sense only when substantial amounts of money are at stake, at least $50,000. At that point, the expense will be more than offset by the two advantages of minors' trusts over custodial accounts: taxes and control. With regard to taxes, the first $5,000 earned by the trust, no matter what the child's age, is taxed at 15%; any amount above that is taxed at 28%.

Control of the income and principal is in the hands of the trustee (normally you) until the child reaches 21, as with an UTMA. But in a minors' trust, your child has 30 to 60 days from the time he or she turns 21 to demand the assets from the trust; if the child fails to do so, the trust continues until whatever time you have specified.

Charitable remainder trusts. You might want to consider a charitable remainder annuity trust if you are about to realize a large capital gain—$20,000 or so—and you want to avoid paying a hefty tax. Say you bought stock for

$10,000 and it is now worth $50,000. In setting up such a trust, stipulate that a beneficiary—usually a child—be paid a fixed amount from the trust's income, say $5,000 a year over four years beginning when he or she reaches 18. A nonprofit institution chosen by you has use of the assets in the trust during its four-year term and then owns them when the trust terminates. The advantages to you: you avoid paying capital-gains tax, you get a charitable deduction (worth $11,033 in this example if your bracket is 28%) over the life of the trust, and your child pays tax on the principal he or she receives at the 15% rate.

Splits and grits. An elaborate yet effective asset-shifting device for wealthy families is a split-interest purchase, commonly known as a split. It is essentially an arrangement in which an adult—usually the parent, although it could be anyone—buys majority interest in an asset and the child buys the rest. The parent then gets the income from that asset for a specified number of years, after which the child receives the property tax-free. Not only is this a cheap way for your child to acquire assets at a fraction of their cost, but it is also a way for a parent or grandparent to eliminate or reduce death taxes. But to set up a split, a child must have money—given by someone other than the person setting up the split—to pay his share.

If your child has no cash to kick into a split, you can consider a grantor-retained income trust, or GRIT. The adults retain the income interest as they do in a split, but they put up the entire purchase amount. What will take true grit is paying the bill from a tax or estate lawyer for setting up either of these arrangements: a nondeductible $1,000 or so.

How to Time Your Gifts

Shifting income to your best tax advantage can be tricky now that children under 14 must pay taxes at the same rate as their parents on investment income over $1,000. When a child reaches 14, such income above $500—but less than $17,850—is taxed at 15%. Nevertheless, properly timed gifts of income-producing property can be an effective way to reduce taxes. The table can be used to figure smaller amounts. For a 10-year-old and a target amount of $25,000, for instance, divide the appropriate numbers in half. Target amounts are estimates of the average cost of tuition, room, and board for a private college when the child is 18, assuming 5% annual increases.

Age of child	Target amount	Gifts						Tax savings
		At birth	Age 5	Age 10	Age 12	Age 13	Age 14	
Newborn	$100,000	$12,500	—	—	$3,453	$20,000	$20,000	$9,458
5-year-old	$70,000	—	$12,500	—	—	$10,119	$42,000	$5,924
10-year-old	$50,000	—	—	$12,500	—	$1,558	$20,000	$3,357

A Consumer Guide to AARP

Chapter Nine

*A*ny group that has grown as large and influential as the American Association of Retired Persons deserves close scrutiny. With membership of 30 million, AARP is the second-largest organized group in the nation after the Roman Catholic Church, which claims a flock of 53 million. Among AARP's swelling ranks are nearly one in every five voters, a fact lost on few campaigners in election year 1988. Indeed, AARP has become in many minds the enforcer of an insatiable and all but invincible gray lobby. For apart from the crush of its numbers, AARP also draws on a seemingly bottomless political war chest.

Keeping those coffers filled is the task of a tax-exempt retail empire that sells products and services ranging from angina medication to tours of Katmandu. AARP Group Health Insurance Program is the nation's largest of its type. AARP Pharmacy Service is the No. 2 private mail-order prescription outlet. *Modern Maturity*, AARP's glossy bimonthly mouthpiece, has the highest average circulation of any magazine, including *TV Guide*. Under its halo as a nonprofit, social-welfare organization, AARP lends its name to eight businesses that generate cash flows of about $10 billion. At last count, AARP's annual net income was $106 million, and ads in AARP publications added another $34 million. Together, that produces almost 60% of its total budget of $236 million.

Many members assume that AARP will always offer terrific deals because of the economies of scale it can bring to an enterprise and because of its presumably purer motives as a nonprofit organization. AARP's advertising reinforces this assumption. A typical marketing brochure for the AARP homeowners insurance program proclaims: "With our low rates and special discounts, your savings could easily reach up to 25% or more!" For irresistibly low annual dues of $5, members get a subscription to *Modern Maturity* and the monthly newspaper *AARP News Bulletin*. They also automatically qualify for discounts of 5% to 25% on car rentals and cut-rate hotel rooms from major chains. As one recruiting come-on accurately promises, "You can save the cost of membership many times over by using just one of the services AARP offers you."

In 1988, *Money* put such promises to the test by comparing AARP's offerings with the competition. On the one hand, we discovered a high-minded service group that enables 400,000 elderly volunteers to donate their services to their communities. At the same time, it is a well-greased marketing machine designed to sell those volunteers and other AARP members a battery of sometimes mediocre products and services, as the following analysis demonstrates.

Mutual Funds for Conservative Investors

Returns of AARP's seven no-load mutual funds, managed by the Scudder Stevens & Clark fund family, have generally been middling. But share prices fluctuate less than those of comparable funds, a sign that Scudder is mindful of the conservative leanings of its AARP

Products and Services AARP Offers

Like many other nonprofit organizations, AARP needs money. But instead of hawking museum replicas, AARP sells $106 million worth of products and services ranging from medications to tours. Operations are run by AARP's partners, which include some of the major names in their fields, from Prudential for health insurance, to Scudder Stevens & Clark for mutual funds and the credit union. AARP also works with the Internal Revenue Service to provide free tax preparation for the elderly and arranges discounts of up to 50% on rental cars and hotels.

Product or Service	Number of participants or policyholders	Proceeds to AARP
Mutual funds	400,000	$1.4 million
Pharmacy	2 million	1.5 million
Homeowners insurance	1 million	3.1 million
Auto insurance	1 million	15.3 million
Health insurance	6.5 million	82 million
Credit union	5,000	None yet
Travel programs	N.A.	3 million
Tax preparation	1 million	None

clientele. Shareholder service is solid and equal to that of most large, no-load groups open to all investors. Management fees are low, but the funds' total expenses tend to be steeper than the competition's. That is because of higher-than-average operating costs resulting partly from AARP's expensive amenities for shareholders, mostly earmarked for aged, novice investors.

For instance, Scudder provides separate telephone lines (including a special line for the hearing impaired) just for AARP. The phone reps are employed by Scudder, but AARP trains them to be sensitive to older people's concerns. In one exercise, for example, reps wear glasses smeared with petroleum jelly to simulate cataracts. "The idea," explains Scudder vice president Davia Temin, "is to remind a phone rep not to tell an elderly caller to read the fine print in the fund prospectus." Since phone staffers are not permitted to offer specific investment advice, they provide the same information anyone might get calling any major no-load family. Other services from AARP/ Scudder, such as recorded 24-hour yield quotations and shareholder newsletters, are also standard for no-load mutual fund groups.

Comments
The seven funds have had middling performances, but their managers keep share-price volatility low.
AARP underprices walk-in drugstores but not all other mail-order pharmacies on all prescriptions.
AARP beats the competition in some localities and loses in others. Shop around among major insurers.
Coverage is costly, especially if you have a less-than-perfect driving record or are in your seventies.
Medigap and long-term-care coverage are generally excellent, but avoid the indemnity policy.
AARP's new mail-order bank offers average savings rates but an inexpensive Visa card with favorable terms.
Many join AARP just for the bargains on car rentals, airlines and hotels. Package tours tend to be costly.
Volunteers help you fill out a simple return for free but don't provide tax planning advice.

Thus, prospective investors should evaluate all funds, AARP's included, to find the ones that best meet their needs. Note that a seven-fund family cannot offer all the categories or provide the full portfolio diversification sought by many investors. There are, for example, no aggressive growth, international, precious-metal, or tax-free money-market funds. Here is a rundown of what AARP does offer:

• Like most fund groups, AARP's family is anchored by a money-market fund. Originally, AARP Money Fund bought only U.S. Government securities, the safest type. The trade-off, though, was a lower-than-average yield. In early 1988, the fund began to buy other high-quality securities, such as AAA-rated corporates, to narrow its yield disadvantage compared to other funds. The move, however, had little impact: AARP's yield of 6.5% in mid-1988 was still about half of a percentage point below that of the average, high-quality money-market fund.

• At the other extreme of the risk spectrum is the Capital Growth Fund, which invests in stocks of fast-rising companies. It has been AARP's star performer, up an average of 18.6% annually from its inception in 1985 through mid-1988. Over the same period, all growth funds rose an annualized 15.5%, on average. AARP's other stock fund, the Growth and Income Fund, buys dividend-paying stocks as well as convertible bonds to help dampen swings in the share price. This fund returned an annualized 16.2% through mid-1988, typical in its category.

• The most popular AARP fund by far is the GNMA and U.S. Treasury Fund, which splits its portfolio between Government National Mortgage Association securities and Treasury bonds. The fund's annualized total return of 10.3% since its launch in 1985 matched the average for all GNMA funds. Another taxable fixed-income fund, AARP's General Bond Fund, invests in high-quality corporates that fluctuate in value more than GNMAs do. This fund has been up 9.1% annualized since 1985 versus 11.4% for the category.

• AARP's two tax-exempt bond funds, the Insured Tax Free General Bond Fund and the Insured Tax Free Short

Term Fund, have also lagged the competition. An investment in Tax Free General grew at an 8% annual rate
through midyear 1988, compared with the category average of 11.7%. The short-term muni fund returned only
5.8%, in a field averaging 7.9%. A major reason for this
subpar performance is that, unlike most muni funds,
AARP's funds buy only insured bonds—ones guaranteed
by a private insurer against default. The cost of the
insurance reduces yields by one-quarter to one-half of a
percentage point. Some mutual fund experts argue that
muni-fund insurance protects too little and costs too
much. While it removes the risk of default, it does not
safeguard shareholders against the far more serious risk
that rising interest rates will cause their share values to
drop. Moreover, competent muni-fund managers can minimize the risk of default at no extra cost by analyzing and
monitoring their bonds. One or two unforeseen credit
problems will have only a small impact on the value of a
well-diversified, uninsured fund.

Good Pharmacy Prices If You Can Wait

The savings from the AARP Pharmacy Service could be
worth the $5 price of admission into AARP all by itself.
There are only two reasons not to consider buying prescription drugs from AARP or from one of its mail-order
competitors: you can't wait a week to receive your medication or you need to consult a pharmacist in person.
Obviously, the AARP pharmacy and its postal-outlet competitors cannot beat the convenience of the local drug-
store. But AARP is next best in speed, aiming for
deliveries within six days. AARP also offers same-day
service at its 12 walk-in centers around the country.

When using a mail-order pharmacy, you typically get its
catalogue and then send in an order form with your
doctor's prescription. Refills may be requested by phone.
The pharmacy will send the bill with your medication.
Unlike the other mail-order pharmacies, AARP offers
braille labeling on containers. But both Medco's National
Pharmacies and Baxter Healthcare feature a 24-hour,
toll-free emergency hotline for consultations with phar-
macists; AARP's 12 toll-free numbers are staffed only
weekdays and from 9 a.m. to 5 p.m. local time.

Comparing AARP Prescription Drug Prices

AARP's pharmaceutical prices are competitive, though not invariably lower than others, such as Medco's National Pharmacies, available to members of the National Council of Senior Citizens, an AARP rival that charges a $12 annual fee ($16 per couple), or Baxter Healthcare's Mature Outlook, a Sears Roebuck discount club with a $9.95 annual fee. America's Pharmacy, the fourth national mail-order service surveyed, sells to the general public. It affixes a 75¢-a-package handling charge; rates from the other three include postage. Chain-store prices at right are averages based on a survey of 70 of them by Medi-Span, an independent firm; quotes assume a 10% senior-citizen discount, which is commonplace. The one advantage of a local economy chain is instant availability. AARP aims for an average arrival time of six days after receipt of an order—a schedule it met in a MONEY spot test. National Pharmacies estimates seven to 10 days delivery, Baxter and America's Pharmacy 10 days to two weeks. Each drug is followed by its generic equivalent. Prices are for 100 tablets.

	Mail order				Chain stores
	AARP Pharmacy Service	National Pharmacies	Baxter Healthcare	America's Pharmacy	
HIGH BLOOD PRESSURE					
Inderal (40 mg.)	$21.55	$21.18	$25.96	$20.77	$21.24
Propranolol (generic)	9.45	8.95	4.26	16.34	12.63
ANGINA					
Persantine (50 mg.)	24.95	24.95	26.62	25.29	28.59
Dipyridamole (generic)	7.95	7.95	3.90	9.60	9.35
ANXIETY					
Valium (5 mg.)	30.65	29.49	32.14	34.55	27.54
Diazepam (generic)	7.75	8.95	2.70	17.49	10.89
ARTHRITIS					
Motrin (600 mg.)	17.95	17.65	24.56	17.21	19.44
Ibuprofen (generic)	10.95	11.99	13.13	11.98	14.19

Members who order prescription drugs from the AARP Pharmacy Service can expect fair and sometimes exceptionally low prices—as well they should, considering the group's ability to buy in bulk. AARP Pharmacy, the nation's second-largest, private mail-order drug operation after Medco's National Pharmacies, regularly stocks some 5,000 brand-name prescription drugs and 825 generics. AARP encourages members to buy generic drugs rather than brand names to get savings—as much as 75%—and this is basically sound advice. Food and Drug Administration studies confirm the safety of generics for most prescription drug users. But patients should consult their doctors before switching from brand names.

Homeowners Should Shop Around

Anyone 50 or older who needs homeowners insurance ought to at least send in a request form published in *Modern Maturity* for a price quote from AARP. (You can't get an estimate unless you are an AARP member.) Then, contrast the cost of coverage AARP sells jointly with The Hartford against rates from several other companies. In some areas and situations, you may find

	Annual premium	
	Jacksonville, Fla.	**Elmhurst, Ill.**
INSURER		
AARP/Hartford	$548	$328
Allstate	374	290
USAA	579	382
Geico	662	378
State Farm	596	294

AARP's homeowners a good buy. But there is no household insurer who offers the best terms across the board (see the table above). Retirees should not be shy about shopping around since insurers consider them preferred risks and consequently discount their rates. An old saw among insurance agents is that if lightning strikes, a retiree is more likely to be home to put out the fire.

Price is the main consideration when choosing homeowners insurance, since coverage is fairly standard. Most homeowners buy the policy known as an HO-3 and, if necessary, purchase extra coverage for their valuables. But the AARP/Hartford policies, unlike those of some competitors, do not cover mobile homes, farms, or houseboats. You will also be turned down if you heat primarily with a wood stove or use more than 25% of your home for business purposes. Also, like some insurers, AARP/Hartford offers a discount on its auto and homeowners policies if you buy the combo. In AARP's case, you get 10% off auto and 5% off homeowners. But half a dozen states, including Massachusetts and New York, prohibit such tie-in discounts.

Comparing AARP Homeowner Insurance Prices

In these two representative examples of annual homeowners insurance prices, AARP/Hartford is in the ball park but isn't the champ among five national competitors. MONEY asked the insurers for premiums on $150,000 of property coverage, $105,000 to $150,000 replacement-cost coverage for contents, and $100,000 of personal liability coverage on three-bedroom, wood-frame houses owned by retired, nonsmoking couples over age 65. All prices assume that deductibles are $250 and that the owners have deadbolt door locks and room smoke detectors. Finer details of coverage differ slightly.

Think twice, however, before signing up for the auto insurance plan offered jointly by AARP and The Hartford. High annual premiums and surcharges levied after traffic violations or accidents spoil the deal for many policyholders, particularly those over 70. Even AARP staffers admit their automobile insurance plan could be improved. "There are significant numbers of people who could do

Auto Insurance Offers Service at a Price

better elsewhere," says Ron Hagen, AARP's director of insurance services.

AARP's only possible edge is the quality of its policy-holder service. In three offices around the country, The Hartford maintains a staff of 2,000 customer service representatives who work exclusively with AARP members. As part of an eight-week training session, new reps are taught by a gerontologist how to respond to the special needs of the elderly. For example, they learn how to enunciate better when speaking on the phone with the hearing impaired.

In the table on page 215 is a comparison of AARP's mail-order auto insurance with policies sold by four nationally respected companies. Three serve the general public: State Farm, Geico, and Allstate. USAA, like AARP, restricts its policyholders to a defined group—in this case, active and former military officers. The companies quoted premiums for hypothetical drivers in St. Petersburg, Phoenix, and Bellwood, Illinois, a small Chicago suburb. AARP did not sell the least expensive policy in any of the nine examples. In four cases, its insurance was the most costly.

When AARP started selling car insurance in 1983, it aimed for premiums as much as 10% below those of State Farm, the nation's largest auto insurer. Today, AARP's premiums often rise well above that target level. In one comparison, AARP charged 80% more than State Farm. Unlike some other insurers, AARP may also assess drivers in their seventies far more than those in their sixties.

AARP takes a particularly tough stance on accidents and traffic violations. If your car gets wrecked or you are caught speeding, you can expect to find a surcharge tacked on to your premiums for the next three years. As a test, the five insurers were asked for the penalties they would impose on a retired, 65-year-old married couple with a 1984 Buick Regal Coupe and a 1982 Buick Skyhawk Limited Coupe if they were fined for driving 15 miles per hour over the limit and if they filed an accident claim during their first year as policyholders. AARP's surcharges were highest or second highest in all but one of the cases surveyed. For example, if the couple filed an accident claim in Bellwood, Illinois, they would see their AARP premiums rise 56%, compared with a 4% increase by State Farm. Add on a speeding conviction and that

	AARP/ Hartford	State Farm	USAA	Geico	Allstate
POLICYHOLDER A					
St. Petersburg, Florida	$685	$381	$402	$537	$444
Phoenix, Arizona	834	528	490	837	668
Bellwood, Illinois	753	478	420	713	591
POLICYHOLDER B					
St. Petersburg, Florida	774	653	612	719	712
Phoenix, Arizona	833	889	677	1,110	1,016
Bellwood, Illinois	705	784	573	865	876
POLICYHOLDER C					
St. Petersburg, Florida	945	746	722	812	884
Phoenix, Arizona	1,070	994	792	1,247	1,230
Bellwood, Illinois	909	905	665	990	1,056

Comparing AARP Auto Insurance Prices

This table indicates the necessity of getting prices from a variety of auto insurers, including AARP. USAA premiums generally were the lowest of the five insurers surveyed, but their policies are restricted to current and former military officers. The second most favorable in our three case studies was State Farm. Our hypothetical Policyholder A is a retired, 75-year-old married male driver whose wife is not covered. He drives a 1984 Buick Regal Coupe. Policyholder B is a retired, 65-year-old married couple with a 1984 Buick Coupe and a 1982 Buick Skyhawk Limited Coupe, both insured. Policyholder C is a 55-year-old married couple in which the husband drives to work and both spouses' cars, a 1984 Buick Regal Coupe and a 1982 Buick Skyhawk Limited Coupe, are insured. In each of these policies, deductibles were $100 for comprehensive and $200 for collision. Coverage included $100,000 of liability insurance, $25,000 for property damage, $5,000 for medical or personal injury protection, and $25,000 of uninsured motorist insurance. Bellwood, Illinois, a small town near Chicago, was included to represent a suburban location.

would raise their AARP premium another 26%. State Farm would not add that surcharge.

Some insurers give big breaks to policyholders with 10-year, clean-driving records. Not AARP. If the couple cited above had no accidents in the previous 10 years, State Farm would waive its surcharge for their first accident claim. AARP would cut their surcharge by 39%, at most. USAA would not levy a surcharge on long-term policyholders after their first speeding violation. AARP would in some states, as would Allstate and Geico.

AARP policyholder discounts are typically provided by other major insurers, too. AARP sales brochures boast of low mileage credits and lower premiums for mature drivers, as well as discounts for defensive-driver training or good safety records. Most are offered by the other surveyed insurers, some of which discount more generously. For example, while AARP cuts premiums 10% for policyholders who also take its homeowners plan, Allstate's homeowners discount is 15%, and Geico reduces premiums as much as 20%. (These discounts are not permitted in every state.)

Two touted features of AARP's auto insurance actually deliver less than meets the eye. AARP guarantees its premium rates for 12 months, while many insurers only lock in rates for six months. But since AARP premiums generally are high initially, a one-year guarantee may be no bargain. AARP also promises that it will automatically renew your policy every year, regardless of your driving record. Exceptions: People convicted of drunken driving or those who have had their licenses suspended or revoked. Robert Hunter, president of the National Insurance Consumer Organization, says poor drivers would probably pay less in their state's assigned-risk insurance plan than they would paying AARP's surcharge-heavy premiums.

Two Good Health Policies and a Clunker

AARP markets three different types of mail-order Prudential group health insurance policies: Medigap, long-term care, and hospital-indemnity. (It does not offer comprehensive major-medical coverage, which is prohibitive for most elderly people.) Of the three group policies, two of them provide excellent coverage for the price and one is a clunker. On average, AARP returns to policyholders 78 cents of each dollar in premiums—guaranteed—compared with the industry norm of about 60 cents. AARP's service also stands out: 200 Prudential claims representatives, working exclusively for AARP members, answer toll-free calls on weekdays.

Most people 65 or older need Medigap coverage for hospital and doctor bills that Medicare ignores, and AARP's bears investigating. Its policy has four variations. Three provide identical coverage (that doesn't include prescription drugs) with annual deductibles for hospital and doctor bills ranging from zero to $200. Prices in 1988 ranged from $143 to $591 a year. The fourth AARP Medigap policy cost an additional $280 a year and reimbursed up to $500 annually for prescription drugs. Like most Medicare supplemental plans, the AARP's drawback is that it pays only those doctor fees Medicare deems reasonable. The difference between Medicare's rates and actual rates can be large. For example, an office visit to an Atlanta internist can cost as much as $150, but Medicare reimbursed you for only $22 in 1988. If you are in excellent health or know that your doctor's fees are within the Medicare guidelines, AARP's Medigap policy should deliver among the best values around.

The exorbitant cost of nursing homes ($24,000 a year, on average) also makes AARP's long-term-care policy worth considering. Like most competing nursing-home and home health-care plans, AARP coverage is limited. The policy, which cost $240 to $1,620 a year in 1988, paid a flat $50 daily benefit—25% below typical nursing-home costs—and stopped paying benefits after only three years. Policies from Aetna, John Hancock, and others offered daily benefits of as much as $100 and pay for up to six years. But premiums ran about $300 to $2,000 annually. In contrast to some plans, however, AARP covers Alzheimer's disease if it is diagnosed after purchase of the policy. Some policies require that you be hospitalized before they will reimburse for nursing-home stays. AARP's doesn't. AARP also defines care broadly: It covers all types of nursing homes as well as at-home care and adult day-care centers.

Alas, AARP's hospital-indemnity policy, like other insurers', is a bad buy. This type of coverage pays a flat, daily benefit for each day you spend in the hospital; AARP charged $120 to $240 a year for $30 to $160 a day in coverage. Since other medical expenses are not reimbursed, this is a limited and uneconomical use of premium dollars.

Supersafe Credit Union

The AARP Federal Credit Union, launched in 1988, may someday become one of the organization's major operations. If just 4% of members join, it would become the nation's largest credit union—and it is already worth a look for anyone 50 or older who needs a Visa card or a money-market savings account. AARP Federal keeps costs down by eliminating walk-in branches. Instead, it operates via a toll-free number and accepts deposits or withdrawals at any of the automated teller machines in the nationwide PLUS network. It is also supersafe because accounts and certificates of deposit are federally insured up to $100,000 by the National Credit Union Administration.

To join, you must pay a separate membership fee of $5 and open a savings account with a minimum deposit of $250. By contrast, banks and thrifts don't charge fees to belong, nor do they require that all customers open savings accounts. But once you are on board, AARP Federal's checking and savings plans are at least equal to the competition. Banks typically demand $500 to $2,000 to open money-market accounts, but you can get a similar AARP account for as little as $250. In either case, you are limited to writing three checks, other than for cash, each month. The AARP credit union also offers four different CDs with maturities of six months to five years.

Perhaps AARP Federal's biggest sales point is its Visa card. The $10 annual fee is lower than the average $14 to $17 at banks, and its 15% annual interest rate is well below the 18% usually charged these days. Also, retired people may find it easier to qualify for the AARP Visa than a similar card from another institution. Despite the Equal Credit Opportunity Act, some lenders do not play fair with older borrowers. "We consistently find some discrimination against the elderly," says Jean Noonan, associate director for credit practices at the Federal Trade Commission. "Some lenders say, 'No job, no credit, no exceptions.' Others give credit, but on much less favorable terms." When you apply for the AARP Federal Visa card, the credit union treats your retirement income like any employee's earnings. If you still don't meet the income threshold to obtain credit—a figure AARP keeps under wraps—AARP Federal will ask for more information about your net worth.

Travel Discounts and Costly Tours

AARP's travel bargains may be a prime reason millions join the organization. The best deals range from car-rental and lodging discounts to the AARP/Amoco auto club. Escorted tours are also available, but tend to be costly. One big advantage in all AARP travel programs is that they are open to members over 50 and their spouses of any age; most airlines and hotels offer senior citizen discounts only to people 62 or older.

Price breaks on renting a car or staying in a hotel just once could more than cover the $5 annual AARP membership fee. Avis, Hertz, and National give AARP members discounts of 5% to 25%, depending on when, where, and what type of car you rent. Eighteen lodging chains, including Sheraton and Holiday Inn, also cut room rates 10% to 50%. American Airlines offers AARP members a 10% discount on some fares. (But anyone over 65 can get 10% off some of American's flights as well as hotel and tour discounts by paying a one-time $25 membership fee to join the airline's Senior Saver Club.) Finally, AARP offers discounts of 5% to 28% on more than 100 cruises available to the general public from Princess Cruises, Holland America, and 12 other lines.

The AARP Travel Service features a diverse menu of about 250 escorted tours for members who want to travel exclusively with small groups of people their own age and their families. (Minimum age: 12.) AARP reviews tour packagers' itineraries, monitors the programs, and follows up on criticisms. To arrange a trip, members call the AARP Travel Service's special toll-free numbers for brochures. They then phone back for booking or ask their own travel agents to do so.

The Travel Service offerings compete most directly with such other packagers of tours for seniors as Grand Circle and Saga International Holidays. AARP provides the widest range of travel choices but generally charges a bit more. Arthur Frommer, the veteran travel writer, notes that tour packages can vary in price by several hundred dollars because of differences in the number of meals that are included, extra excursions, and the quality of the accommodations. He suggests that if you want to take a seniors' trip, pick two comparable tours and then ask the operators to explain precisely why their prices differ.

Frommer adds that tours catering specifically to elderly travelers rarely offer the most economical packages. But they do typically provide special services targeted to an older age group. For example, AARP asks prospective travelers to fill out questionnaires on hearing, vision, allergy, mobility, and other problems. If a trip to India, for example, seems too ambitious for an AARP member, a Travel Service agent might suggest a less demanding itinerary. All three operators guarantee that hotels they book have elevator service and that their groups avoid long hauls by bus or on foot, key considerations that tour packagers to the general public may ignore.

Tax Preparation for Simple Returns

You have nothing to lose by trying AARP's free Tax-Aide program. But you don't have to be a member to take advantage of this service as long as you are over 60. Tax-Aide is part of the larger Internal Revenue Service program called Tax Counseling for the Elderly (TCE). The IRS coordinates training of the 30,000 AARP and the other 38,000 TCE volunteers who assist in filling out returns from February 1 to April 15 or beyond for late filers. The tax counselors set up shop in neighborhood churches, schools, and libraries—and make house and hospital calls to shut-ins.

Tax-Aide may be a boon if you need straightforward guidance on a simple income tax return. But its volunteers, unlike accountants, will not suggest tax planning strategies or offer year-round consultations. If a Tax-Aide counselor makes a mistake costing you money, AARP will not pay the tax penalty and interest, as H&R Block and some other commercial tax preparers will. The risk of a costly mistake appears small, though. According to the IRS' figures, TCE volunteers erred on only 5% of the 1040 forms they worked on for 1987. (The IRS does not break out separate error rates for AARP Tax-Aide volunteers.) Note that the 5% TCE error rate beats that of IRS employees paid to assist the public (6%). U.S. taxpayers in general had a 9% error rate.

Index